*An Argument Open to All*

# An Argument Open to All

Reading *The Federalist* in the
Twenty-First Century

## SANFORD LEVINSON

Yale UNIVERSITY PRESS
*New Haven & London*

Yale University Press books may be purchased in quantity for educational,
business, or promotional use. For information, please e-mail
sales.press@yale.edu (U.S. office) or sales@yaleup.co.uk (U.K. office).

Designed by James J. Johnson.
Set in Miller Roman type by Newgen North America.
Printed in the United States of America.

Library of Congress Control Number: 2015940161
ISBN: 978-0-300-19959-8

A catalogue record for this book is available from the British Library.

This paper meets the requirements of
ANSI/NISO Z39.48-1992 (Permanence of Paper).

10 9 8 7 6 5 4 3 2 1

*For Michael Walzer, on the occasion of his eightieth birthday*

# Contents

## PART 3.

*Why "Confederation" Is Both "Odious" and an "Imbecility"*   55

## PART 4.

*The State and the Machinery of Death (or, at Least, Defense): Standing Armies*   83

## PART 5.

*How Does One Pay for the Services Supplied by the Union?*
*On Taxes and the Taxing Power* 109

## PART 6.

*To Err Is Human (and Perfect Clarity Is Chimerical)* 133

# PART 7.

## *On the Limits of the "Rule of Law"*   147

# PART 8.

## *National and State Prerogatives*
## *(and Maintenance of a Federal Political Order)*   155

# PART 9.

## *Veneration versus Reflection*   181

# PART 10.

## *Institutional Design: The Legislature*   189

# PART 13.

## *On the Executive*   253

# PART 14.

## *The Roles of the National Judiciary*   297

# PART 15.

*Reprise: The Importance of Institutions and the Necessity of a Strong National Government*   321

*An Argument Open to All*

# Publius, Our Contemporary

## *An Introduction*

- "[M]en are ambitious, vindictive, and rapacious." Only those willfully ignorant of "the uniform course of human events" and "the accumulated experience of ages" should expect "harmony between a number of independent, unconnected sovereignties in the same neighborhood."
- Because "[t]he circumstances that endanger the safety of nations are infinite, . . . no constitutional shackles can wisely be imposed on the power to which the care of [that safety] is committed."
- "It is in vain to oppose constitutional barriers to the impulse of self-preservation. It is worse than in vain; because it plants in the Constitution itself necessary usurpations of power, every precedent of which is a germ of unnecessary and multiplied repetitions."

These are surely provocative, even troubling, assertions. At the very least, they challenge one of the central premises of liberal constitutionalism—that government must be limited in its power in order to preserve the primary good of liberty. So who would say such things? The answer is "Publius," the nom de plume adopted by Alexander Hamilton, John Jay, and James Madison when crafting the eighty-five essays that we know collectively as *The Federalist*.[1] We might, of course, read them only as ways of understanding eighteenth-century thought, secure in the knowledge that we think differently (and presumably better) now. But we might also read them as insights into basic political reality, very much including that of the twenty-first century.

*The Federalist* is, without doubt, the best known, most widely read and analyzed extended work of American political thought. A host of books and articles by historians, political theorists, lawyers, and others devote themselves to uncovering the ultimate meaning of some particularly canonical essay among the eighty-five. Prime examples include *Federalist* 10, famous for its theory of "factions," or 78, in which Hamilton defends judicial review. Yet other works seek to describe the intellectual

1

influences on the three authors. Do their arguments owe more to Hume than to Locke, more to the unnamed Machiavelli or Thomas Hobbes than to the often-named Montesquieu? Did the thoughts expressed in the essays represent a broad "consensus," at least of American political elites of the time? Or, on the contrary, was Publius unusual in his viewpoints as well as his intelligence? Or we might wonder how many people, located where, and at what time (before or after key ratification votes in several states, for example), actually read any of the essays and had their minds changed as a result? That *we* today find them of great interest is no evidence at all for their influence at the time they were written.

Some authors question Madison's or Hamilton's sincerity, especially given what each had said at the Philadelphia Convention, which had concluded only months before (and whose proceedings were kept remarkably secret), let alone the views expressed later in their important political careers. There is also the independent question of how the essays fit into the general corpus of Madison's and Hamilton's thought. Anyone with specific biographical interests must attend to Ray Raphael's powerful question: Why should we believe that these particular essays, published over the roughly eight-month period between October 27, 1787, and May 28, 1788, uniquely capture the authors' complex body of thought? "[I]f Hamilton was indeed wise and brilliant," Raphael asks, "when exactly was that so? When he penned his essays as Publius or when he was touting a stronger, more centralized government both before and after that time?"[2] With Madison, the question runs in the opposite direction. The arguments about the seemingly inevitable inadequacies of state government and thus the necessity of a strong national government that he articulated in *The Federalist* differ dramatically from those he made especially eleven years later, when he wrote the Virginia Reports objecting to the Alien and Sedition Acts of 1798. Presenting *The Federalist* as dispositive evidence for their thought is like analyzing the political thought of presidents by focusing exclusively on their campaign speeches or inaugural addresses. There is no doubt something to be learned from them, but it would be palpably foolish to rely on them as guides to what the presidents "really" thought or, even more, how they would behave in office.

The eighty-five essays that make up *The Federalist* were part of a self-conscious political campaign to elicit support from wavering delegates, particularly in New York State. All three authors were well aware of pru-

dential considerations with regard to specific arguments they were making (and, just as important, those they left unsaid). One may truthfully describe *The Federalist* as one of the great campaign documents of all times,
prepared in a very particular context by politically savvy individuals. Indeed, part of what is most illuminating about the essays may well be the
importance of adjusting, for good and for ill, to the necessities presented
by concrete circumstances. They never pretended to have the luxury of
presenting a picture of a truly ideal government.

This volume, however, has almost nothing to do with addressing or,
even more certainly, resolving any of the questions set out above. Instead,
what follows are eighty-five short—and highly "presentist"—essays on
each of the separate contributions by the fictive Publius. By ignoring the
actual human beings hiding behind the mask of Publius, we can simply
elide almost all of these issues. The strength of Publius's arguments in be-
half of the Constitution—let alone their present relevance—do not at all
depend on our knowledge as to who actually wrote the essays in question.
Publius himself suggests as much in the powerful conclusion to *Federalist* 14, about the importance of thinking for oneself rather than submitting to ideas attached to the prestige of "names." If Publius has something
interesting to say to us today, as nonhistorians trying to make our way in
the twenty-first century, that is entirely independent of the identity of the
person penning the words.

Each of my essays is between 800 and 2,300 words. That is not, needless to say, enough space to do justice to many (perhaps any) of the original
essays. Instead, in respectful homage to their origin as eighteenth-century
op-eds designed for public consumption and debate, I conceive of my
own essays in a similar spirit. Each focuses on a limited number of major
points and asks the same basic question: What does this essay contribute
to our understanding of twenty-first-century politics? At the very least,
Publius addresses many *questions* that still unsettle us; but what about
his *answers*? Perhaps they too remain compelling; if not, then perhaps
we can learn something important by rejecting them. The purpose of the
original essays was to spur thought and action by their eighteenth-century
readers. Though I hope my own essays have a respectable shelf life, I have
no illusions about being read 225 years from now. I do hope, though, that
they can generate useful thought (and perhaps even action) about our contemporary political situation.

Just as relatively few modern readers begin at *Federalist* 1 and read straight through to 85, I would be surprised if most readers of this book read it straight through. There is repetition among Publius's own essays, perhaps because their authors knew it was foolish to assume that someone picking up the newspaper that day—or seeing a copy perhaps weeks later—would have read and remembered all the essays that preceded it. Although I have tried to minimize the repetition in my own essays, it has surely not been eliminated entirely, for which I beg the reader's indulgence. Although I certainly hope that the whole is greater than the sum of its parts, I have tried to make each of my essays "freestanding"; ideally, each should be understood without the reader having perused all of what came before. I do hope, though, that everyone will read at least the first essay, on *Federalist* 1, as it announces the major theme of the book, to which I refer regularly in later essays.

I cannot emphasize strongly enough that this project has nothing at all to do with establishing an "original understanding" of the Constitution that can be viewed as the equivalent of commands for judges and others trying to interpret the Constitution. As it happens, I have strong reservations about the entire originalist enterprise. For starters, as any close reading of *The Federalist* makes clear, there are perhaps fatal tensions in some of the arguments, sometimes within even a single essay and more certainly *among* the various essays. (And it is surely relevant to the enterprise of originalism that the uneasy alliance between Madison and Hamilton collapsed early in the Washington administration amid bitter disagreements over the basic meaning of the Constitution they both endorsed.) Moreover, as the essay on *Federalist* 37 shows, there are other reasons, rooted in the very nature of language, for doubting the cogency of the attempt to divine definitive understandings either of the complex words or concepts that make up the Constitution. But these reservations are the topic for another, very different book.[3]

Instead, I am interested in whether *The Federalist* speaks to us *today,* as members of the American political community or, for that matter, as a foreign reader who has been led to believe in the potential importance of *The Federalist* with regard, say, to designing a new constitution in one of the many countries undergoing varieties of "regime change," which includes the drafting of new constitutions. One of the themes that will emerge in many of the essays is that Publius had only limited faith in what we might term a "legalized" Constitution, that is, one consisting of commands whose meanings, when ambiguous, should be resolved by judges whose authority gives them primacy over all other interpreters. It is not that Publius did not see a useful role for judges; he spells it out particularly in *Federalist* 78. But it would be a huge error to ignore the extent to which Publius relied far more on politics, in the highest sense of that term, including a widely shared commitment to "prudence." There is almost no reason to believe that he would commend racing off to courthouses to find out what judges might declare to be the one true meaning of the Constitution.

Some might find in *The Federalist* normative guidance on designing our collective futures; others might find themselves skeptical about the arguments presented and so come to believe that we need to deviate from, rather than simply follow, the decisions made well over two centuries ago in Philadelphia. In two other books I have written, *Our Undemocratic Constitution: Where Our Constitution Goes Wrong (and How We the People Can Correct It)*[4] and *Framed: America's 51 Constitutions and the Crisis of Governance,*[5] I have set out my criticisms of the Constitution and advocated a new constitutional convention to address its weaknesses. I will not rehearse those arguments here.

Rather, my point is that every one of the essays that make up *The Federalist* contains something that should spark our interest today. Sometimes the connections between then and now are glaringly obvious, as is true of the three excerpts at the beginning of this introduction, taken, respectively, from *Federalist*s 6, 23, and 41. We live in a time, after all, when governmental agencies like those devoted to "national security" and "central intelligence" appear to defend basically unlimited power when used in the service of what the last excerpt called "the impulse of self-preservation." In other instances, contemporary relevance might be harder to discern, though I believe that it is still there when each given essay is examined carefully. Thus, I hope that by the end of the book readers are persuaded that it has been worthwhile to pay careful attention to at least parts of all of the essays. It would have made this book prohibitively long to include the original essays within the text, but they are easily available in many different print and online editions.[6] I certainly hope that this book encourages readers to return to the original texts.

The referent for "our interest" may be quite broad. Many countries around the world are actively (often controversially) engaged in drafting new constitutions. Since 2000 alone, these have included Tunisia, Egypt,

Bolivia, Iraq, Kenya, Hungary, and the European Union, to name only a partial and necessarily mixed list. Indeed, in the aftermath of the referendum in Scotland on secession from the United Kingdom, there is serious talk of convening a "constitutional convention" that would set out the explicit terms of a far more federal UK than is now the case.

For better or worse, those charged with drafting new constitutions often look to *The Federalist* for insights, not least because organizations like the American Bar Association are quick to send the drafters copies and to insist they are worth reading. I agree with the ABA that the essays are worth reading, though not because they are especially useful as a how-to guide to constitution writing in the twenty-first century. Instead, what is most striking about the essays as a whole is their decidedly unsentimental analyses of what Publius deems political realities. Many of those analyses have decided implications for anyone, American or foreign, interested in the relationships between governmental institutions and the challenges actually facing political systems. In any event, I hope that this book, and its own 85 essays, might contribute to the important work of drafters who are rightly worried about the state of contemporary political (dis)order and might be tempted to look at *The Federalist* for insights, whether positive or negative.

Contexts inevitably matter when reading (or writing) a book. We may speak more or less the same language as Publius and even inhabit, in some sense, the same country. But we necessarily approach his subjects with our own sensibilities and what Publius would describe (and commend) as the lessons of our own experience. We are in the position of the theatergoer who has already seen *King Lear*. The first scene is overladen with our knowledge that act 5 will feature dead bodies and ineffable sadness. Similarly, we know things that Publius, however intelligent and well-informed, simply could not have known and that color the use we make of what he wrote. So I invite you to explore *The Federalist*, written long ago in the late eighteenth century, and contemplate how it speaks to our very different situations in the twenty-first century.

# PART 1

## *Something Must Be Done to Save the Union*

## On the Frequency of "Reflection and Choice" by "We the People"

IN HIS FIRST PAPER, introducing what we know as *The Federalist,* Publius tells his audience that "it seems to have been reserved to the people of this country, by their conduct and example, to decide the important question, whether societies of men are really capable or not of establishing good government from reflection and choice, or whether they are forever destined to depend for their political constitutions on accident and force." No sentence more marks Publius as a child of the Enlightenment. He calls on his readers to join him in an unsentimental, intellectually ruthless evaluation of their political situation. One can imagine Thomas Jefferson agreeing with this sentence, even if one is confident that Publius would have dismissed Jefferson's suggestion that we engage in a "revolution" every nineteen years.

Publius begins the essay by referring to the "unequivocal experience of the inefficiency of the subsisting federal government." Later, in *Federalist* 15, he will label as an "imbecility" the government established by the Articles of Confederation in America's first (and largely forgotten) constitution. He is obviously defending the proposed constitution as a decided improvement. Were this book about the history of America during the 1780s, we could inquire at some length into its actual degree of "inefficiency" or "imbecility." Some people certainly disagreed and believed that the United States could survive and prosper without the drastic changes proposed by the Philadelphians, and some, albeit relatively few, historians share these inclinations.

These genuine cleavages of opinion among political elites—those capable of being elected to ratifying conventions—were reflected in the quite narrow margins by which the Constitution was approved in several state ratifying conventions. The pros and cons were only ten votes apart in New Hampshire and Virginia, and New York's politically decisive ratification was by a vote of 30–27. Rhode Island, which had rejected the Constitution in a popular referendum, finally held a convention that ratified the document—on May 29, 1790, more than a year after George Washington took his oath of office as our first president—by the less-than-inspiring vote of 34–32. Its decision to join the Union may have been encouraged by hints that Massachusetts and Connecticut would jointly invade and carve up the state should it insist on remaining independent (which would mean that Newport, then a leading port, would remain a haven for smugglers wishing to avoid American tariffs).

But it is not this book's purpose to adjudicate historical debates. I am more than happy to stipulate that Publius was absolutely correct in his dire description of the challenge facing citizens of the young country. After all, it is dire situations that most call for both "reflection and choice," rather than thoughtless adherence to conventional wisdom.

The central question is whether we still believe, well into the third century after October 27, 1787, when Publius's initial essay was published, that it makes sense to subject American constitutionalism to the standards of "reflection and choice." Can we as Americans—or anyone living elsewhere in the world—make informed and reflective choices about what is necessary for "establishing good government"? Or are we trapped by contingencies of "accident and force"—including what political scientists call the "path dependence" generated by prior choices—that make a hollow mockery of claims to political autonomy?

The American Revolution was in large measure fought over claims by the British that Parliament possessed full sovereignty over their North American colonies. Its triumph—and the triumph of the vision, set out in the Declaration of Independence, of government by consent of the governed—was sharply manifested in the first three words of the Preamble to the 1787 Constitution. "We the People" would have full authority to "ordain" a new political order. That is what it means to be a free people, at least in 1787.

But Publius was not praising unfettered *will*, which could be arbitrary and unjust. Instead, what dignified the American experience and made it of world-historical importance is the *reflection* that precedes choice. The citizenry must be offered good reasons, to be accepted or rejected on the basis of the quality of the arguments. Thus Publius promises, near the conclusion of his essay, to "frankly acknowledge to you my convictions, and I will freely lay before you the reasons on which they are founded. . . . My arguments will be open to all, and may be judged of by all. They shall at least be offered in a spirit which will not disgrace the cause of truth."

Even two centuries later, we can find Publius's promise deeply inspirational, speaking to what Lincoln called "the better angels of our nature."

When would-be democracies emerge from authoritarian backgrounds, cynics sometimes speak of a principle of "one person, one vote, one time." The winners, they suggest, will use the power gained in a presumptively legitimate election to entrench themselves in power. We must ask ourselves if we look at what happened in 1787–1788 in a similar way: Was it a unique event of government created by "reflection and choice"? If so, it presumably becomes incumbent on the citizenry thereafter to accept without further reflection what was done then.

But perhaps it presents a model for "We the People" *throughout* our collective lifetime. This would suggest the possibility of emulating the Framers first by asking probing questions about the "efficiency"—perhaps even "imbecility"—of the government established by their Constitution and then offering improvements, even radical ones (as was the Constitution relative to the Articles), for contemporary "reflection and choice."

The history of the United States since George Washington's inauguration in 1789 certainly features additional episodes of "reflection and choice." There have, for instance, been some important textual amendments. One might wonder if *all* of them meet the criteria of uncoerced "reflection and choice." After all, the landmark Thirteenth and Fourteenth Amendments were generated by an extraordinarily bloody war and, in the case of the latter, a military "reconstruction" that dictated as one of its conditions the ratification of the proposed amendment by the defeated Confederate states.

Full consideration of this question would take us too far afield from the central question, which is the meaning of Publius's injunction for us today. But other amendments, even if less transcendentally important, are nonetheless significant and were added to the text after public discussion and choice. At the national level, though, few people now alive can remember such "reflection and choice." In terms of actual consequences for the operation of the American political system, the last truly significant alteration was the Twenty-second Amendment, added in 1951 to remove any temptation that a president emulate FDR by running for a third term in office. One could imagine Bill Clinton running for his seventh term as president in 2016 if the amendment did not clearly forbid that!

Today, what would we need in order to take seriously the possibility of "reflection and choice" in a discussion of the adequacy of the United States

Constitution? Let me suggest some answers, though they are certainly only the beginning. First, we must assume that the Constitution *ought* to be subjected to full and fearless critique. One might hope that it survives the critiques and reinforces the common belief that it is truly splendid; but, at least for the period of "reflection and choice," we must suspend any such assumptions and instead take seriously the possibility that we have blinded ourselves to deficiencies, some of them perhaps extremely serious. A second assumption is that "We the People" are in fact *capable* of such an inquiry, so those who embrace the Publian creed of full candor in argument will be received by an audience who, even if they ultimately reject those arguments, will do so in a spirit of good faith by presenting their own reasons that can equally be subjected to critical review.

I will return to these themes. As we shall see, one can scarcely read *The Federalist* as expressing great faith in what we today might view as "democracy." Still, Publius *is* expressing his faith that there exist among his readers a critical mass with the proper disposition and abilities, and that it is worth taking the pains to write the collection of essays we know as *The Federalist* in an attempt to engage them. Although he doubts the motives of at least some of the new Constitution's opponents, he professes to concede that some oppose it in good faith, motivated by the same desire he has—to serve the public interest. Why, then, shouldn't he expect them to change their minds when presented with arguments that address their concerns and demonstrate why they have little reason to worry?

Publius in *Federalist* 1 seems to believe in the existence of an American public that can be trusted to discuss and then decide absolutely basic questions at the heart of governance. Do we think that is possible today, or is it a quixotic, even potentially dangerous fantasy?

FEDERALIST 2

## *How Much* Pluribus *within a Single* Unum?

*F*EDERALIST 2 FOCUSES ON the extent to which the United States has gained its unity by virtue of nature's bounty, including extensive rivers. But, Publius adds, "With equal pleasure I have as often taken notice that Providence has been pleased to give this one connected country *to one* *united people—a people descended from the same ancestors, speaking the same language, professing the same religion, attached to the same principles of government, very similar in their manners and customs,* and who, by their joint counsels, arms, and efforts, fighting side by side throughout a long and bloody war, have nobly established general liberty and independence" (emphasis added).

If we were interested in historical truth, it would be easy to demonstrate the utter fatuity of this declaration, just as, incidentally, one might express similar skepticism about the assertion in the first sentence of the Declaration of Independence that the various colonies consisted of "one people" entitled to secede from the British Empire and take its rightful place, as a single people, among the nations of the earth. Many distinguished historians have shown that those who came from elsewhere (not to mention, of course, the Native American tribes who already inhabited the land) were descended from a wide variety of ancestors, including hundreds of thousands of slaves coercively brought from all over Africa. They most certainly did not all speak the same language. Benjamin Franklin, for example, was appalled by the presence of German speakers in Pennsylvania; just as certainly, they did not profess the same religion, even if one decides to ignore the difference between Catholics and dissenting Protestants; and they scarcely could be described as "very similar in their manners and customs." Among the settlers from Great Britain alone, never mind those from other parts of Europe, there were remarkable variations of background. To assume homogeneity simply because of common British origin would be like assuming in today's America that there are no interesting differences among long-established residents of, say, Maine, New Mexico, North Dakota, or Georgia. Finally, they were hardly "attached to the same principles of government"; think only of the significant number, whom we tend to forget, who cast their lot with King George III and after defeat resettled in Canada, Jamaica, Great Britain, and, in the case of some former slaves, Sierra Leone.

One might dismiss the Loyalists and exiles from post-Revolutionary America as "un-American," but one can scarcely direct this epithet at those who engaged in often-bitter debates in Philadelphia, where three delegates refused to sign the Constitution, or at the ratifying conventions afterward, or at some of the pamphlets and speeches rendered "out of doors" in public gatherings. It would be unfair to tax Publius with knowledge of a future civil war, but that event further calls into question his optimism about homogeneity and concord in America.

For my purposes, it doesn't matter that Publius was a terrible sociologist. What makes his assertion worth our attention today is whether we share his presumed belief that the success (or failure) of the American political experiment (and perhaps similar experiments elsewhere) *does* depend on a requisite degree of homogeneity. Indeed, the correct word may be "homogeneities," as he includes ancestry, language, religion, and broader culture as the source of "manners and customs." The disciplines of American history and political science after World War II were rife with analyses emphasizing the importance of "consensus" on basic political issues and the existence of a distinctive "civic culture" that differentiated the United States from less lucky, more divided countries. Many political scientists thought the existence of such social and cultural phenomena rendered the particularities of formal political systems (or constitutions) almost irrelevant.

It takes little reading of modern newspapers or political speeches to realize that there are many "*Federalist*-2 Publians" in twenty-first-century America, who are concerned—perhaps even terrified—that the American "We" is becoming irreparably fragmented. Our national motto, *E pluribus unum*, suggests that whatever their apparent differences, Americans ultimately achieve a necessary unity. How is this to be attained? Some believe that it is enough to share a commitment to the political vision outlined in the Preamble or a willingness to be bound by decisions reached through the institutional procedures the Constitution has established. Others believe more is required, that, for example, there should also be a commitment to accept English as the only "American" language. Whatever else they may think about learning from the French, the proponents of this view presumably applaud the declaration in Article 2 of the French Constitution of 1958 that "[t]he language of the Republic shall be French." No nonsense about "multiculturalism" and the recognition of multiple languages within the polity, as one finds, for example, in Canada or in what is often called the world's largest democracy, India.

Similarly, the late Harvard political scientist Samuel P. Huntington published in 2004 as his last book *Who Are We? The Challenges to America's National Identity*.[1] He adopted a "Publian" reading of our history, asserting that "the American people who achieved independence in the late eighteenth century were few and homogeneous: overwhelmingly white (thanks to the exclusion of blacks and Indians from citizenship), British, and Protestant, broadly sharing a common culture, and overwhelmingly committed to the political principles embodied in the Declaration of Independence, the Constitution, and other founding documents."[2] Huntington despaired that this world was irredeemably lost. America is now fully multiracial—both African and Native Americans are full citizens, for starters—with many ethnicities and religions represented in the American "mosaic." In his book he noted the increasing multilingualism generated primarily by the vast new numbers of Spanish-speaking immigrants, who he feared were far less likely to leave their initial language than were Asians, another increasing part of the American mosaic. Huntington noted that the Union of Soviet Socialist Republics was no more, destroyed by the secession of groups rejecting rule by "foreign" Russians. And even a full decade ago he noted as well that Great Britain has become considerably more "devolved" particularly with regard to Scotland. One suspects he would not have been surprised to learn that nearly 45 percent of Scottish voters would in 2014 support secession from the Union with Great Britain that was formally established in 1707.

After writing that "No society is immortal," Huntington goes on to quote Rousseau: "If Sparta and Rome perished, what state can hope to endure forever?"[3] Thus Huntington suggested that we should not blithely assume that even the post–Civil War United States would maintain itself into the indefinite future. He explicitly rejected the wisdom of relying only on what might be termed "constitutional attachment," describing this as the "classic Enlightenment-based, civic concept of a nation" in which "nationalism," lacking any other commonalities, was predicated entirely on commitment to abstract propositions. "History and psychology, however, suggest that this is unlikely to be enough to sustain a nation for long."[4] Instead, he called for renewed emphasis on the "core culture" that he believed dominated in 1787. Although he emphasized that his call for returning to an "Anglo-Protestant culture" did not mean privileging "the Anglo-Protestant people"—non–Anglo-Protestants could assimilate to that culture, just as immigrants to France are expected to take on the trappings of "Frenchness," beginning with language—critics accused him of nostalgia for an America controlled by persons of his own Anglo-Protestant background. Harsher analyses were offered as well.

One need not agree with Huntington's analysis in order to wonder if there are in fact limits to the heterogeneity that a society can welcome if it would try to achieve what the Constitution calls a "Republican Form of Government." Does such a government require a version of "We the People" that, at the very least, shares important ideological presuppositions, even if they are expressed in different national languages? Consider the limitation of American law, going back to the initial naturalization law of 1795, that no one shall be eligible for naturalization—in effect being "reborn" as a full "American" to replace one's former civic identity—unless the applicant for citizenship has not only been resident within the United States for at least five years and shown him- or herself to be "a person of good moral character," but is also, and crucially, "attached to the principles of the Constitution of the United States, and well disposed to the good order and happiness of the United States."

In one of the most eloquent judicial opinions in the history of the United States Supreme Court, which invalidated punishment of Jehovah's Witnesses who refused to salute the American flag, Justice Robert Jackson wrote, "If there is any fixed star in our constitutional constellation, it is that no official, high or petty, can prescribe what shall be orthodox in politics, nationalism, religion, or other matters of opinion, or force citizens to confess by word or act their faith therein. If there are any circumstances which permit an exception, they do not now occur to us." One might wonder how this magnificent credo of American liberty coexists with the demand that would-be citizens demonstrate attachment "to the principles of the Constitution." Can these "principles" ultimately be reduced to the nonorthodoxy so eloquently expressed by Jackson, or is there something more, such as acceptance of certain substantive commitments?[5]

Most of us, I suspect, are hesitant simply to hope for the best with regard to those who wish to enter the United States, whether as resident aliens, who by definition have no wish to become citizens, or, even more so, as citizens with the right, among other things, to vote. I know that I have qualms about certain sizable groups of immigrants who come from undemocratic, indeed anti-democratic, countries and, because they live together in this country and recreate their own versions of their former cultures, may be contemptuous of some of the assumptions required to operate a republican form of government. This may include, for example, a genuine commitment to the "good order and happiness of the United States" and its multiple groups and not only one's own kith and kin. Of course, one might argue that it is far too late in the day to posit the actual relevance of the republican vision, that our political system is so wholly committed to interest-group politics that it is completely legitimate for a voter—or a public official?—to be concerned exclusively with his or her private interests, including those "partial" groups one identifies with, in contrast to a completely fictitious "We the [one] People of the United States."

As Huntington noted, these concerns are not limited to the United States. As a frequent visitor to Israel, I have wondered more than once if the significant immigration from the former Soviet Union was altogether good for Israel, inasmuch as many of those immigrants appear to have little commitment to pluralistic democracy. (This is, incidentally, even more true of those labeled as "ultra-Orthodox" or "Haredi," some of whom reject the legitimacy of the state of Israel on the ground that only the Messiah can legitimately establish such a state.) Israel, it should be noted, differs from the United States in granting immediate citizenship, under the Law of Return, to any Jew who declares that he or she wishes to be a part of the Jewish homeland. This means, among other things, that newcomers can vote almost immediately. There is nothing like the American requirement of a five-year residence before one becomes a citizen, in which one purpose of the delay is, presumably, to give the newcomer time to assimilate. One of the more obscure clauses of the Constitution requires that naturalized citizens wait even longer—seven and nine years, respectively—before they are eligible to serve in the House of Representatives or the Senate. (They remain permanently ineligible to become president.)

Perhaps the success of the United States is sufficient to render irrelevant the fact that Publius was simply wrong about the actual composition of American society in 1787. So does this entail that his belief about the significance of homogeneity was completely without merit?

## FEDERALIST 3

### Federalism and Foreign Policy

IN FEDERALIST 3, PUBLIUS STRESSES the degree to which a single united nation will be better equipped to participate in international affairs and contribute to what he deems the central task of any government:

"providing for [the] SAFETY" of the citizenry. Interestingly, he doesn't argue that a larger nation will find it easier to raise armies and navies should war break out. Instead, he emphasizes the costs to a sound foreign policy—and thus the greater likelihood of war—should the thirteen states fragment into multiple nations, or even should they retain the Articles of Confederation and barriers to unity it imposed.

Distrust of states—and a fragmented polity—is a pervasive theme in *The Federalist*. Publius argues that "the prospect of present loss or advantage may often tempt the governing party in one or two States to swerve from good faith and justice," a tendency that, if not controlled, could provoke discord and full-scale war with the young country's many potential enemies. Fortunately, he says, "those temptations, not reaching the other States, and consequently having little or no influence on the national government, the temptation will be fruitless, and good faith and justice be preserved." We can take comfort in the fact that "the national government, not being affected by those local circumstances, will neither be induced to commit the wrong themselves, nor want power or inclination to prevent or punish its commission by others."

Publius draws a sharp distinction between local or state interests, whose impact should be minimized to whatever degree possible, and the truly national interests that will presumably be instantiated in the decisions of the government's leaders under the Constitution. Creation of this government does not guarantee international peace and concord, but it makes it more likely, which is no small matter.

Federalism, even in the realm of foreign policy, which is Publius's main concern, has scarcely disappeared as an important concern today. Even if a particular state's decisions cannot, by themselves, spark war with another country, it is not at all unlikely that it could so antagonize a given country that it seriously complicates American foreign policy. Consider only two issues recently presented to the United States Supreme Court—both, as it happens, involving Mexico.

One case involved the clear violation by Texas of an international treaty, signed by the United States, promising that criminal defendants who are citizens of a foreign country have a right under international law to have their embassy notified of their being in legal peril. A Mexican national, José Ernesto Medellín, in 1997 was convicted and sentenced to death by the state of Texas for a brutal murder. The Mexican embassy was never informed of Medellín's arrest. It is certainly possible that the embassy would have given him better legal counsel than he received on his road to death row. Mexico sued the United States in the International Court of Justice (sometimes called the World Court), which held that Mr. Medellín's rights had indeed been violated and that, at the very least, he should not be executed before having the opportunity to demonstrate that the clear violation of his treaty rights might have prevented his receiving an effective defense. Against the request by the Bush administration that Texas honor the verdict, the state laconically noted that the administration of criminal justice was *its* prerogative and not the prerogative of the national government, still less the World Court. It chose to ignore both the World Court and the entreaties of the Bush administration, which then sued, arguing that federal treaty obligations took precedence over state prerogatives. The Supreme Court disagreed, ruling in effect that Texas had a right to administer its criminal justice system as it saw fit, including executing a prisoner who everyone agreed had been denied his treaty rights and, in the process, antagonizing Mexico.

The second case is probably better known, inasmuch as Arizona led many states in passing onerous laws directed against unauthorized aliens, who, by definition, had violated American law either in their initial crossing into the United States or in remaining beyond the limited time authorized by a visa. It is estimated that there are well over 10 million such persons in the United States, many of them clustered in America's Southwest in border states with Mexico. Civil-liberties groups and the United States itself challenged the constitutionality of the Arizona laws that, for example, permitted police to demand that anyone arrested for any reason, including traffic stops, prove their citizenship. The national government argued that Arizona's policy, clearly directed against Mexican citizens who entered that state, generated tensions with Mexico to the detriment of American national interests. Arizona in effect argued that it was being forced to pay an inordinate price to safeguard these purported interests and that it had both the duty and the right to prefer the interests of Arizona's own citizens, who were increasingly antagonistic to the presence of unauthorized aliens in the state. (Similar laws, some of them even more draconian, were passed in Alabama and Georgia.) In a 5–3 decision, the Supreme Court struck down aspects of the Arizona law on the ground that they were indeed "pre-empted" by national laws, which is simply

lawyer-talk for granting the national government supremacy over conflicting state laws. But it left in place other parts of the law, including the
police's ability to ask for identification.

Publius claims "that a cordial Union, under an efficient national government, affords them the best security that can be devised against HOS-
TILITIES from abroad." Although we are properly conscious of the special
importance of *armed* hostilities, there are, of course, many other forms
of hostile action. The United States has been engaged for many years
in attempts to stanch the traffic of drugs across its border with Mexico.
American authorities have little direct power to control actions by Mexico
and must rely on eliciting the cooperation of the Mexican government—
and the Mexican people, which to at least some extent may depend on
the perceptions that the United States is acting in "good faith and justice"
rather than "swerv[ing]" from these paths or, more to the point, allowing
its constituent states to swerve. The extent of the rights to autonomous
action enjoyed by American states has been highly controversial from the
beginning, with the capacity, as demonstrated most dramatically in 1861,
to rend the nation and generate the most violent hostilities. And as Publius recognized, endorsing a strong notion of states' rights may have grave
implications for American foreign policy.

### FEDERALIST 4

## *"Concerning Dangers from Foreign Force"*

IN *FEDERALIST* 4, PUBLIUS CONTINUES to emphasize dangers posed
by the fact that the United States lives within an international system
of states. Here he presents the starkest vision of that order. "It is too true,
however disgraceful it may be to human nature, that nations in general
will make war whenever they have a prospect of getting anything by it. . . ."
The United States, he continues, will inevitably appear to threaten the
interests of several powerful countries: "With France and with Britain we
are rivals in the [cod] fisheries," and further tensions would certainly be
raised as the United States sought entry into trade with China and India. It therefore must always be watchful of countries that may believe
they can "get something" by hindering the United States. What Publius
called "inducements to war" were almost literally everywhere. Presumably

potential adversaries would begin with everyday diplomacy, but underlying serious diplomacy, as Clausewitz would so famously write, is often the threat of war. Although he was too tactful to say so, Publius may have viewed treaties with other nations as what he would describe in a later essay as "parchment barriers," to be breached whenever it was thought advantageous to do so. Peace—and protection of vital American interests—required strength, which he believed could come only through union.

Publius noted, for example, the considerable advantages the United Kingdom enjoyed over a mere alliance among England, Wales, and Scotland. "What," he asked, "would the militia of Britain be if the English militia obeyed the government of England, if the Scotch militia obeyed the government of Scotland, and if the Welsh militia obeyed the government of Wales?" If the Constitution were not ratified and America were ultimately divided into "three or four independent governments—what armies could they raise and pay—what fleets could they ever hope to have? If one was attacked, would the others fly to its succor, and spend their blood and money in its defense?" Even worse, perhaps, was the danger that one of these separate countries—perhaps called New England, Atlantica, and Dixie—would be "flattered into neutrality" should an attack by a European adversary occur, perhaps because of "specious promises or . . . by a too great fondness for peace," which would lead them "to decline hazarding their tranquillity and present safety for the sake of neighbors, of whom perhaps they have been jealous, and whose importance they are content to see diminished?"

What does this have to do with us today? The answer is simple. If we put to one side the fact that Great Britain reentered American soil during the War of 1812, capturing part of Maine and burning down the national capital, we can say that the United States successfully staved off a foreign attack until December 7, 1941. Today, of course, the key date that "will live in infamy" for many Americans is September 11, 2001, a very different kind of attack by an equally different kind of enemy (who, among other things, was not organized into a standard-form state). One element that links both of those episodes, though, is America's expansion well beyond the limited borders Publius assumed in 1787. Another linkage, even more obvious, is the development of modern technology, which makes the United States vulnerable to adversaries located far away. Those who, for example, describe Iran, especially should it produce nuclear weapons, as a major threat to American national security surely do not envision Iran's sending an army of warships into New York Harbor or even interdicting our ships as they ply the international oil trade. And we are increasingly aware that hackers working from thousands of miles away can do more potential harm to the American economy and generate more feelings of insecurity than even a "standard-model" terrorist armed with a firearm.

Not that the modern international system is altogether different from the one described by Publius. Those who describe themselves as unsentimental international-relations "realists" have little trouble agreeing with his statement that "nations in general will make war whenever they have a prospect of getting anything by it." What makes our own world different is the increasing importance of nonstate groups like Al Qaeda to wreak havoc and, along the way, induce further degrees of paranoia by those adopting a Publian perspective.

The fall of the Berlin Wall and the liberation of Eastern Europe in 1989, followed by the collapse of the Soviet Union in 1991, generated a number of fantasies that, a quarter century later, can be described as "post–Cold War triumphalism." The United States was viewed as the "new Rome," a unique superpower capable of bending the entire world to its will through its economic and military might. That vision has been left in shreds, especially after the near-collapse of the international economy in 2008 and the realization that American military intervention (even when supported by "coalitions of the willing") promised at best only temporary and uncertain success. We are, for better and worse, part of an international, globalized economic order, where the weakness of the euro or the diminishment of China's willingness to buy bonds from the United States can have ominous effects on what we continue to describe as the "domestic" economy. And our military budget, larger than those of the next eight nations combined, turns out to be less dispositive than we thought. Modern presidents, of whatever political background, must cobble together complex and fragile alliance systems designed to forestall adverse behavior by common enemies, whether "nations" in a conventional sense, or modern movements that are fully capable of opportunistic relocation to whatever country will, voluntarily or not, give them havens.

The question is whether the international system that long ago compelled the transformation of the modest and aptly named Articles of Confederation into a far stronger entity called the *United* States of America now requires similar moves toward a wider, transnational political order.

One can think of the North American Free Trade Agreement, which created a free-trade zone among Canada, the United States, and Mexico, as a successor to the free-trade zone created in 1787 stretching from Massachusetts (which then included much of what is now Maine) to Georgia. Or one can look at some of the more utopian hopes for the United Nations or, more modestly, at the North Atlantic Treaty Organization, created in 1948 to stave off the menace of the Soviet Union (and, not at all coincidentally, to integrate what was then called "West Germany" into that particular alliance system).

Still, as Publius suggested, the problem with alliance systems is that they ultimately rely on the "parchment barriers" of treaties. Will a country really risk its death and destruction because allies are being attacked? But even when nations find compliance in their interest, they may resist putting their armed forces under foreign command, making integrated security efforts unwieldy and inefficient.

There is a paradox inherent in many of Publius's arguments. His immediate concern was the fragmentation of the fledgling nation under the Articles of Confederation and the need, therefore, to exalt the benefits of union. But the argument for union may have no logical stopping point. If greater unity is needed to resist potential aggression by Great Britain or France, then why doesn't it follow, in another historical period, that the United States, Great Britain, and France should join together in a genuinely common political enterprise in order to provide a unified response to China or some other common rival? The Atlantic and Pacific Oceans no longer provide automatic security. Almost everyone today recognizes the necessity of what George Washington dismissed as "entangling alliances." Shouldn't we at least consider the possibility that such alliances will—and *should*—ultimately lead to stronger forms of political unification that will, in their own way, replicate the vital transformation of 1787–1788?

## FEDERALIST 5

### *In Union There Is Strength*

IN *FEDERALIST* 5, PUBLIUS CONTINUES the major theme enunciated in *Federalist* 4: the great advantages of union and the concomitant dangers linked with the presence of multiple countries within the existing Confederation. He was particularly worried about the breakup of the Confederation into what he labeled "NORTHERN" and "SOUTHERN" (emphasis in original) confederacies. "Different commercial concerns" might generate different international as well as local interests. As we know, union was not enough to forestall the development of these different concerns. The United States was threatened with at least the theoretical possibility of terminal discord when South Carolina in 1828 tried to "nullify" what it labeled the "Tariff of Abominations," which protected developing northern industry by placing significant tariffs on the importation of goods from Great Britain directed at southern markets. Partly because the putative states' rights advocate Andrew Jackson threatened military intervention if South Carolina carried out its threat to defy national law, South Carolina basically capitulated, though the sense of grievance generated by this triumph of nationalism bore full and bitter fruit in 1861. It is clear, then, that union could not prevent war, whether we call it the Civil War or the War Between the States.

Publius's dour vision is confirmed by American wars against Canada and Mexico. As we have seen, his almost Hobbesian vision of the international political system easily suggests that a would-be hegemon would not be deterred by international borders—"parchment barriers" of a different kind, perhaps, but ultimately just as symbolic and unreal. (Think of Vladimir Putin in 2014 vis-à-vis Ukraine.) And the United States, which lusted after Canada throughout the nineteenth century, invaded that country/colony of Great Britain not only during the American Revolution itself but also, more importantly, early in the War of 1812 (when we burned down the capital of "Upper Canada," an action that some historians think explains the British burning of Washington, DC, later in the war). We also invaded later, but again unsuccessfully. Mexico, of course, was a different story. The Mexican War of 1847 was very clearly a "war of choice" initiated by Jackson's successor, James K. Polk, as part of his expansionist agenda. Out of it came what we today call the "American Southwest," including all or parts of Texas, New Mexico, Arizona, Nevada, Colorado, Utah, and California. Later in the century, the United States would gain Puerto Rico in the aftermath of the Spanish-American War. Multiple interventions in Central America would also be an important part of twentieth-century American foreign policy, though unaccompanied by formal integration as American territory.

Perhaps most interesting—even poignant—for the modern reader is the very beginning of the essay, where Publius quotes a July 1, 1706, letter from Queen Anne to the Scottish Parliament concerning the hoped-for acceptance of the Treaty of Union that would formally unite the still-independent countries of England (which had been joined by Wales in 1536) and Scotland. "An entire and perfect union," wrote the Queen, "will be the solid foundation of lasting peace: It will secure your religion, liberty, and property; remove the animosities amongst yourselves, and the jealousies and differences betwixt our two kingdoms. It must increase your strength, riches, and trade; and by this union the whole island, being joined in affection and free from all apprehensions of different interest, will be ENABLED TO RESIST ALL ITS ENEMIES." A truly United Kingdom, she argued, was "the only EFFECTUAL way to secure our present and future happiness, and disappoint the designs of our and your enemies, who will doubtless, on this occasion, USE THEIR UTMOST ENDEAVORS TO PREVENT OR DELAY THIS UNION."

Queen Anne's hopes were realized, of course. What lends poignancy to her letter is that the "affection" among the constituent parts of the United Kingdom has always kept the kingdom far short of perfection, and contemporary British politics has featured a variety of "devolutionist" movements by which significant powers have been translated to the Scottish Parliament and the National Assembly for Wales. A 2011 referendum in Wales, for instance, gave 63 percent support to the proposition that the Welsh Assembly should be able to make binding laws in some twenty policy domains without having to procure assent from the British Parliament in London. Even more interesting is the vote held in 2014 within Scotland, in which a significant minority supported withdrawing entirely from the United Kingdom and resuming full-scale Scottish independence.

Do any of Queen Anne's arguments still have purchase in the twenty-first century? Can anyone seriously argue that Great Britain is threatened with the kinds of invasions that make union between England and Scotland necessary for defense? Does British membership in NATO not suffice? As the countries of Europe become more integrated into the European Union, however fitfully, will the United Kingdom have much ability to protect trade within its territory? After all, it is the great achievement of the European Union, originally conceived as a "free-trade zone," that the United Kingdom can no longer discriminate against products (or even immigration) from any EU country, just as the 1787 Constitution prevented

New York from discriminating against goods imported from New Jersey or North Carolina.

Paradoxically or not, the integration of European countries into the European Union seems to have generated a variety of autonomy or even secessionist movements, as with Catalonia and the Basque regions of Spain, or Flanders within Belgium, not to mention the possibility of British secession from the EU itself as a result of the desire of many contemporary Britons to discriminate against immigration from the Continent. As the fear of external warfare diminishes, attention can return to the actual extent to which the countries organized around putative necessities of defense will necessarily maintain their unity in a radically different world. Threats to national security have not disappeared, but they take quite different forms today. Once again, the need for "reflection and choice" rears its head.

FEDERALIST 6

## *Humankind as "Ambitious, Vindictive, and Rapacious"*

IN VIVID PROSE AND muscular argument, Publius makes even clearer his skepticism that a world of competing disunited states—here he is envisioning the collapse of the "United States" into separate entities—can provide a basis for anything other than endless war. "A man must be far gone in Utopian speculations," he warns, "who can seriously doubt that, if these States should either be wholly disunited, or only united in partial confederacies, the subdivisions into which they might be thrown would have frequent and violent contests with each other." To deny this is "to forget that men are ambitious, vindictive, and rapacious." It therefore takes a willful ignorance of "the uniform course of human events" and "the accumulated experience of ages" to expect "harmony between a number of independent, unconnected sovereignties in the same neighborhood."

It is worth noting that Publius, here as elsewhere, is making a universal statement about the nature of "men." There is no notion of what has come to be called "American exceptionalism" with regard to basic human character. One must design institutions to try to alleviate the implications of that character—thus the emphasis in these essays on the importance of unity and the potentially catastrophic consequences of fragmentation—

but the underlying structure of human nature remains as a constant for Publius.

The universalist aspect of Publius's diagnosis of the human condition has significant implications if *Federalist* 6, or *The Federalist* more generally, is read by a foreign audience. We in the United States can easily read Publius to offer a rationale for our contemporary defense budget, under which, even with congressionally mandated "sequestration" and, therefore, automatic budget cuts, in 2014 the United States continued to spend "more on defense than the next eight countries combined."[1] It's a cruel world out there, and the United States should be willing to spend whatever is necessary to defend our national interests, or so many would argue. But foreign readers can also draw from Publius the identical message: They too need to fear predatory would-be hegemons and have the same interest in beefing up their own defenses against countries, including "neighbors," that could easily turn out to be threats. After all, as Lord Palmerston, the British foreign secretary memorably put it in an 1848 speech to Parliament, "We have no eternal allies, and we have no perpetual enemies. Our interests are eternal and perpetual, and those interests it is our duty to follow."[2] To suggest that "friendship" can significantly trump "interests," he had said earlier in his speech, is a "romantic notion."[3] This has often been paraphrased as a maxim that states in the international system have no friends; they have only interests. One can only assume that Publius would agree.

So why should any other country trust American professions of "friendship" to take precedence over cold calculations of what is in the interest of the United States? In any event, it is readily understandable why the leaders of other countries, upon reading Publius, might believe that they too need to enhance their own national security, whether this involves threatening to build nuclear weapons or simply attempting, through alliances with other countries, to balance the power now perceived to be held by the United States or, increasingly, China.

Franklin Roosevelt famously declared that the "only thing we have to fear is fear itself," especially if the fear generated runs on banks lest one lose all of one's deposits. Putting to one side whether FDR's injunction was empirically accurate, it is clear that many political campaigns, including recent presidential elections in the United States and all too many abroad as well, are organized around various tropes of fear. Those exhibiting insufficient fear are often dismissed as naive utopians whose callowness should disqualify them from holding political office. Perhaps Publius believed that the Constitution might contribute to the "pursuit of Happiness" or to maintaining the "Blessings of Liberty" that the new country's Declaration of Independence and Preamble to the Constitution, respectively, announced as their founding aspirations. But the real foundation for his argument is his commitment to another part of the Preamble, providing for the "common defence,"[4] and his belief that anything short of a newly enlarged and vastly more powerful national government would fail in that aspiration.

There is no escape from Publius's near-paranoia. Lest we rely on singular virtuous leaders, he takes care to discredit Pericles, whose ancient funeral oration to his fellow Athenians, with its invocation of "courage, sense of duty, and a keen feeling of honour," is sometimes assigned even today to students as exemplifying the necessary character for maintaining a republican form of government. But Publius's Pericles, because of "private pique" or fear that he might be prosecuted for theft of a statue, drives Athens into wars that ultimately destroy its democracy.

For Publius, it makes no difference how governments are structured or what the basis of their legitimacy is. He notes the presence of "visionary or designing men, who stand ready to advocate the paradox of perpetual peace between the States, though dismembered and alienated from each other." Thus they suggest that "[c]ommercial republics, like ours, will never be disposed to waste themselves in ruinous contentions with each other. They will be governed by mutual interest, and will cultivate a spirit of mutual amity and concord." Were he more like Vice President Biden, Publius might simply dismiss such arguments as "malarkey." He concludes his essay by citing the French philosopher l'Abbé de Mably, who wrote that "NEIGHBORING NATIONS . . . are naturally enemies of each other unless their common weakness forces them to league in a CONFEDERATE REPUBLIC, and their constitution prevents the differences that neighborhood occasions, extinguishing that secret jealousy which disposes all states to aggrandize themselves at the expense of their neighbors." Absent a move to unity, one can expect only continued warfare, and even in times of "peace," endless fear of renewed hostilities. Moreover, in the twenty-first century, we live, for better and worse, under a much broader notion of "neighborhood" than did de Mably or his American admirer.

Publius takes no refuge in what we today call "democratic peace." As political scientist Sebastian Rosato has written, "the democratic peace theory—the claim that democracies rarely fight one another because they share common norms of live-and-let-live and domestic institutions that constrain the recourse to war—is probably the most powerful liberal contribution to the debate on the causes of war and peace."[5] Among other things, it "provides the intellectual justification for the belief that spreading democracy abroad will perform the dual task of enhancing American national security and promoting world peace." This belief has undergirded American foreign policy from Woodrow Wilson's time through Franklin Roosevelt to George W. Bush and Barack Obama. Rosato is among the political scientists who find the theory to be disconfirmed by what Publius called the "lessons of . . . experience" (though, to be sure, other political scientists disagree).

Publius provided a good reason to support the amalgamation of New York and North Carolina into a new and strengthened United States of America governed by the institutions established by the new Constitution. But he seems to provide no reason for anyone in our own time to rest secure in the belief that the "good old Constitution"—or even the strength of the United States in the twenty-first century—is enough to overcome this century's pervasive fear.

Publius gives us no grounds for optimism. As Ronald Reagan famously said of dealing with the Soviet Union, "Trust, but verify." Perhaps we should place Reagan in a distinctly Publian tradition that, at the end of the day, minimizes the value of trust in favor of endless vigilance. For Publius, then, a principal virtue of a constitution is that it lets us—and all other readers, wherever located—prepare for never-ending conflict, which can, of course, take a variety of forms, including economic as well as military.

## FEDERALIST 7

### *Endless Sources of Conflict (and War),*
### *Even within the United States*

IN THE PREVIOUS ESSAY, Publius cited all of human history, from Pericles on, coupled with a universal theory of human nature—"ambitious, vindictive, and rapacious"—to support his argument that would-be autonomous states or countries could not escape the ravages of war. In

*Federalist* 7 he turns more particularly to the thirteen states that initially joined together in the Articles of Confederation (and, of course, had earlier joined together to overthrow British rule) and are now being asked to recognize the deficiencies of the Articles and endorse the new, far more centralized, government proposed by the Philadelphians.

Once again, his theme is the threat of endless conflict and ultimately warfare in the absence of unity. If most historians of American political thought emphasize the influence of such political theorists as Locke, Hume, and Montesquieu on the generation of those who wrote and adopted the Constitution, this essay reminds us of the importance of Thomas Hobbes. It was Hobbes who depicted life in a state of nature as "nasty, brutish, and short," because of the threat presented by one's neighbors in the absence of a state that could guarantee security. As Hobbes noted, even the strongest individuals had to sleep, thus making them vulnerable to "rapacious" acts. The only protection, he argued, was the creation of an extraordinarily strong "Leviathan-state," whose potentially absolute powers would guarantee at least the protection of life, whatever the attendant costs to liberty or pursuit of happiness.

What might go wrong, then, if the Constitution were rejected in favor of maintaining the Confederation or, more likely, the dissolution of the United States into several republics? Some of Publius's answers seem safely locked into the circumstances of 1787. This is certainly true, for example, of his concern that failure to ratify the Constitution might lead to fatal discord among the states concerning the vast "western lands" to which they made conflicting claims. Most of these lands were in fact ceded to the national government; indeed, one of the last acts of the Congress established under the Articles was to pass the famous Northwest Ordinance, which ultimately generated the states of Ohio, Indiana, Illinois, Wisconsin, and Michigan. But what if the Union dissolved into constituent states or several "confederacies" of various states? "In the wide field of Western territory," he wrote, ". . . we perceive an ample theatre for hostile pretensions. . . ." Even if he may have been right, what does that have to do with us today, at least within the United States?

We might ask the same question about another of his examples, the possibility of trade wars, particularly with regard to the ability of seaboard states like New York in effect to impose high import fees on the ultimate consumers living in states lacking similar deepwater ports. Many people argue that a central purpose of the Constitution was the creation of a free-trade zone designed to prevent such trade disputes (and their escalation into violence); this explains, for example, the Constitution's prohibition of almost all import fees levied by states, as against those imposed by the new national government.

We will have occasion later to contemplate the fact that the national government under the Articles had no power of "direct taxation." All it could do was to issue "requisitions" against the states, basically a plea for voluntary payment of dues to remain in the Union. Many states behaved as the United States did for many years with regard to its dues to the United Nations. "Not this year, thank you," was often the response, and, like the UN, the Confederation government could do nothing other than complain. Since the Constitution solved this problem, only historians remain interested in the operation of the requisition system.

Perhaps we get closer to contemporary relevance with Publius's comment that "it is an observation as true, as it is trite, that there is nothing men differ so readily about as the payment of money." Trite or not, this observation applies whether one is paying out money or hoping to receive it. Our contemporary politics are dominated by an almost pathological opposition by some to the very idea of paying taxes. It turns out that "taxation with representation" is hardly more popular than "taxation without representation." The key point is to avoid taxation at all. Yet even as one resists the paying out of taxes, there is equal incentive to strive to maximize one's influx of money. To the extent that government tax policies, and consequent expenditures, almost inevitably have "redistributionist" tendencies, there is ample cause for discord. Some of this discord involves individuals or social classes—the "haves" against the "have-nots"—but some can involve states themselves.

The late New York Senator Daniel Patrick Moynihan often brought up the extent to which states like New York received far less in federal programs than did other, smaller states, which benefited mightily from disproportionate power granted them particularly in the Senate (and therefore to some degree in the Electoral College). As Moynihan pointed out, it is a mistake to think of New York as a "rich state," though it surely contains more than its share of rich persons. But in 1999, only New Mexico had a greater percentage of its citizens living in poverty than New York did. Still, one discovers that small, rural states receive substantially far more per capita federal expenditures than do the large, urban states in which most Americans actually live.

Paradoxically or not, one finds that the greatest political opposition to federal spending and the concomitant support for a leaner, meaner national government comes from the states who are the *beneficiaries* of redistributive policies of "taxing and spending" rather than the states that might wish to describe themselves as benefactors (or, perhaps, *victims*). One need only contemplate the consequences for the Great Plains and Upper Midwest states if, for example, Congress changed federal agricultural programs to eliminate the government's vast subsidies on wheat, soy, or corn.

But we should ask ourselves if adoption of the Constitution necessarily solved the structural problem Publius identified, which, simply put, is the propensity of "sovereign states" to use their powers to benefit their own citizens, whatever cost might be inflicted on "outsiders." Consider in this context state "economic development commissions," whose goal can often be described as recruiting companies from their present locations in some other state. The recruitment mechanisms often include the promise not only of "business-friendly" policies—including hostility to unions—but also tax abatements and other forms of what economists call "tax expenditures" that mean that the incoming companies will pay little, if any, taxes. The arrival of these companies creates new jobs in the receiving state, but only by eliminating existing jobs in another state. From a national perspective, it is not at all clear that such competition, however desirable from a certain business perspective, does anything to promote a healthy national economy. Many economists speak of a "race to the bottom" provoked by "beggar-thy-neighbor" competition among states. To be sure, this competition has its defenders, most notably George Mason Law School Professor Michael Greve, who sees it as a valuable way of minimizing both the regulatory and the tax burdens placed on business in general and, therefore, a way of "disciplining" states that might be too hostile to business interests.[1] Greve and others think the resulting "business-friendly" environment brings general prosperity. For Greve, the advantage of federalism is that it serves precisely to maintain the "hostile pretensions" that worried Publius, in part because they cut against the kind of national unity and subordination to a truly common enterprise effacing a feeling of membership as well in the state and its own particular commitments that might cut against the ostensible national goals.

Perhaps it is enough that we do not, in the twenty-first century, genuinely fear that war will break out among the states. Publius would count this as a great success of the new Constitution. But is it utopian to hope for more?

## *On the Rise of a Militarized State*

PUBLIUS CONTINUES TO argue that a truly United States offers far better prospects for maintaining security and liberty than does adherence to the Confederation and the likelihood of ultimate dissolution into three separate countries along the Atlantic coast. He posits that "[s]afety from external danger is the most powerful director of national conduct," which, as we saw, is little more than an extension of the central insights of both Hobbes and Locke, that people are motivated to live under organized government because it offers them security against threats by ill-motivated others. To provide adequate security against "external danger" requires establishing "standing armies" of military personnel always ready to defend the country against invasion. One of the most controversial features of the 1787 Constitution was its legitimation of such an army, as opposed to sole reliance on militias composed of sturdy yeomen who could be mustered when dangers presented themselves. Publius, like George Washington, had little faith in such militias, whatever their place in American myth. Both understood the virtues of a well-trained professional military.

Yet Publius, who is certainly politically sagacious enough to know that many of his readers will be wary of a standing army, offers as a central advantage of the new Constitution, and the attendant unity of the constituent states, that the threat of foreign invasion would be so remote that a *large* standing army would be basically unnecessary. Thus he reassures his readers that the highly advantageous geographical position of the United States, separated from Europe by an ocean, renders unnecessary "to our security" what he calls "[e]xtensive military establishments." But "if we should be disunited, and the integral parts should either remain separated, or, which is most probable, should be thrown together into two or three confederacies, we should be, in a short course of time, in the predicament of the continental powers of Europe—our liberties would be a prey to the means of defending ourselves against the ambition and jealousy of each other." Such fragmentation would generate, "in a little time," the establishment "in every part of this country the same engines of despotism which have been the scourge of the Old World."

We need not revisit the sad tale of the disintegration of the United States into the bloodbath of 1861–1865 in order to see a continuing relevance for Publius's arguments. Although for well over a century we were protected by the Atlantic Ocean and the even vaster reaches of the Pacific Ocean from most direct involvement with foreign powers—the War of 1812 to the contrary, and it was viewed, correctly or not, as a victory for the young nation—it is equally true today that we are enmeshed in hosts of alliances, entangling or not. Often these alliances are explained in terms of America's purported commitment to help other countries achieve the blessings of democracy. But it would be foolish to deny the element of self-defense that undergirds alliance systems. To treat, as for example NATO does, an attack on one as an attack on all, with requisite response from all members of the alliance, is to try to preserve an inevitably uncertain peace by raising the stakes for those who might be tempted to invade a country deemed insufficiently strong to defend itself.

At least since the end of World War II, with the rise of NATO and other formal and informal alliances, the United States has maintained a strong standing army to guard against threats deemed contrary to vital American interests, whether or not they involve invasions of the homeland. The United Nations is, among other things, a mechanism for collective defense. The first American war after the UN was established, the action in Korea, occurred without a formal declaration of war by Congress. President Truman claimed that the United Nations Charter compelled the United States to defend South Korea against North Korean aggression, which was viewed as a proxy for a more fundamentally aggressive move by the forces of international communism led by the Soviet Union.

"The perpetual menacings of danger," writes Publius, "oblige the government to be always prepared to repel it; its armies must be numerous enough for instant defense. The continual necessity for their services enhances the importance of the soldier, and proportionably degrades the condition of the citizen. The military state becomes elevated above the civil." This militarization of the political order leads, inevitably, to "frequent infringements" of the presumptive rights of the citizenry. "[B]y degrees the people are brought to consider the soldiery not only as their protectors, but as their superiors."

How is this relevant to us in the twenty-first century? It is not enough simply to note that millions of Americans are employed by the military, and millions more serve the military as contractors. Nor is the percentage of the gross domestic product consumed by so-called defense spending necessarily telling. The current percentage is about one-third of the 14 percent that it was in 1953, at the conclusion of the Korean War. Rather, the relevance is that the military has become "valorized." It is not only that ambitious politicians often use the mantra of "supporting our troops" to justify military spending and weapons systems whose primary virtue is that building them provides jobs for the politicians' constituents. Those who serve in the military are automatically deemed "heroes," even as the politicians who rhetorically embrace them often cast scorn on, say, public schoolteachers or express absolute indifference to budget cuts that might decimate those who serve the poor.

Diane Mazur, a former Air Force officer who now teaches at the University of Florida Law School, in her book *A More Perfect Military: How the Constitution Can Make Our Military Stronger*, bewails a number of cases decided by the Supreme Court that treat the military as an institution not only set apart, but also *better* than civilian institutions in important ways. Also worth noting is a 1992 article, "The Origins of the Military Coup of 2012," written by Charles Dunlap, while still a colonel in the United States Air Force, that describes a fictional coup sparked by military officers disgusted by what they saw as the decadence of civilian life and institutions,[1] and having been trained to take seriously, as a central function of the modern military, the task of nation-building rather than simply fighting wars. In Dunlap's fiction, the military leadership decides that it is the United States itself that needs rebuilding; the declaration of permanent martial law is upheld by a popular referendum.

A 2011 essay in the journal *Daedalus* described the "chasm" that has developed between the roughly 1 percent of the American population directly involved in the military and the 99 percent civilian population that leads a far different life. "The entire military," writes Robert Goldrich, "has become a refuge for those who question the basic orientation of civilian society and do not wish to live within many of its central boundaries," including automatic subordination to civilian authority regardless of the personal identity of those imbued with the authority of office (such as president of the United States).[2]

Dunlap described his piece as "emphatically not a prediction," and fortunately it wasn't. He wrote it to express his skepticism about the shift in the military's mission from war fighting to nation-building. But one can certainly wonder if Publius's insights, coupled with Dunlap's concerns, might not be worth very much taking into account today. Perhaps "standing armies" themselves are less the real danger than the development of a political culture that emphasizes the ubiquity of threats coupled with a loss of faith in civilian values and leaders in favor of the discipline and values of the military. What should we think, for example, of a 2014 Gallup Poll that found the military by far the most admired institution within American government, securing the "confidence" of 74 percent of the American people? This is especially alarming when we compare it to the approval levels of other national political institutions. Even the Supreme Court registered only a 30 percent confidence level, one point higher than the presidency and a full 23 points higher than Congress.[3] A greater percentage of Americans have confidence in the military than in the legislative, executive, and judiciary branches combined. It is hard to see this as good news for democracy.

Perhaps there is no cause for concern, and we can safely dismiss *Federalist* 8 as an eighteenth-century relic or simply disregard it as a clever piece of propaganda designed to elicit support for the Constitution from those tempted to maintain the system established by the Articles of Confederation. But perhaps Publius's arguments are very much worth attending to today. How, though, can we have a truly mature conversation about the dangers he points to if we regard the military as composed almost entirely of "heroes" and stand ever ready to accuse its critics of being insufficiently supportive of our troops, naively inattentive to the dangers facing the country, and, therefore, a presumed threat to national security?

# PART 2

## *Bigger Is, in Fact, Better*

FEDERALIST 9

# *The New (and Improved) Science of Politics*

W ITH HIS EMPHASIS on the pervasiveness of conflict and the dire
consequences attached to failure to ratify the proposed constitution, Publius is scarcely a fount of general optimism. Yet as in his first
essay, where he endorses Americans' capacity to exercise "reflection and
choice" in how they wish to be governed, in *Federalist* 9 the Enlightenment optimist peers out at us, telling us, for example, that "[t]he science
of politics, . . . like most other sciences, has received great improvement."
He is no acolyte of "ancient wisdom" or even "tradition." Instead, he happily informs us that "[t]he efficacy of various principles is now well understood, which were either not known at all, or imperfectly known to the
ancients." Among these are the "regular distribution of power into distinct
departments; the introduction of legislative balances and checks; the institution of courts composed of judges holding their offices during good
behavior; the representation of the people in the legislature by deputies of
their own election." These, he proclaims, are "wholly new discoveries, or
have made their principal progress towards perfection in modern times."

Publius's central target here, as in later essays, is Montesquieu and his
followers, who believed that what the Constitution called a "Republican
Form of Government" could exist only in small, homogeneous communities. Political theorists often identify "republican" political theory not only
with Montesquieu but with the Florentine Machiavelli, who wrote admir-
ingly, if often despairingly, of the efforts by Italian city-states to maintain
the tenets of civic republicanism. It is no coincidence that Publius begins
this essay with sneering references to "the history of the petty republics
of Greece and Italy" and the "sensations of horror and disgust at the distractions with which they were continually agitated, and at the rapid succession of revolutions by which they were kept in a state of perpetual vi-
bration between the extremes of tyranny and anarchy." The last thing we
should do is adopt Florence—or for that matter, ancient Athens—as our
model, given the "tyranny and anarchy" that inevitably lie down that unfortunate road.

Instead, we should accept the good news brought by the new political science: There "are means, and powerful means, by which the excellences of republican government may be retained and its imperfections lessened or avoided." Contrary to Montesquieu and his adherents, these means include "the ENLARGEMENT of the ORBIT within which such systems are to revolve, either in respect to the dimensions of a single State or to the consolidation of several smaller States into one great Confederacy." Publius will develop this argument most famously in *Federalist* 10, but here he clears the ground by calling for the reversal of our accustomed linkage between smallness and the attainment of a "Republican Form of Government."

We will have several occasions to sketch out the continued relevance of Publius's optimism on this point, as well as the problems it raises. What is crucial for now is his faith placed in "the science of politics." He was writing well before the creation of the modern university system and its division into sometimes rigidly separate disciplines. Today's universities, of course, divide the social sciences into disciplinary specialties, including a department of political science. Most such departments share the view that knowledge about how best to design government is cumulative and thus progressive. Publius confidently (and probably correctly) thought that his generation knew more than the greatest thinkers of antiquity, not least because, as Isaac Newton wrote in a 1676 letter to Robert Hooke, "If I have seen further it is by standing on ye sholders of Giants." One need not denigrate past giants in order to proclaim that even without similar powers, we can see further than they did precisely because we have the advantage of coming later. And, of course, it often happens that a later giant wins undying fame by demonstrating the errors of an earlier one. So it is, Publius suggests, with Montesquieu, the political theorist most often cited in *The Federalist*. Intellectual giant though Montesquieu may be, Publius confidently asserts, he was simply wrong in insisting that small is better if one is trying to attain and maintain a republican form of government. To be sure, Publius also suggests that Montesquieu might actually agree with the new wisdom, but at the end of the day (or the essay), the accuracy of his reinterpretation of the French philosopher is quite beside the point. He is rejecting what philosophers sometimes call the "argument from authority" in favor of what we can ascertain from our own experiences.

It is surely possible that political scientists claim too much for their own "science." But what about "science" more generally? American politics in the twenty-first century have become characterized by often-savage debate about the merits of scientific thinking itself. Sometimes this debate is phrased as "religion" versus "science." Sometimes, more moderately, it takes the form of skepticism about a specific finding claiming the mantle of "science." Some critics of what is sometimes denigrated as "scientism" have adopted a leaf from postmodernist theorists, who emphasize that *all* claims about the world are constructed stories and none can establish a truly verifiable connection with the world "as it really is." Thus, these critics claim, scientism itself has attributes of religious faith, including its submission to the authority of ostensibly great scientists or to the consensus of a particular scientific discipline, as with, for example, the presence of a significant, perhaps even potentially catastrophic, threat of climate change caused, at least in part, by activities of humans. How is reliance on such a consensus different, critics ask, from relying on the teachings of great theologians or the magisterium of the Roman Catholic Church about such basic questions as when human life begins? (Perhaps needless to say, most critics of science-based consensus would scarcely offer as the basis of an invidious comparison the Catholic Church or theologians in general.)

Publius obviously lived in a different intellectual milieu from our own. Yet his invocation of the authority of the "new and improved" political science also makes him recognizably one of us—or at least similar to many of us likely to be reading this book. As a political scientist (as well as lawyer) myself, I scarcely want to deny the value of such systematic inquiry. Evidence-based reasoning seems distinctly preferable to reliance on intuition, conventional wisdom, or religious beliefs. I substantially agree with Oliver Wendell Holmes Jr. that law should be based far more on "experience," including empirical argument, than on arid "logic" seemingly above mundane evidence. Still, one important lesson of history is the repeated decline and fall of theories that once seemed unassailable. There is no doctrine of "scientific infallibility," and it is well to remember, as Oliver Cromwell insisted, that "we may be mistaken" even in our most confident judgments.[1] Still, we must do the best we can with the intellectual insights we have, given that the alternative is intellectual paralysis. Nothing would be less "Publian" than throwing up one's hands and accepting the status quo because of the possibility that future experience will invalidate one's presuppositions.

## Can Moral or Religious Education Overcome Natural Tendencies toward Faction?

THERE CAN BE LITTLE doubt that *Federalist* 10 is the best-known of the eighty-five essays, and it has certainly received the most attention. It is famous for its discussion of "faction," that is, the propensity of people to organize around their own selfish interests, and thus to subordinate the proper concern for the "public good" that Publius sees as necessary for a properly operating "Republican Form of Government." But the essay is notable as well for its insistence that there is no genuine remedy for faction, inasmuch as selfishness is hardwired into our psychology. The best one can hope for is to figure out ways, through adept institutional design, to limit its effects. I discuss what might be called the "Publian anxiety" at length in my book *Framed,* and it would be pointless to repeat the analysis here.

Instead, I want to focus on a single sentence, part of Publius's general discussion of the impossibility of eliminating the factious disposition, particularly if we treasure liberty: "If the impulse and the opportunity [to engage in factious conduct] be suffered to coincide, we well know that neither moral nor religious motives can be relied on as an adequate control." Few statements could pose a greater challenge to what many Americans would like to believe. Going back to Parson Weems's biography of George Washington (the source of the story about young George and the cherry tree, which purportedly revealed his inability to tell a lie), we Americans like to believe we can discern in our would-be leaders the moral dispositions that will enable them to resist the temptation to collaborate with factions opposed to the public interest. And many Americans, of course, believe that "religious motives" are especially trustworthy barriers against political sin. Millions of Americans—perhaps even the majority—would be appalled if the next president broke with the custom of adding "So help me God" at the end of the presidential oath, and instead simply asked his or her fellow citizens to rely on a personal promise to comply with the duties set out in the Constitution. This perspective helps to explain why 43 percent of respondents to a June 2012 Gallup Poll said they would not vote for an atheist for president—a higher percentage than those who said they would not vote for a Muslim.

But Publius casts cold water—what Justice Holmes in another context termed "cynical acid"[1]—on the wisdom of relying on "moral or religious motives" to prevent people from lining their own pockets. In the political context, we might fear the most abject corruption, such as literally stealing from the public treasury. But far more likely, and debilitating to a republican form of government, is a willingness to subordinate one's concern for the public interest to advantaging one's political party and the electoral constituency—or "base"—it relies on.

Publius actually emphasizes religion when outlining the various "interests" that threaten the attainment of a politics of the "common good." "A zeal for different opinions concerning religion" can become the basis of a political party that seeks to use the coercive force of government, whether through taxation or outright oppression, against those deemed to hold the wrong religious views. To be sure—and this is an obvious problem with trying to define the common good—some no doubt believe that it *would* serve the common good if everyone shared their own sense of "true religion." The overly zealous Puritans who exiled Roger Williams to Rhode Island or who hanged four Quakers for repeatedly challenging Christian orthodoxy clearly believed this. And the supporters of a modest tax in Virginia to pay religious ministers—the object of Madison's great 1784 "Remonstrance on Religious Liberty" in opposition—clearly believed the state would benefit from the added teaching of religious principles that public funds would support. Indeed, George Washington, who rarely attended religious services or overtly invoked Christianity, nonetheless told the country in his Farewell Address:

> Of all the dispositions and habits, which lead to political prosperity, Religion and Morality are indispensable supports. . . . Let it simply be asked, Where is the security for property, for reputation, for life, if the sense of religious obligation desert the oaths, which are the instruments of investigation in Courts of Justice? And let us with caution indulge the supposition, that morality can be maintained without religion. Whatever may be conceded to the influence of refined

education on minds of peculiar structure, reason and experience both
forbid us to expect, that national morality can prevail in exclusion of
religious principle. . . .[2]

One could support Williams or attack public funding of religion by
invoking certain principles of "toleration" or "liberty." Far more subversive
is the suggestion that religious "zealotry," besides being a threat to the "domestic tranquility" announced in the Constitution's Preamble as one of the
great purposes of government, would also prove ineffective at staving off
factious misconduct, the "latent causes" of which are "sown in the nature
of man." And, after all, even patriotism, the presumably public-spirited
loyalty to one's country, can be perceived as a kind of faction from a more
universal perspective. Valorization of one's own country can easily lead to
the denigration of those who are not members of that community and the
consequent dismissal of their own interests.

Consider in this context Mark Osiel's brilliant and disturbing analysis
of torturers in Argentina during the "dirty war" of the late 1970s.[3] Many
individuals who knew that torture was wrong were nonetheless persuaded
to engage in it by military and political leaders who said it was necessary
to protect the state, with added support from Roman Catholic priests who
defined the dirty war as a "holy war" against terrorism. One might write
a similar book on the "war on terror" that followed September 11, which
featured not only the torture of detainees but—as importantly with regard
to Publius's theme—justifications by political leaders at the highest level,
supported by highly educated lawyers. David Halberstam's classic book on
America's misadventure in Vietnam was tellingly titled *The Best and the
Brightest*. The finest education is no guarantee of sound judgment.

Publius offers little cause for optimism about limiting the ravages of
faction, inasmuch as they follow from basic human social psychology. He
has good reason to be anxious. But we are, of course, not in identical positions inasmuch as we have the presumptive advantage of nearly 230 years
of additional experience. Is it chimerical to believe that the United States
Constitution, even buttressed by "moral" or "religious" education, can
provide adequate protection against our "latent" natures and the propensity to self-preference over the common good? It is, alas, all too possible,
looking back at the course of American history, to think that skepticism is
warranted, even if one believes the Constitution provides some marginal
protection.

## FEDERALIST 11

### *It's a Harsh and Competitive World Out There*

Iɴ *FEDERALIST* 11, Publius returns to the dangers facing the thirteen states from abroad and the utility of union in confronting those dangers. This essay focuses on commercial competition and the desire of rapacious European countries to exploit their advantages over the weak American states. Along the way, Publius notes the advantages for *internal commerce* among the states from the national free-trade zone created by the new Constitution. This contrasts with the Articles of Confederation, which allowed a variety of impediments to the free movement of goods. But the principal theme is international competition. How, for example, can the new country protect itself from being exploited by stronger nations with more substantial fleets?

One way is through "prohibitory regulations" that will "oblige foreign countries to bid against each other, for the privileges of our markets." Access to these markets is a precious good, and foreign countries should not believe it will come without a price. But such regulations, which by definition impose costs on foreign countries and their commercial interests, are scarcely self-enforcing. They must be supported by physical resources that make their enforcement plausible, and this means building a strong navy. Such a "powerful marine" will have two main purposes. The first is to provide ships to move American goods around the world and, presumably, bring goods back to the United States on American "bottoms." The second is to build ships that can, if need be, defend American shipping interests, particularly in the West Indies, from interference by British, French, and Spanish ships.

The United States cannot afford to remain what Publius terms an "insignificant" state—as measured, among other ways, by maritime resources. This condition would leave it "a prey to the wanton intermeddlings of all nations at war with each other; who, having nothing to fear from us, would with little scruple or remorse, supply their wants by depredations on our property as often as it fell in their way. The rights of neutrality will only be respected when they are defended by an adequate power. A nation, despicable by its weakness, forfeits even the privilege of being neutral."

Once again, Publius shows a strong streak of what will later be labeled by theorists of international relations as a "realist" view of the international system, where competition among separate states compels any country that wishes to avoid being exploited—or conquered—to build its military capacities. Without such capacities, countries are inevitably vulnerable. With them, as Publius almost exuberantly concludes, one can overcome the "arrogant pretensions of the Europeans. . . . Let Americans disdain to be the instruments of European greatness! Let the thirteen States, bound together in a strict and indissoluble Union, concur in erecting one great American system, superior to the control of all transatlantic force or influence, and able to dictate the terms of the connection between the old and the new world!" There is, of course, ambiguity in this last sentence. Is the point to overcome the ability of *any* country to "dictate the terms" of commerce, or is it to ensure that it is the United States that does the dictating? Consider that Commodore Perry's famous aggressive encounter with Japan, by which that country was forced to open itself up to American traders, occurred only sixty-five years later.

Who might read *Federalist* 11 with special interest today? Might it not be a country like China, for generations the victim of foreign exploitation backed by other powers' "powerful marines"? No doubt Chinese leaders viewed these countries, including the United States, as engaging in "wanton intermeddlings," sometimes as the consequence of their wars with one another, sometimes in concert, but always with disdain for China's own interests in development and autonomy. China during that era might well have been described as "despicable in its weakness."

Obviously, that day has passed, and now one can read sobering analyses of China's growing naval capacities and the techniques by which it limits access to its domestic markets by foreign countries eager to reach its one billion potential customers. The American Bar Association, as noted in the introduction, often suggests that foreigners read *The Federalist* in order to be inspired to create institutions that will guarantee liberty and support the rule of law. But the various essays within *The Federalist* contain decidedly mixed messages. Whatever Publius's general commitments to such values may have been, it is hard for us as modern readers to blind ourselves to the hard-headed realism that counsels not only political union but also the building up of a navy that will enable the country to defend itself and flourish in a basically heartless system of commercial competition. Perhaps Publius speaks to twenty-first-century Americans, but he may speak as well, and even more powerfully, to foreign readers as to what *they* must do within this system to protect themselves against the United States and its commercial allies.

## FEDERALIST 12

### *Commerce and State Finance*

PUBLIUS SOUNDS very twenty-first century when he writes, very near the beginning of *Federalist* 12, "The prosperity of commerce is now perceived and acknowledged by all enlightened statesmen to be the most useful as well as the most productive source of national wealth." The last phrase has a double meaning: He is referring not only to the aggregate wealth of members of the community, who will presumably thrive from their participation in what would come to be called "commercial society," but also to the effect of a thriving commercial sector on the government's ability to finance itself.

The first meaning is captured by Publius's emphasis on "[t]he assiduous merchant, the laborious husbandman, the active mechanic, and the industrious manufacturer," all of whom "look forward with eager expectation and growing alacrity to [the] pleasing reward" of increasing prosperity that will accompany "their toils." The second, though, is close behind, inasmuch as Publius also emphasizes that "Commerce . . . must of necessity render the payment of taxes easier, and facilitate the requisite supplies to the treasury." A prosperous commercial society was, for Publius, a win-win situation, providing benefits to its citizens as well as necessary funds to the government that must ultimately exercise stewardship over the society. As he reminds us toward the end of the essay, "A nation cannot long exist without revenues. . . . [They] must be had at all events."

Publius knows his America very well. He recognizes people's reluctance to pay taxes. This is illustrated in our own time by Grover Norquist's remarkable success in getting almost all Republican congressmen and senators to sign a pledge that they will oppose any and all increases in federal taxes. A modern pundit might consider Publius prophetic for his comment that "it is evident from the state of the country, from the habits of the people, from the experience we have had on the point itself, that it is impracticable to raise any very considerable sums by direct taxation." To be sure, the national government today does raise immense sums of money through direct taxation, including, most importantly, the federal income tax. But government almost always needs more money than at least some citizens and their elected representatives think it does, and anyone concerned with public finance, as Publius most definitely was, must constantly search for ways of adding to the public fisc that will generate minimal opposition.

The answer, for both Publius and the national government for the next century, was to gain revenue "indirectly," particularly through customs duties placed on imports. To be sure, such duties were ultimately passed along to consumers in the form of higher prices, but the all-important collection of revenues to finance government would already have taken place. A side benefit of such duties, of course, was the "protection" offered nascent local producers and industries against unfettered competition from abroad. Any contemporary country tempted to adopt Publian policies with regard to its own imports would be met by strong American opposition, given that it is generally thought to be in our interest to maximize "free trade" and the concomitant ability to ship our own goods abroad.

Given the importance of customs duties in 1787 for sustaining the government, Publius returns to his central theme, the necessity of union. The reason is simple: A union will provide a free-trade, customs-free economy for those within it, even as it finances itself by collecting duties from outsiders. But failure to create a union would mean, among other things, that the constituent states could never hope to raise sufficient taxes through import duties, because smuggling between the disunited states would be too easy. "The relative situation of these States; the number of rivers with which they are intersected, and of bays that wash their shores; the facility of communication in every direction; the affinity of language and manners; the familiar habits of intercourse;—all these are circumstances that would conspire to render an illicit trade between them a matter of little difficulty, and would insure frequent evasions of the commercial regulations of each other." Under the Articles of Confederation, some states did try to impose tariffs on commerce from other states; but Publius suggests these states were kidding themselves if they genuinely believed that they could effectively regulate interstate trade. There would be too many incentives and opportunities to evade such laws.

How much happier would be the financial future of a union "[i]f . . . there be but one government pervading all the States, there will be, as to the principal part of our commerce, but ONE SIDE to guard—the ATLANTIC COAST." Ships coming from abroad "would rarely choose to hazard themselves to the complicated and critical perils which would attend attempts to unlade prior to their coming into port," and, of course, there are a limited number of primary ports—Boston, Newport, New York, Philadelphia, Baltimore, and Charleston—each of which could easily monitor arrivals and collect the appropriate duties. "A few armed vessels," Publius notes, "judiciously stationed at the entrances of our ports, might at a small expense be made useful sentinels of the laws." This part of the United States Navy would easily pay for itself by deterring efforts to evade customs duties.

Publius concludes his essay by noting that "the necessities of the State . . . must be satisfied in some mode or other." Yet even Publius, who certainly advocated to a stronger notion of the state than, say, Thomas Jefferson, would have been astounded by what most of us today view as "necessities of the State." Indeed, our most fundamental political disputes are often about the proper size and domain of the national government and the amount of money required to finance such a government. We are well beyond a time when we can simply look to imposts on foreign commerce to finance the national government. The value of *Federalist* 12 in the twenty-first century is as a reminder that, as economists are fond of saying, there is no free lunch. The goods—and even the bads—of government must be paid for. This requires tax revenue, not to mention the endless bickering and strife connected with deciding who should pay how much and when. Publius fully recognized that many people would rather evade taxes than pay them, and that any wise government must confront this reality.

Given the remarkable sweep of services we now demand from a national government, it is not surprising that taxes remain a volatile issue. Moreover, as the United States has become far more inclusive in its politics, it is also the case that governmental spending often has redistributive implications. Haves are asked to finance the needs of have-nots, and the politics of redistribution in America, as many historians have noted, is inextricably connected with the politics of race, as well.[1]

The last presidential candidate to campaign on a forthright promise to raise taxes was Walter Mondale, who carried his home state of Minnesota and the District of Columbia against Ronald Reagan in 1984 and lost everywhere else. In 2012, Barack Obama pledged to raise the taxes of "the top 1 percent" of the American public, which meant, by definition, that the remaining 99 percent would not have to pay more for what they received from the national government. Publius was happily able to envision collecting "enough" revenue through a method that the citizenry would find almost painless. No doubt contemporary secretaries of the treasury (or presidents) envy him for that.

## FEDERALIST 13

## *Economies of Scale*

*F*EDERALIST 13 is remarkably short, only 959 words. It continues the basic theme of the prior essays, the advantages of union and the costs of either adhering to the Articles of Confederation or, more likely, breaking up into two or three separate countries. Publius spends much of this essay's four paragraphs arguing that two countries (New England, New York, New Jersey, and probably Pennsylvania in one, and all the states south of Pennsylvania in the other) are far more likely than the three that were often suggested (in which the mid-Atlantic states would form a separate union).

This is of little contemporary interest. More relevant for the twenty-first-century reader, however, is Publius's emphasis on what might be termed economies of political scale. The previous essay argued that a single union would find it easier to raise revenues. Here he says that there are economies attached to being part of a single union. The most obvious example is the military. He has already noted that a disunited group of states would require far more ships and crews in order "to guard the inland communication between the different confederacies against illicit trade." If, in addition, "we also take into view the military establishments which it has been shown would unavoidably result from the jealousies and conflicts of the several nations into which the States would be divided," it is obviously far more economical to avoid this duplication of expenses, and the easiest path is union under the new Constitution. Those who would reject it on the grounds that it would be expensive to build a new national capital or pay for national officials are simply bad accountants. Bigness is in many ways less costly. Far better, for example, to have to hire one ambassador to a given country rather than two, three, or thirteen.

We have already seen Publius's enthusiasm for "the extended republic." He expresses not a scintilla of regard for smaller (and thus more local) governments and societies. They are breeding grounds for factions; they are also drains on the public fisc, requiring needless duplications of effort, whose financial costs could far more profitably be spent elsewhere. Publius argues eloquently why a single national government trumps two or three separate ones on a variety of measures. But do these arguments apply when that ostensibly single government finds itself enmeshed in a web of international commitments?

The great narrative of American history, for better and for worse, is expansion, ultimately into the mid-Pacific and the Caribbean. Those who spoke of "manifest destiny" clearly believed the United States could not be cabined into its original territory, even as doubled by Jefferson's Louisiana Purchase in 1803. Few argue today for the return of unabashed American imperialism. Ironically, those who describe as needless many expenditures attached to national standing armies are likely to oppose what they regard as an overemphasis on maintaining "sovereignty." Such critics surely are not proud that the United States today spends more on its military than do all other significant countries combined.

Others, however, note that as a percentage of gross domestic product, the military budget of the United States, approximately 4 percent of GDP, ranks eighth overall, well below such countries as Myanmar (26 percent), Jordan (10 percent), and Georgia (8.5 percent).[1] And China has a half million more active members of its armed forces than does the United States. In any event, one might well see these worldwide expenditures as a telling indictment of humanity's ability to waste precious resources and believe also that the move toward ever-larger political units would liberate us to spend those resources far more productively. After World War II there was much interest, at least in some circles, in "world government," no doubt sparked by the founding of the United Nations and by what we would today regard as utopian hopes for that institution. Today almost no one is heard speaking in favor of any such project.

Publius does an excellent job of explaining why the American government must become bigger, in every way, than it was under the Articles of

Confederation. But we are entitled to ask what the upper limit of that big-ness is and how we will know when it has been reached.

## FEDERALIST 14

### *Publius and Permanent Revolution (or, at Least, Improvement)*

FEDERALIST 14 is another much discussed essay. Its principal aim is to refute Montesquieu and other political philosophers who argued that a "Republican Form of Government" required a relatively small ter-ritory and homogeneous population (recall *Federalist* 2). Publius auda-ciously argues that Montesquieu and his devotees got it exactly backward: Small territories (such as the American states) and homogeneous popula-tions were far more likely to generate tyranny of the majority, defined as a popular faction's ability to exercise its power in its own interest at the cost of oppressing minorities. An extended republic offered far more protec-tion, by making it considerably more difficult—ideally, impossible—for a local faction to gain national power. As noted in the last essay, the most interesting question generated by the support for an "extended republic" is whether there are limits on the extension.

I want to focus on *Federalist* 14's final paragraph, not only because of its inherent interest but also because I personally find it to be the most truly inspiring passage in all of the eighty-five essays. Publius begins his conclusion by calling for the rejection of "the unnatural voice" that "petu-lantly tells you that the form of government recommended for your adop-tion is a novelty in the political world . . . ; that it rashly attempts what it is impossible to accomplish." This is no good reason to reject the vision of an extended republic that underlies the Constitution. Publius describes "the glory of the people of America, that, whilst they have paid a decent regard to the opinions of former times and other nations, they have not suffered a blind veneration for antiquity, for custom, or for names, to overrule the suggestions of their own good sense, the knowledge of their own situation, and the lessons of their own experience[.]" He invokes the American Revolution itself as exemplifying the "precedent" for innova-tive action. Without the visionary leadership of the revolutionaries, "the people of the United States might, at this moment" be "laboring under the weight of some of those forms which have crushed the liberties of the rest of mankind." That did not happen, because American patriots "pursued a new and more noble course. They accomplished a revolution which has no parallel in the annals of human society. . . . They formed the design of a great Confederacy, which it is incumbent on their successors to improve and perpetuate." One might describe Publius as one of the great "idea entrepreneurs" of all time, encouraging his readers, in modern parlance, to "think outside the box" and to reject the conventional wisdom that linked preservation of republican government to small territories alone.

This certainly echoes Publius's call, in the very first *Federalist*, to engage in "reflection and choice" about the kind of government America will need in order to attain the great goals set out in the Preamble to the Constitution. Now he calls for his readers to reject "a blind veneration for antiquity, for custom, or for names," the latter, presumably, a reference to the so-called genetic fallacy by which the validity of an argument is thought to rest on the prestige of the persons invoked in its favor. Instead, his readers should always judge arguments by the evidence that can be adduced to support them.

If the Publius of *Federalist* 10 reveals his anxieties about faction and tyranny, in *Federalist* 14 he seems to speak instead with what Ralph Waldo Emerson would later memorialize as the spirit of "self-reliance" based on thinking for ourselves and rejecting all modes of conventional wisdom that cannot pass the test of our "own good sense" and the "lessons of [our] own experience." One can, of course, find many such assertions in those we consider our greatest leaders. Consider only Abraham Lincoln in his annual message to Congress in 1862: "The dogmas of the quiet past, are inadequate to the stormy present. The occasion is piled high with difficulty, and we must rise—with the occasion. As our case is new, so we must think anew, and act anew. We must disenthrall ourselves, and then we shall save our country." We might refer to this as one of Lincoln's many "Publian moments," measured by his willingness to offer his own distinctive "reflection and choice" as to what the United States needed at present rather than pronounce himself simply the faithful devotee of the "dogmas of the past."

What would be the consequences if we taught the conclusion of *Federalist* 14 (and Lincoln) to the young as representing what it means to be an American committed to the enterprise of "self-government"? And what would it mean to reject their inspirational quality? Do we really want our children—and the adults they will turn into—to believe that they must submit to decisions made in the past, however admirable those making the decisions might have been in many ways? Does something about contemporary American society—and others across the world?—make it ill-advised, or worse, to advocate today the almost exuberant spirit of intellectual independence that Publius expressed?

Part of having learned the "lessons of . . . experience" involves being able to determine when prior decisions need to be revisited, in order to escape the costs of path dependence and adherence to traditional ways of doing things even when the potential consequences appear dire. Even the most devoted admirer of the 1787 Constitution presumably agrees that it was desirable not only to abolish slavery via the Thirteenth Amendment but also, in the previous Twelfth Amendment of 1803, to correct the glitch in the Electoral College that brought the country to the brink of civil war because of the tie vote between ostensible running mates Thomas Jefferson and Aaron Burr. (The new amendment allowed the electors to specify their choices for president and vice president, unlike the original plan, in which they picked their top two choices for the presidency.) It would be astonishing if the United States Constitution had become so perfect as to need no new corrective amendments.

So we must ask ourselves if it was *only* Publius's generation that had a duty to improve the institutions of American governance in order to perpetuate its central goals, as set out in the Preamble. If this seems to be a dubious proposition, then we must be willing to honor their example not by mindless adherence to their own decisions of 1787, but by standing in their shoes (or on their shoulders) and asking what improvements are necessary in our own time.

# PART 3

*Why "Confederation" Is Both
"Odious" and an "Imbecility"*

# FEDERALIST 15

## "The Imbecility of Our Government"

Until now Publius has primarily been endorsing the benefits of union, trying to fend off those who would risk the disintegration of the existing United States into two or three separate countries. Some opponents of the Constitution certainly agreed that disintegration would be unfortunate, but they believed the Articles of Confederation were adequate both to preserve union and to safeguard the presumptively vibrant state governments whose sovereignty was protected by the Articles themselves. In *Federalist* 15, Publius directly attacks this premise. His rhetoric shows no holding back, no concession that it might be a close case whether to abandon the Articles only six years after their 1781 ratification in favor of the audacious Constitution drafted in Philadelphia. For Publius there is only one reasonable answer: Junk the Confederation and accept the new Constitution.

"We may indeed with propriety," Publius proclaims, "be said to have reached almost the last stage of national humiliation. There is scarcely anything that can wound the pride or degrade the character of an independent nation which we do not experience." His list of examples ranges from the uncertain ability to repay the debts owed "to foreigners and to our own citizens contracted in a time of imminent peril for the preservation of our political existence" to Great Britain's failure to honor the terms of the Treaty of Paris relating to the surrender of important forts, which "are still retained, to the prejudice of our interests, not less than of our rights." But it is futile to think of truly resisting the British noncompliance when "[w]e have neither troops, nor treasury, nor government." Similarly, the new country is in no position to remonstrate against Spain's refusal to allow "a free participation in the navigation of the Mississippi." However important commerce may be "to national wealth," it has reached its "lowest point of declension" because of the de facto trade wars among the ostensible members of the Confederation. There is more. His bill of particulars portrays "national disorder, poverty, and insignificance . . . , the dark catalogue of our public misfortunes." Because of the "imbecility of

57

our government," America's ambassadors, who at the time included John Adams in London and Thomas Jefferson in Paris, are what he terms "mere pageants of mimic sovereignty."

Astonishingly, though, some people were still defending the Articles and criticizing the necessity of adopting the new Constitution. "This renders a full display of the principal defects of the Confederation necessary, in order to show that the evils we experience do not proceed from minute or partial imperfections, but from fundamental errors in the structure of the building, which cannot be amended otherwise than by an alteration in the first principles and main pillars of the fabric." We cannot hope to rectify our desperate situation simply by doing some incremental remodeling and rehab. Instead, Publius the architect is telling us in effect, "Tear it down and start over. Fortunately, I have the blueprints for the new national household in my hand."

Given the call in the twenty-first century in some quarters for a national government that, after being deprived of tax revenues, can then be drowned in a bathtub, it is tempting to revisit the arguments Publius offers for an empowered national government that could, crucially, *directly* regulate (and tax) its residents instead of pathetically pleading with the states to do so. He calls upon "that best oracle of wisdom, experience" to support a genuine "national government, or, which is the same thing, of a superintending power, under the direction of a common council." Publius directs withering scorn at any expectation that states will subordinate their own self-interest, which is in effect just another "faction" inimical to the general good, to that of the common union. "Each State, yielding to the persuasive voice of immediate interest or convenience, has successively withdrawn its support, till the frail and tottering edifice seems ready to fall upon our heads, and to crush us beneath its ruins." It is ironic indeed that contemporary supporters of states' "rights" or "sovereignty" against a strong national government attempt to wrap themselves in Publius's mantle. It surely provides them little warmth.

One need not be a latter-day anti-federalist to believe that our modern national government is not living up to the promises in the Preamble. Pundits and editorialists across the political spectrum regularly describe American politics as "dysfunctional" or even "pathological." Two distinguished political scientists, Thomas Mann and Norman Ornstein, who had earlier written a critique of Congress entitled *The Broken Branch,* chose to call their most recent book, published in 2012, *It's Even Worse Than It Looks*. It has become a cliché of presidential campaigns that the nonincumbent criticizes our "broken system" and promises to reform it.

What is missing from most such analyses is what Publius does in *Federalist* 15, which is to connect his political critique to the inadequacies of the Articles of Confederation. But connecting dots, however important and necessary, does not complete the task. One must also convey the lessons taught, and that requires explicit choices as to the rhetoric one uses and the evidence one submits. Does one always use the most temperate language, paying full heed to what one's opponents might say? Or, instead, does one engage those opponents in a savage game of thrust and parry? Ecclesiastes might remind us, quite rightly, that there is a time for temperance. But there are also times when temperance must be forgone if one is truly and rightly worried that the inertial force behind any status quo— even one, as with the Articles of Confederation, ratified by the last of the original thirteen states only six years before—will make change difficult. The line between public education and demagogy is often quite thin, and, no doubt, Publius's opponents in 1787 might well have viewed his language as having crossed that line. Do we?

We will see later, when considering *Federalist* 40, that more than inertial force made changing the Articles difficult; amending them required unanimous approval of all state legislatures. Adherence to this rule would have doomed the enterprise of necessary change, and it was simply ignored. But even if the Articles had been easier to amend, it would still be necessary to overcome whatever sentimental attachment there might be to America's first constitution. Dismissing the government it created as an "imbecility" surely helped undermine that attachment.

The United States Constitution, of course, has far more inertial force behind it. It is often described as the central document of America's "civil religion," with some of the same sacred qualities that attach to the Bible, Torah, or Koran. It also, of course, benefits from association with such giants as Madison and George Washington, whose role as president of the Philadelphia Convention was almost as important, at least symbolically, as his service as the first president under the new Constitution. There had, in fact, been eight "presidents" of the Congress established under the Articles of Confederation, but most are unknown save to specialists in American history. One of those whose name is likely to be recognized,

John Hancock, never actually made it down to New York, where Congress met, following his selection in 1786 (succeeding Richard Henry Lee, the other nonobscure president).

But what if one believes that the various discontents and dysfunctionalities that plague contemporary American politics are linked to the Constitution (even as amended by the so-called Reconstruction Amendments in the aftermath of the Civil War)? To what extent should one tug at the sleeve of recalcitrant listeners and insist, perhaps even loudly, that they should at least consider the possibility that the Constitution they have been taught to revere is itself an "imbecility" in important aspects and in need of a full-scale checkup and diagnosis, with the possibility that fairly radical surgery may be required?

FEDERALIST 16

## Why Confederation Is "Odious" and a National Government Is Necessary

CONSIDER THAT THE United States was, at the time Publius was writing the essays that became *The Federalist*, operating under the Articles of *Confederation*. By the eighteenth century, "confederation" was a notion well known to political theorists and practicing politicians. Its first great proponent among political theorists was the German philosopher Samuel von Pufendorf, who grappled with one of the central questions of both theory and practice: Why would an existing, presumptively autonomous, state wish to limit its autonomy by entering into a political union with another such state? The answer, not surprisingly, is that the international system may threaten the autonomy particularly of small states; the whales (or sharks) can do all right by themselves. We have, of course, already seen a form of this argument in Publius's earlier comments about the importance of union.

But there are many forms of union, and "confederation," a system in which only a small handful of functions are assigned to a higher political authority, is surely one of them. The most obvious of these functions is defense. One might think of the North Atlantic Treaty Organization, an "entangling alliance" by which the United States has pledged to come to the defense of any of its partners should they be attacked; or, perhaps more to the point, the United Nations. President Truman used the UN to justify his unilateral decision to order American troops to defend South Korea upon an invasion from North Korea in June 1950. The United States, he argued, was committed to obeying the request by the General Assembly to protect South Korea from aggression outlawed by the new United Nations Charter.

Whatever one thinks of this argument, or of the United Nations or NATO generally, no one believes that these organizations' jurisdictions extend into the full range of political issues, or that either has any authority over the behavior of individuals within their member nations. Their writ extends only to the *governments* that comprise the larger confederations. The United Nations can levy dues, for example, and for many years the United States was notoriously deficient in meeting this obligation. No one suggested that the United Nations could respond by levying taxes against American citizens.

The importance of *Federalist* 16 is to criticize—indeed, sharply to condemn—as unacceptable the reliance on such a limited conception of "confederation" to save the United States from a dire fate. Publius regards "confederation" as "the parent of anarchy." History, he argues, teaches that "delinquencies in the members" of a confederacy "are its natural and necessary offspring; and that whenever they happen, the only constitutional remedy is force, and the immediate effect of the use of it, civil war." In case we have not yet gotten the point, he calls confederation an "odious . . . engine of government." We have already seen his earlier arguments about the duplication of expenses for armed forces should the United States not move toward fuller unity. Here, more than ever, he suggests that "civil war" is an almost certain outcome, even within a confederation formed to prevent the likelihood of warfare among completely independent entities.

Even if war is not the outcome, it is certainly likely that the constituent states will refuse to cooperate with requests from the national government that they consider onerous. (The government, of course, will not describe them as "requests," but with no means of enforcement, that is all they are.) Small states can perhaps be coerced, but this is a chimerical hope with regard to larger states, or even small states that are willing to band together in their recalcitrance. Publius's vision of the national government's life under "confederation" is either frequent use of military force or a descent into impotence.

Thus the key paragraph:

> . . . [I]f it be possible at any rate to construct a federal government
> capable of regulating the common concerns and preserving the gen-
> eral tranquility, . . . [i]t must carry its agency to the persons of the
> citizens. It must stand in need of no intermediate legislations [from
> the states]. . . . The government of the Union, like that of each State,
> must be able to address itself immediately to the hopes and fears of
> individuals; and to attract to its support those passions which have
> the strongest influence upon the human heart. It must, in short, pos-
> sess all the means, and have a right to resort to all the methods, of
> executing the powers with which it is intrusted, that are possessed
> and exercised by the government of the particular States.

Not only can the new national government pass laws directly affecting each and every person residing in the United States; equally important, the states cannot interfere with the enforcement of these laws. To
put it in a slightly different way, any attempted interference would be the
equivalent of "an open and violent exertion of an unconstitutional power"
equivalent to revolution. The reference to "unconstitutional" action by a
state elicits Publius's one reference to judicial authority before his consideration of the judiciary, which begins only near the very end of the series,
at *Federalist* 78. It is significant that the judiciary is mentioned as a means
of disciplining *states* that might be tempted to renege on the constitutional bargain. That is, "[t]he success" of a particular bit of state resistance
"would require not merely a factious majority in the legislature, but the
concurrence of the courts of justice. . . . If the judges were not embarked in
a conspiracy with the legislature they would pronounce the resolutions of
such a [legislative] majority to be contrary to the supreme law of the land,
*unconstitutional and void*" (emphasis added).

Anyone familiar with American politics during the American Revolution certainly realized that such "exertions" could sometimes succeed,
rendering irrelevant the claims from British lawyers and judges that the
American patriots were behaving "unconstitutionally" in failing to submit to British authority. Publius thus concludes his essay by referring "to
those mortal feuds which, in certain conjunctures, spread a conflagration
through a whole nation" and suggests that "they do not fall within any ordinary rules of calculation. When they happen, they commonly amount to
revolutions and dismemberments of empire. No form of government can
always either avoid or control them. It is in vain to hope to guard against

events too mighty for human foresight or precaution, and it would be idle to object to a government because it could not perform impossibilities."

There is nothing merely academic about Publius's rejection of confederation in favor of a truly empowered national government that can reach ordinary individuals through legislation and subsequent enforcement. After all, one of the great dramas of American politics between 2010 and 2012 involved the reaction in some states to the "mandate" established by the Affordable Care Act ("Obamacare"), which required almost all residents to purchase or otherwise obtain medical insurance, subject to payment of a penalty if they did not comply. Several states have tried, in effect, to nullify the law by proclaiming their ability to free their citizens of any duty to obey it. Thus Virginia passed a law stating that "No resident of this Commonwealth . . . shall be required to obtain or maintain a policy of individual insurance coverage. No provision of this title shall render a resident of this Commonwealth liable for any penalty, assessment, fee, or fine as a result of his failure to procure or obtain health insurance coverage." Whatever one thinks of the policy behind this statute, Publius was absolutely correct in suggesting that the purported state law would be of no effect whatsoever, assuming that the national government has the power to pass the law in the first place, which the Supreme Court has confirmed. States do indeed have powers of their own regarding the parts of the statute that require state participation in, for example, the Medicaid program or the creation of "exchanges" to provide information about medical insurance possibilities. As Heather Gerken and Jessica Bulman-Pozen have tellingly written, "uncooperative federalism"[1] is an important part of the American political fabric, for good or for ill. But this is altogether different from imposing a liability on ordinary people themselves.

Were we still merely a confederation, the national government would either have no power to regulate the health-care system or, even if it had the notional power, would be unable to reach actual individuals and could, in effect, only hope for voluntary state compliance with those laws reaching state institutions. But partly through Publius's efforts, we moved from being a "confederation" into a brand-new form in which two different levels of government, both nation and state, could pass legislation affecting ordinary individuals and, in case of a conflict between them, the national government would always prevail, save for a genuinely revolutionary situation. As I suggested earlier, Publius helps to explain not only the monumental shift in American governance in 1787–1788, but also similarly monumental shifts that are giving the European Parliament increasing authority to pass similarly "direct" legislation without having to go through the intermediary step of receiving support from the European Union's constituent states. Perhaps one day—though certainly after my lifetime—similar arguments will transform the United Nations into a genuine world government.

FEDERALIST 17

## *The Political Sociology of Federalism (Part I)*

HAVING SHARPLY denounced the Articles of Confederation and called for the creation of a far stronger national government that can regulate and tax the citizenry directly, without requiring the approval of state governments, Publius must now answer the obvious question: Will the national government created by the new Constitution be *too* powerful? His answer, not surprisingly, is no. But his arguments are rooted far more in political sociology than in the parsing of the Constitution's text, which he does not even mention here. The equally obvious question for us in the twenty-first century, particularly within the United States, is whether his assertions, even if arguably true in his time, have real purchase for our own.

Publius begins by addressing the objection that the new Constitution "would tend to render the government of the Union too powerful, and to enable it to absorb those residuary authorities, which it might be judged proper to leave with the States for local purposes." His response does not take the form offered by most constitutional lawyers, which is that the Constitution creates only a limited government of assigned powers, so that one should look carefully, for example, at the delineation of powers set out particularly in Article I, Section 8. Instead, Publius professes himself unable to discover what temptation the persons entrusted with the administration of the general government could ever feel to divest the states of the authorities of that description. "The regulation of the mere domestic police of a state," Publius asserts, "appears to me to hold out slender allurements to ambition."

One might note the rhetorical effect of the word "mere," as if the ordinary work of states is beneath the attention of national politicians. Thus, he continues, "Commerce, finance, negotiation and war seem to comprehend *all* the objects that have charms for minds governed by that passion; and all the powers necessary to those objects ought, in the first instance, to be lodged in the national depository" (emphasis added). Again we might admire the audacity of suggesting that "all" of the objects, taken together, do not in fact cover the entire waterfront. Thus, Publius writes that "[t]he administration of private justice between the citizens of the same state, the supervision of agriculture and similar concerns—all those things, in short, which are properly provided for by local legislation—can never be desirable cares of a general jurisdiction." He thus dismisses as "improbable that there should exist a disposition in the federal councils to usurp the powers with which they are connected; because the attempt to exercise those powers would be as troublesome as it would be nugatory; and the possession of them, for that reason, would contribute nothing to the dignity, the importance, or the splendor of the national government." So, the message to worried critics of the Constitution is, in effect, to lighten up. Given post–New Deal developments, one might wonder if he would offer such complacent advice today!

As we have already seen, Publius takes a decidedly unsentimental view of human nature, and all of his arguments are nested in his understanding of what actually motivates human beings. Why, for example, will individuals who are presumably leaders of their own communities, perhaps even the governors of their states, choose to leave hearth and home, the localities and people they know best, in order to travel to a new national capital by distinctly uncomfortable stagecoach and participate in the national government? Can one count simply on an abstract sense of civic duty? Not really. Instead, Publius alludes to the new national leaders' ambition to play roles on the national (perhaps even international) stage, and ultimately to achieve glory and honor. Men (and Publius, of course, was assuming a completely male-dominated political universe) ultimately wished to be remembered for their achievements as warriors or statesmen, and perhaps be memorialized through great public monuments. Interestingly, he never suggests that men will pursue political power to increase their private wealth.

What will protect states from an overreaching national government is not particular constitutional limitations but the unimportance, from the lofty perspective of the Publian national leader, of what state governments do. What "dignity," either of government or, more to the point, of political officials themselves, attaches to the mundane concerns of state government? Publius in effect insults state governments, describing their handiwork as insignificant, in order to reassure their partisans that they have nothing to worry about from newly empowered national officials. One might wonder why anyone concerned about preserving state autonomy would find this argument reassuring.

"[L]et it be admitted," Publius acknowledges, "for argument's sake, that mere wantonness and lust of domination would be sufficient to beget that disposition" of governmental overreach. What, then, can save states from overreaching national power? The answer is that "the people of the several States," to whom national officials are ultimately accountable, "would control the indulgence of so extravagant an appetite," presumably by throwing the rascals out of office should they attempt to use national power too aggressively. But why would one expect this to happen? The answer, again, lies in social psychology. "It is a known fact in human nature," Publius asserts, "that its affections are commonly weak in proportion to the distance or diffusiveness of the object. Upon the same principle that a man is more attached to his family than to his neighborhood, to his neighborhood than to the community at large, the people of each State would be apt to feel a stronger bias towards their local governments than towards the government of the Union; unless the force of that principle should be destroyed by a much better administration of the latter."

The national government will be both literally and metaphorically a distant entity. National officials might be notables whose names are known to the general populace, but they are far less likely than state officials to be friends and neighbors. Even if people profess an esteem for their national leaders, these distant figures are unlikely to enjoy the same affection as those who are closer and more familiar. So long as state government maintains an "administration" satisfactory to the public, it will possess the political capital to fend off national overreach. But there is obviously what lawyers call a "negative pregnant." That is, what if it is "government of the Union" that turns out to exemplify the "much better administration"? And what if the friends and neighbors in state government, perhaps because one knows them too well, are found unsatisfactory with regard either to competence or, more ominously, their character? (James Madison, for example, when he served in the Virginia House of Delegates in the 1780s, was appalled by the caliber of his associates.) Should that happen, "the people of the several States" will presumably transfer their loyalties to the larger government. And, one might add, it is altogether likely that the leaders of that government might discover that the activities of state government aren't so "mere" after all, and are in fact well worth the national government's attention.

One might say, either happily or with chagrin, that this has in fact been the narrative arc of American politics over the past two centuries. There has been an ever-stronger shift of power to the national government as national officials, motivated by either raw ambition or a dedicated commitment to the national interest, steadily use their constitutional powers to limit state autonomy. These developments are often debated in highly legalistic terms—think only of the recent national debate over the remarkable exertions of national power in the Affordable Care Act, most of which were upheld in a highly controversial 5–4 decision by the Supreme Court. But Publius's major point is that such questions are (and should be) ultimately resolved not by the abstractions of legal (or "constitutional") argument, but instead by the complex decisions of the general public as to the degree to which they genuinely trust public officials.

Even if the arc of American history has been decidedly bending toward greater assertions of national political authority, it has scarcely taken a smooth path. We fought a Civil War that killed more than 2 percent of the national population and have suffered as well many lesser illustrations of the ineluctable tensions between localist and nationalist visions of governmental power. They are scarcely absent today. Following the reelection of President Obama, several hundred thousand Americans signed petitions indicating their desire at least to think of withdrawing from the United States. In a country of 320 million, where, as the "population clock" of the United States Census tells us, a new person is added every fifteen seconds,[1] a few hundred thousand have little sway. But the real question, both in 1787 and now, is whether the proper response to such petitions lies in strictly legal arguments—"what you propose to do is simply illegal, and that's the end of it"—or in trying to demonstrate that the national government is worthy of our loyalty and affection, not least because of the quality of its administration with regard to the issues most of us care about. Surely, such a demonstration, and the concomitant feelings attached to it, is far more important than reliance on what might well be dismissed as arid legalism.

## FEDERALIST 18

### *Ancient History as Caution*

I T IS CERTAINLY TEMPTING to dismiss the modern relevance of *Federalist* 18, which concentrates on the sad history of two "confederacies of antiquity," both Greek. The first was the Amphictyonic Council, the second the Achaean League. Publius, as he often does, exhibits impressive knowledge of ancient history. One doubts that anyone in public life today is competent to assess his analysis of the two confederacies. (Nor were most of his contemporary readers.) What is important, though, is that Publius exhibits no nostalgia for them. His point, as noted by the historian J. R. Pole in his excellent edition of the essays, is that "both to avert the distractions of internal disorder, and for external defense, Americans need an even higher level of unity enforced by a central government." One might regard this as relatively unimportant for contemporary America, which is, after all, governed by the distinctly more powerful national government and Constitution that supplanted the Articles of Confederation. But it is interesting to examine the essay against the background of developments in the European Union.

According to Publius, "It appears that the cities had all the same laws and customs, the same weights and measures, and the same money." It would be an exaggeration to describe all of twenty-eight countries that now belong to the EU—the latest is Croatia, which joined on July 1, 2013—as sharing the same laws and customs, but they are all increasingly bound by trans-European laws and directives, including decisions of both the European Court of Justice and the European Court of Human Rights. And, of course, nineteen of these countries are, for better or worse, part of the Eurozone. (All have long since become metric, making the United States the lone holdout among major countries.) But for the Achaean League, these commonalities, linked as well to common structures of governance, were not enough. Publius concludes his lesson in ancient history: "I have thought it not superfluous to give the outlines of this important portion of history; both because it teaches more than one lesson and because, as a supplement to the outlines of the Achaean constitution, it emphatically illustrates *the tendency of federal bodies, rather to anarchy among the members, than to tyranny in the head*" (emphasis added).

One must always remember—and this is one of the confusing aspects of the nomenclature adopted by both proponents and opponents of the new Constitution—that Publius uses the word "federal" to refer to what political theorists and political scientists would call "confederal" institutions. I cannot emphasize too often the importance of the "first constitution" of the United States and of its utter replacement by the new Constitution, which Publius is defending. As we have already seen with his sharp critique of state autonomy in *Federalist* 10, one might even be forgiven for reading the final sentence as a cautionary note about the distinctly new form of federalism that *The Federalist* is gamely defending. It is difficult to read Publius as ever expressing any great concern about the possibility of "tyranny in the head" of the new governmental system; he is far more concerned about the possibility of "anarchy among the members" and, even more important, the necessity of establishing a single strong state that can stand up against foreign adversaries. The Amphictyonic Council, for example, failed because "[e]ven in the midst of defensive and dangerous wars with Persia and Macedon, the members never acted in concert, and were more or fewer of them, eternally the dupes, or the hirelings of the common enemy." Only in genuine unity is there strength, and such unity requires developing forms of government, with suitable powers, capable of resolute action. One can doubt whether Europe, for all its remarkable strides toward "union" in the aftermath of World War II, has moved beyond being a "league" or "confederation."

I suggested above that *Federalist* 18 might be simply anachronistic for American readers, given the decision made (at least by eleven states) in 1787–1788 to ratify the Constitution. But a recurring question, very much part of our own lives, is the extent of power we are willing to cede a central government that evermore defines its principal task as protecting Americans from foreign threats, some coming from other sovereign states, others from nonstate entities like Al Qaeda, and still others, such as cyber attacks, whose origins may never be known. During the administration of

George W. Bush, there was a strong public reaction against the disclosure that John Poindexter, the director of DARPA's Information Awareness Office, was trying to develop a program of "total information awareness." Disclosures by Edward Snowden during the Obama administration of "metadata" gathering by the National Security Agency suggest that Poindexter was simply ahead of the curve, and it remains to be seen whether most Americans will simply accept the reality of what has come to be called the modern "national surveillance state." One can wonder if we should be as complacent as Publius was in 1788 about the possibility of "tyranny in the head."

## FEDERALIST 19

## *The Defects of Multiple Sovereigns*

*F*EDERALIST 19 AND 20 both continue the principle theme set out in *Federalist* 18, which is the invidious comparison of earlier federations or leagues with the new system to be established by the Constitution. Unlike the previous essay, which concentrated on ancient history, 19 focuses primarily on the Germanic empire that grew out of the collapse of the earlier, ninth-century empire presided over by Charlemagne. While it appears to have established a stronger central government than that seen in ancient Greece, it was not sufficient to the task of maintaining peace and security. The reason is simple: "The fundamental principle, on which it rests, [is] that the empire is a *community of sovereigns*" (emphasis added). This reality ultimately "render[s] the empire a nerveless body; incapable of regulating its own members; insecure against external dangers, and agitated with unceasing fermentations in its own bowels." Later, Publius argues that "[t]he impossibility of maintaining order, and dispensing justice among these sovereign subjects" led to the empire's fragmentation. It needed, but never achieved, a "proper consolidation."

I argued that the previous essay, whatever its meaning for contemporary Americans, had a decided message for Europeans interested in the future of the European Union. This essay speaks as well to Americans, especially at a time when the majority of the Supreme Court is dominated by conservatives who seem infatuated with the notion of "state sovereignty"—to say nothing of less august political leaders, many identified with the Tea Party, who are similarly inclined to attack the national government's claims by asserting the sovereign status of states within the union. Thus Chief Justice Roberts, writing an opinion that was properly viewed as gutting the Voting Rights Act of 1965, referred frequently to the retained "sovereignty" of states. The act required certain states with a history of discrimination to obtain "preclearance" by the Department of Justice when changing established modes of voting, in order to make sure the proposed changes would not in fact make it more difficult for members of racial minorities to exercise the franchise. This requirement, supported by Congress and Democratic and Republican presidents alike, offended the sovereignty of these states, wrote the chief justice for a five-justice majority.

Perhaps the most dramatic use of "state sovereignty" language occurs in Justice Scalia's dissent in *Arizona v. United States,* which involved that state's attempt in effect to make its own policy with regard to possible undocumented aliens, independent of federal immigration laws. The majority held that most of the Arizona laws being litigated were preempted, meaning that the national government indeed is supreme over the states when regulating any subject that is properly within its domain of authority, as immigration most certainly is. (There are some exceptions if the state laws do not touch on significant national interests.) Justice Scalia wrote an exceptionally strong dissent that began: "The United States is an indivisible 'Union of sovereign States.' Today's opinion, approving virtually all of the Ninth Circuit's injunction against enforcement of the four challenged provisions of Arizona's law, deprives States of what most would consider the defining characteristic of sovereignty: the power to exclude from the sovereign's territory people who have no right to be there. Neither the Constitution itself nor even any law passed by Congress supports this result. I dissent." There is, in fact, an 1837 case that could easily be cited in support of this view, but its importance is precisely that the majority, most of whom were appointed by Andrew Jackson, were far more respectful of notions of "state sovereignty" than was, for example, John Marshall. Such notions were at the heart of the great struggle over secession in 1860–1861, which involved not only obvious force of arms but very serious constitutional arguments about the ability of a "sovereign state" to withdraw from the Union. (I will say more about secession later in this book.)

"Sovereignty talk" certainly did not disappear from constitutional discourse after Appomattox. But there is a certain irony in seeing "state sovereignty" attributed to the Framers as a foundational value, especially if we include Publius among them. But who really cares what he believed? The question is what *we* today should think about the questions he raised. At the very least, it is difficult, perhaps impossible, to read Publius as an admirer of any truly vigorous state "sovereignty." He appears to be far closer to what Patrick Henry, the Constitution's most outspoken opponent during the Virginia ratifying convention, feared and attacked: someone committed to a "proper consolidation" that would allow the United States to escape the limits of confederal—or perhaps even "federal"—status and instead become a strong nation with a government commensurate to the challenges it faced. To a remarkable degree, even in the twenty-first century, the United States seems rent by many of the same disputes that presented themselves during ratification. That Publius was a partisan of "consolidation" is not a reason to adopt that position today (or perhaps even then). But his arguments certainly should not be dismissed as mere relics of the past.

## FEDERALIST 20

### *The Dutch Provide the Final Cautionary Example*

PUBLIUS FINISHES HIS tour of comparative governments (all of them found wanting) by looking at the Dutch republic, another "confederacy of republics" that alas, "confirm[ed] all the lessons derived from those which we have already reviewed." The concluding paragraph of *Federalist* 20 summarizes "[t]he important truth, . . . that a sovereignty over sovereigns, a government over governments, a legislation for communities, as contradistinguished from individuals . . . is subversive of the order and ends of civil polity, by substituting VIOLENCE in place of LAW; or the destructive COERCION of the SWORD, in place of the mild and salutary COERCION of the MAGISTRACY" (emphasis in original).

The Dutch constituent republics were presumptively governed by the States General, made up of approximately fifty "deputies appointed by the provinces." The States General have broad powers, but significantly, the assertion of these powers requires "unanimity and the sanction of their constituents." Once again, the results are dismal: "Imbecility in the government; discord among the provinces; foreign influence and indignities; a precarious existence in peace, and peculiar calamities from war." But there is an additional important lesson: "In critical emergencies, the States-General are often compelled to overleap their constitutional bounds," especially with regard to the ostensible requirement of unanimous consent to treaties. "A weak constitution," Publius writes, "must *necessarily* terminate in dissolution, for want of proper powers, or the usurpation of powers requisite for the public safety" (emphasis added).

Later, I shall discuss more fully the implications of the word "necessarily" and the general topic of emergency powers in our own time. It is worth noting for now the degree to which Publius echoes (without citing) Machiavelli, whose most substantial work of political analysis is not *The Prince* but the *Discourses* on Livy's treatment of ancient Rome. "Among all the other Roman institutions," Machiavelli argued, the dictatorship "truly deserves to be considered and numbered among those which were the source of the greatness of such an empire, because without a similar system cities survive extraordinary circumstances only with difficulty." Dictatorship was central to Rome's success because "[t]he usual institutions in republics are slow to move . . . and, since time is wasted in coming to an agreement, the remedies for republics are very dangerous when they must find one for a problem that cannot wait." When emergency—or apparent emergency—strikes, there must be political leadership to recognize the situation and make immediate decisions without fear of bureaucratic hindrances, the need for time-consuming attempts at consensus building, or the many veto points common to representative government. "Republics must therefore have among their laws a procedure . . . [that] reserve[s] to a small number of citizens the authority to deliberate on matters of urgent need without consulting anyone else, if they are in complete agreement. When a republic lacks such a procedure, it must necessarily come to ruin."[1]

What causes this ruin? Machiavelli identifies two possibilities. First, republics can come to ruin by stubbornly "obeying their own laws" even when these laws prevent the measures necessary to save the country. Here, perhaps unusually, political leaders follow the law (as they understand it) with what might otherwise be admirable strictness, even as they are driving the political order over a cliff. Far more common, as Publius himself suggests, is the willingness of political leaders, faced with exigent circumstances, to publicly announce that they must break the law to save the republic. This is Machiavelli's second cause of ruin: "breaking laws in order to avoid" disastrous consequences. The problem is that breaking laws in urgent circumstances creates a precedent for breaking them again where the urgency is less clear (or nonexistent); and it encourages political leaders to retain unconstitutional norms even after the emergency has passed. What starts as emergency measures may become normalized.

We know that Publius detested the Articles of Confederation and the "imbecility" it led to. Perhaps he believed that the 1787 Constitution presented a completely satisfactory cure for the problems manifested under the Articles and the foreign examples that he devoted three essays to examining. This would require viewing the national government as *always* having the requisite powers to confront the challenges before it, whether domestic or foreign. There would never be any worry that states might be able to proclaim "sovereign" authority, even if only "residual," after whatever grants of sovereign power were made to the new national government.

Recall the earlier discussion of the Medellín case, which involved the enforcement of United States obligations under treaties entered into with foreign countries, including Mexico. Medellín lost his case in a 6–3 decision, with Chief Justice Roberts writing the majority decision, and Justice Breyer, joined by Justices Ginsburg and Souter, dissenting. Suffice it to say that the majority held that most international treaties are not "self-enforcing," so that even after signature by the president and ratification by two-thirds of the Senate, it was usually necessary for both houses of Congress to pass independent legislation making treaties applicable to the states. The president's displeasure at Texas's defiance of the International Court of Justice was a mere factoid without legal relevance. As one might surmise, Justice Breyer begged to disagree on both of these points. He concluded a powerful dissent by suggesting that the message sent by the majority's decision was that "the Nation may well break its word even though the President seeks to live up to that word and Congress has done nothing to suggest the contrary."[2] Even though Justice Breyer is no "originalist" who believes in slavish adherence to purported "original intent" of the Framers, he might well have cited Publius's critiques of the German and

Dutch federations for the proposition that the concerns expressed there are present today as well, and therefore worth taking seriously whether or not one feels "obligated" to adhere to Publius's wishes simply because he asserted them.

## FEDERALIST 21

### *On the Importance of Sanctions*

PUBLIUS IN *FEDERALIST* 21 continues his relentless criticism of the government—or, more accurately, the lack of any government worth the name—established by the Articles of Confederation. Here he emphasizes "the total want of SANCTION to its laws. The United States as now composed, have no powers to exact obedience, or punish disobedience to their resolutions. . . ." Publius is here touching on a fundamental debate about the meaning of "law." Does it consist only of demands issued by some governmental entity, or must these demands be backed by power? Such power, obviously, can take many different forms, ranging from seizure of property to incarceration to the threat of death. It is, for Oliver Wendell Holmes Jr., precisely the risk of running into such power—what Publius capitalized as "SANCTION"—that constitutes "law." Holmes offers the intellectual construct of "the bad man,"[1] who is wholly devoid of any notion that "the law" should be obeyed simply because it *is*, after all, the law. (Readers may think, in this context, not only of armed robbery, but also of their own habits regarding jaywalking, observing speed limits, or, perhaps, even other aspects of "the law.") It is common to distinguish between the "law on the books" and the "law in action," the latter referring to the actual willingness and ability of state officials, who include, in this context, the cop on the beat, to impose sanctions on those who would disobey. Sometimes the relevant sanctions come after full-scale trial and sentencing. But they can also include the inconvenience if, for example, a police officer pulls over a driver for whatever reason.

One need not believe that "bad men" have entirely taken over society. But there are surely enough to require the threat of state power to deter bad behavior or, if they are not deterred, at least catch wrongdoers and prevent them from doing further harm. The point, for Holmes, is that "a bad man," motivated by sheer selfishness, desires "to avoid an encounter with the public force." (Just think of the near ubiquity of drivers slowing down if they see a police car, even if, perchance, they are within the speed limit.) Thus, writes Holmes, "a man who cares nothing for an ethical rule which is believed and practised by his neighbors is likely nevertheless to care a good deal to avoid being made to pay money, and will want to keep out of jail if he can."

So who are the "bad men" Publius is worried about, and why is it so important that the new national government be able to visit adequate "sanctions" upon those who might defy its commands? Interestingly, they turn out to be groups of individuals in a given state—or even the "usurpation of rulers" within those states, who might threaten "state constitutions" and the "liberties of the people" presumably meant to be protected by those constitutions. Once more we see that to be a "federalist," a warm supporter of the new Constitution, is to underline the threat posed by the existence of states in a federal political order. In effect, the national government has to have sufficient power to be able to suppress potential "despotism" within states. Only "the inordinate pride of state importance" would blind one to this realization.

We have scarcely resolved the issue of the comparative importance of nation and state in our polity today, including, of course, the degree to which we want to enhance the national government's ability to "sanction" those it considers law breakers. Such controversies can take the abstract form of debate over which level of government should be responsible for enforcing what kinds of laws. Should a bank robber, for example, be vulnerable to both state and federal prosecution for what in effect is the "same" crime (of knocking over a particular bank)? The Supreme Court has held that since two "sovereigns"—both the state and national governments—are involved, each may choose to try a defendant for breaking its own law. Such questions may raise "double jeopardy" questions for the legal theorist—or the person unlucky enough to face trial in both state and federal courts—but most ordinary citizens take little interest in them.

That is surely not the case, however, with regard to *conflicts* between the laws of state and national governments. There might be deep differences between national and state governments—or the wider society presumably represented by the former and the more local one that constitutes the latter—as to how one defines "liberty" and, therefore, "usurpation." The most dramatic example in our history obviously involved slavery. In much of the country by the 1850s, preventing the forced return of fugitive slaves to their home states was viewed as virtuous, not simply the violation of federal law that it often was. Federal force was essential in many communities for maintaining the rights of out-of-state slaveholders.

It is not difficult to think of more-recent examples, perhaps less morally freighted than chattel slavery, but not necessarily less controversial than slavery was in the decades before 1865, when most presidents, congressional leaders, and Supreme Court justices either held slaves themselves or were politically sympathetic to the claims of slaveholders, if only to keep the union together. For some, the best analogue is the endless debates over abortion, in which one side defines itself as protecting "the right to life" and the other says it is protecting the fundamental liberty of a woman to engage in "reproductive choice." But one can place some of the debates over the "mandate" to purchase health insurance in this context. If one does not have such insurance, then the sanction is payment of a tax. To be sure, like all taxes, it helps to raise revenue, but there is also no doubt that it is meant to serve as a penalty that will induce many people to purchase insurance rather than have to pay it. Interestingly enough, the tax is not very onerous; a rational "Holmesian" might calculate that the costs of the tax are less than the benefit received through insurance and thus might not comply with the "mandate." But that is just to say that it may be a peculiar sort of "mandate." As Holmes suggested in his seminal lecture on *The Path of the Law,* the "bad man" treats *all* laws as simply pricing systems, setting out only the costs of disobedience but otherwise not being truly "obligatory."

Less freighted, perhaps, are current debates over drugs. Should marijuana, for example, be the subject of national regulation (and "sanction"), or should this be left to states? As of 2015, four states plus the District of Columbia have passed laws purporting to "legalize," at least under state law, the recreational use of marijuana. An additional nineteen states have legalized at least some non-recreational use, usually linked to medical treatment.[2] One problem is that existing federal law, as construed by the Supreme Court, clearly supersedes all such state laws and turns anyone who takes refuge in them into a potential criminal. And there are some notable examples of individuals "sanctioned" by the national government, even against defenses that they were protected by state laws supporting, for example, the medical use of marijuana.

Quite remarkably, then Attorney General Eric Holder announced, after the Colorado referendum legalizing marijuana in that state, that the United States would refrain from invoking clearly constitutional national laws so long as the Colorado vendors behaved responsibly, meaning that they made no sales to anyone underage. Why did Holder do this? Is it because, as with same-sex marriage, he came to believe that the national laws prohibiting sale of marijuana were unconstitutional? There is no reason to believe this. He far more likely believes, as may the former marijuana user President Obama, that the "war on drugs" has largely been a costly, even catastrophic, failure. Far from protecting "domestic Tranquility," it may have served more as a source of family breakdown, as children, parents, and siblings have been torn from their families and incarcerated, frequently for long terms, in federal prisons. There are, obviously, many convicts serving sentences or out on parole from *state* convictions, but the central issue is precisely the degree to which we want "one size fits all" national policies or, instead, are willing to accept what might be regarded as a patchwork quilt of state policies. If the latter, what is illegal in one state may well be legal in another, and even if two states agree on criminalization, they may have quite different answers as to the appropriate "sanction."

## FEDERALIST 22

### *Publius as Majoritarian*

*F*EDERALIST 22 IS THE last of the essays whose primary purpose is to set out the "most material defects" of the existing political order under the Articles of Confederation. Almost all are traceable to the lack of a sufficiently powerful national government capable of overcoming the fragmentation, inefficiencies, and occasional out-and-out hostility generated by the Articles' inadequate organization of the separate states. The tone of this essay is well captured by a single sentence: "It must be by this time evident to all men of reflection, who can divest themselves of the prepossessions of preconceived opinions, that it is a system so *radically vi-cious and unsound,* as to admit not of amendment but by an entire change in its leading features and characters" (emphasis added). Earlier, Publius offers as an illustration of the "system of imbecility in the Union" the na-tional government's need to rely on "requisitions and quotas" imposed on states that frequently chose not to comply.

My commentaries on the remaining sixty-three of Publius's essays will obviously address many of the specific changes the Constitution in-stantiates. It may be particularly interesting, though, to conclude these commentaries on what might be termed the "critical," rather than "con-structive," essays by Publius by looking carefully at one particularly strong theme. In my own recent writings on the United States Constitution, in-cluding a book pointedly entitled *Our Undemocratic Constitution: How the Constitution Goes Wrong (And How We the People Can Correct It),* I argue that the Framers were suspicious of "democracy" and committed to minimizing the possibility of genuine majority rule. Whether or not Publius is a twenty-first-century democrat (which he certainly is not), it is illuminating to realize that he could, at least on occasion, be a vigorous proponent of majority rule.

Consider his acerbic dismissal of the "right of equal suffrage among the States," by which Rhode Island or Delaware gets "an equal weight in the scale of power" with larger states such as New York or Virginia. "Every idea of proportion and every rule of fair representation conspire to con-demn" this principle. "Its operation contradicts the fundamental maxim of republican government, which requires that the sense of the majority should prevail." Publius condemns as "sophistry" the "reply" that we should accept the formal equality of the "sovereign states," as is true today, for example, in the General Assembly of the United Nations, where Fiji and the United States have equal voting power. This "logical legerdemain," he writes, cannot "counteract the plain suggestions of justice and common-sense" that rule should be in the hands of the majority of the people and most definitely not a majority of particular states that may comprise only a "a small minority of the people of America." In a rare footnote, Publius notes that "New Hampshire, Rhode Island, New Jersey, Delaware, Geor-gia, South Carolina, and Maryland are a majority of the whole number of the States, but they do not contain [even] one third of the people." In 2010, nine states had half the population,[1] though it is possible that by the

2020 census, this may change. But even if demographic changes bring the number of states with half the population up to ten—there is no plausible possibility that the number would be greater—that would still mean that the united support of the remaining forty states would still represent only a minority of the population. A majority of the U.S. Senate, which adopts the principle that Publius so clearly despises, could be cobbled together from states with only slightly more than 20 percent of the population. One could get to the two-thirds majority needed to ratify a treaty or to over-ride a presidential veto with senators representing less than 35 percent of the populace. Publius suggests that the "larger States would after a while revolt from the idea of receiving the law from the smaller. To acquiesce in such a privation of their due importance in the political scale, would be not merely to be insensible to the love of power, but even to sacrifice the desire of equality. It is neither rational to expect the first, nor just to require the last. The smaller States, considering how peculiarly their safety and wel-fare depend on union, ought readily to renounce a pretension which, if not relinquished, would prove fatal to its duration."

The Senate is far more anti-majoritarian in actual operation than a simple calculation of the numbers suggests. Even after some modification of the filibuster system in 2013, it remains part of the Senate's operative rules that it requires the acquiescence of sixty senators before pending legislation can even be brought to the floor or, more to the point, voted on. Thus one regularly reads that bills go down to defeat in the Senate by, say, fifty-five in favor to forty-five against. The fifty-five "aye" votes, which often represented far more than a majority of the total population, were outvoted by the remaining forty-five. As Publius writes, "To give a minor-ity a negative upon the majority (which is always the case where more than a majority is requisite to a decision), is, in its tendency, to subject the sense of the greater number to that of the lesser." Given the necessity that "[t]he public business must, in some way or other, go forward," one must accept that "a pertinacious minority can control the opinion of a majority," with the practical consequence that "the majority, in order that something may be done, must conform to the views of the minority." This entails "te-dious delays; continual negotiation and intrigue; contemptible compro-mises of the public good." That is when the system "works." "[U]pon some occasions things will not admit of accommodation; and then the mea-sures of government must be injuriously suspended, or fatally defeated."

Such situations "must always savor of weakness, sometimes border upon anarchy."

Could Publius travel to our time, one could all too easily imagine his saying "I told you so." What might most amaze him, though, is not simply that the Senate has now survived more than two centuries with no change in the malapportionment ordained by the 1787 Constitution itself, but that American political culture so calmly accepts the legitimacy of the principle that Publius so strongly—and I think correctly—denounces. There is, for better or worse—I would say the latter—no spirit of "revolt" demanding that the national government conform to the "fundamental maxim of republican government." Perhaps the most fundamental question facing any contemporary analyst of American politics is how this acquiescence might be explained. Was Publius simply wrong? Do "We the People" in fact benefit from placing such veto power in the hands of a minority of our population? Or perhaps, at the end of the day, it has not mattered all that much whether our institutions accord with the "fundamental maxim" of majority rule. Perhaps only academic political theorists really care about such matters, while ordinary Americans are properly concerned only about the quality of the decisions that emanate from these institutions. More ominously, though, most Americans may instead believe we have paid a very high price for the anti-majoritarian makeup of the Senate, but that nothing can be done. Even if "revolt" *would* be justified, in some abstract sense, one quickly realizes that it would be doomed to failure.

The well-known "serenity prayer" (generally attributed to Reinhold Niebuhr) begins with a plea to "grant me the serenity to accept the things I cannot change." There is much to be said for this hope, but we should recognize how much it conflicts with the tone of Publius's critique of the American system, which does not stop at mere "amendment" but recommends "an entire change in its leading features and characters." Or perhaps the central point is that Publius believed that he—or the collective "We the People"—*could* change things, where we are far more pessimistic. In any event, there is nothing remotely "serene" about his stance toward the world. Americans had earlier engaged in violent revolution against the British; now Publius advocates scrapping the Articles of Confederation and replacing them with a radically different Constitution. What does it mean in the twenty-first century to be faithful to the Publian vision of politics set out in 1787?

# PART 4

## *The State and the Machinery of Death (or, at Least, Defense)*

### *Standing Armies*

# FEDERALIST 23

## *"Common Defence" and (Un)limited Government*

PUBLIUS HAS EXPRESSED a remarkable rhetorical level of hostility toward the government established by the Articles of Confederation and its ineffectiveness. After this systematic accentuation of the negative, Publius turns to positive modes of argument emphasizing the "necessity" of a Constitution that will establish a sufficiently "energetic" government commensurate with the challenges facing the new country. *Federalist* 23 offers a forthright list of these challenges: "The principal purposes to be answered by union are these[:] the common defense of the members; the preservation of the public peace as well against internal convulsions as external attacks; the regulation of commerce with other nations and between the States; the superintendence of our intercourse, political and commercial, with foreign countries." Like political leaders down to the present, Publius emphasizes "[t]he authorities essential to the common defense." They include, as specified in the Constitution, the ability to raise and support armies and navies and to establish rules to govern them. So far, so good. It is difficult to imagine anyone seriously opposing Congress's ability to do this, even granting that there will always be disputes about the size of the army and navy and the number of dollars devoted to them. But then come the sentences that still have the power to startle:

> These powers ought to exist without limitation, BECAUSE IT IS IMPOS-
> SIBLE TO FORESEE OR DEFINE THE EXTENT AND VARIETY OF NATIONAL
> EXIGENCIES, OR THE CORRESPONDENT EXTENT AND VARIETY OF THE
> MEANS WHICH MAY BE NECESSARY TO SATISFY THEM. The circumstances
> that endanger the safety of nations are infinite, and for this reason no
> constitutional shackles can wisely be imposed on the power to which
> the care of it is committed. . . .
>
> This is one of those truths which, to a correct and unprejudiced
> mind, carries its own evidence along with it; and may be obscured,
> but cannot be made plainer by argument or reasoning. It rests upon
> axioms as simple as they are universal; the MEANS ought to be propor-
> tioned to the END; the persons, from whose agency the attainment of
> any END is expected, ought to possess the MEANS by which it is to be
> attained. (All capitalizations and boldface in original.)

It is often said that the essence of the United States Constitution—
some would say of any proper constitution—is that it establishes a limited
government. One of the most common mantras today is that the national
government is a "limited government of assigned powers." To reject this
limitation is, for many, to countenance the Leviathan state of Thomas
Hobbes, whereas many Americans pride themselves on the quite different
heritage drawn from John Locke, whose social contract establishes a far
more limited government than its Hobbesian counterpart.

One way of preserving the notion of "limited government" is by proclaiming that it can't just do whatever it might wish to do. A common, and
unproductive, contemporary debate involves whether the national government could require everyone to eat broccoli (though, obviously, no such
attempt has been made). But what limits, if any, *are* placed on government
when it makes decisions within a domain where it clearly has power and,
just as importantly perhaps, public support? Publius seems to suggest a
simple answer: none. To be sure, he is writing about the 1787 Constitution,
which notably lacked a Bill of Rights. Some of the support for the initial
amendments to the Constitution undoubtedly came from people who accepted Publius's description of national governmental power but, unlike
him, were scared by its implications and therefore wished to limit government even when it was acting for the "common defence." But anyone
familiar with contemporary debates about defense, especially in the wake
of the attacks on September 11, 2001, knows that the Publian argument
is alive and well, including within the chambers of several members of
the United States Supreme Court. Publius's argument is literally a deadly
serious one.

For Hobbes especially, but for Locke as well, the most basic function
of government is providing "security" for individuals who properly fear
the prospects of a "nasty, brutish, and short" life in the "state of nature."
Americans had special reason to feel such concerns. The settlement of the
so-called New World was accompanied by almost endless warfare. Historian Bernard Bailyn called his remarkable book on seventeenth-century
settlements *The Barbarous Years,* a title that is amply vindicated by the
multitude of wars he recounts, especially between settlers and Native
American tribes. But Americans had also participated in a war between
1756 and 1763 that was only the North American front of a wider conflict
between Great Britain and France, which was itself a part of a quasi world
war. The American Revolutionary War, which began in 1775 and lasted

until the Treaty of Paris in 1783, also had overtones of the seemingly end-less struggle between Great Britain and France. After all, the Revolution was importantly aided by French loans and the active participation of the French Navy. No one writing in 1787 could possibly believe that tranquility had come to Europe, or that the United States, even if protected from the two great European adversaries by the Atlantic Ocean, could rely on be-ing insulated from world events. The British would, of course, burn down Washington in 1812, and there would be important and often brutal armed struggles between the United States military and various Native American tribes until the end of the nineteenth century.

So the question, then as now, is whether the United States, when fac-ing what it thought were fundamental or even "existential" challenges, would be forced to fight "with one hand tied behind its back," to use a mod-ern idiom, because of limits on the national government's powers. Publius seems to find this a ludicrous notion. If we accept that one end of govern-ment is, as the Preamble states, to "provide for the common defence," then we must, he argues, accept any and all means conducive to this end. Ends justify means.

Many persons quail when presented with such arguments, but the stock response must be that if the validity of proposed ends does *not* justify means, what does? If national defense is the ultimate end of all govern-ments that hope to maintain popular support, then is it entailed that *all* means are justified? This suggests that the only limits on national power are prudential, where public officials come to the conclusion that certain means would not, in fact, be useful to the goal of national defense. This means, by definition, that they *would* be acceptable if the officials con-cluded in good faith that the gains outweighed the costs (however those costs are defined).

There is, of course, nothing merely "academic" about such questions. Readers can easily think of examples, both past and present, in which American public officials flouted what many consider "basic American values," including constitutional norms, in the name of national security. The most notorious such example during World War II was the placement of 120,000 persons of Japanese ancestry, roughly half of them American citizens, in what one member of the Supreme Court described as "a con-centration camp."[1] Congress (and President Reagan) ultimately apologized and even paid modest reparations some four decades later, though, cru-cially, they did not concede that the action was unconstitutional, only that it was unwise and unjust. Today's debates center on such issues as torture and drone attacks. Many critics argue that such actions are in fact counterproductive; they may generate more opposition to American interests than they stifle. Yet all such arguments accept the basic premise of the defenders of such actions: that the proper frame for deciding their rightness or wrongness is an evaluation of their costs and benefits to the state.

Far more fundamental are critiques that accept that a given means may be "efficacious" but call for it to be rejected nonetheless. "Let justice be done though the heavens fall" is one common slogan in such situations. Publius appears to find such sloganeering beside the point. Do we? If not, are we willing to live with the consequences, even if they include significant threats to the United States?

2012 was the fiftieth anniversary of the Cuban Missile Crisis. There are many things one might say about those "thirteen days" when John Kennedy and the so-called ExComm (the Executive Committee of the National Security Council) that he brought together wrestled with the American response to the discovery of Soviet nuclear missiles in Cuba. Here we need only note the almost complete lack of interest during those thirteen days in any constitutional limitations on the unilateral exercise of presidential power. Kennedy was remarkably uninterested in consulting with members of Congress, let alone seeking congressional approval for what might have triggered a nuclear cataclysm. According to Theodore Sorensen, Kennedy believed there was a one-in-three chance that American resistance to the Soviet adventurism in Cuba would lead to nuclear war. We obviously survived, and Kennedy won many plaudits for his coolness under immense pressure. Did Kennedy's actions during the crisis vindicate Publius's argument about the need for unlimited government when the national defense is thought to be at stake? Or is one of the "lessons of . . . experience" that nothing succeeds like success, whatever the risks taken or norms violated?

## FEDERALIST 24

### *The Inconvenience of Militia Service*

IT IS NO SURPRISE that after beginning his list of the constitutional order's "principal purposes" with "common defense," Publius next turns to discussing how the new country should organize its military. One of the more controversial aspects of the proposed Constitution was its embrace of a standing army, something many political thinkers of the time saw as a threat to "republican liberty." That liberty in turn depended on the willingness of ordinary citizens—the "virtuous yeomanry"—to emulate Cincinnatus by leaving their plows and farms to pick up muskets in order to defend their liberty against would-be tyrants. Once the struggle was over, ideally with the militia's victory, they would return to their plows.

Like most leaders of the American Revolution, including George Washington, Publius thought it foolish in the extreme to rely on a citizen-militia. It was even more foolish to reject the obvious value of having a professionally trained standing army that could instantly respond to threats and remain on the job however long the task required, without fearing that their crops would fail or that their families would be condemned to privation. Today, of course, we have long since grown used to our powerful standing military. As of 2010, there were approximately 1.4 million full-time members of the United States Army, Marines, Navy, Air Force, and Coast Guard; the 2010 register included an additional 850,000 non-full-time military personnel, the two largest groups being 358,200 enrolled in the Army National Guard and 205,000 members of the Army Reserve. Perhaps the winding down of American participation in Iraqi and Afghan wars will diminish these figures. Moreover, the "sequester" passed by Congress (and accepted by President Obama) that requires significant cuts in almost all federal programs, including the defense budget, has its own impact. Thus Secretary of Defense Chuck Hagel, prior to his leaving office, proposed cuts that would shrink the Army to pre–World War II levels.[1] Still, it is hard to imagine that the standing armed forces, in all of their many forms, will sink significantly below 2 million people, which would require a full 10 percent cut from the 2.25 million level of 2010.

Members of these reserve forces are sometimes called "weekend warriors" because they commonly train one weekend per month, plus an extended training period of two weeks each year. We are most aware of them, at least in peacetime, when the National Guard is called up in response to natural disasters like hurricanes. In what has been described as "the largest domestic deployment in National Guard history, 50,000 troops" were sent to various Gulf States following Hurricane Katrina in 2005. But they are also frequently called upon to participate in conflicts abroad. Over "200,000 Guard troops" were sent overseas to Iraq and Afghanistan in the years after September 11, 2001; at times, they constituted roughly "half of all combat brigades in Iraq."[2]

Do these deployments exemplify the "working partnership" between the standing army and the weekend warriors, or might we adopt Publius's more cautionary words about citizen militias? Writing in 1787, he emphasizes the "constant necessity for keeping small garrisons on our Western frontier. No person can doubt that these will continue to be indispensable. . . ." Today we are told by presidents and defense secretaries of both parties that we must keep up garrisons throughout the world, given the almost ubiquitous threats facing the United States, and that we need an ever-ready military force available for deployment. Although exact numbers are hard to come by, the Department of Defense indicated that there were approximately 250,000 military personnel serving abroad during the Christmas holidays in 2013.[3] The United States may have more than 200,000 military personnel in bases (or fighting active wars) in approximately 150 countries (though some may be lodging only relative few personnel).[4] As Publius writes, the necessary troops "must either be furnished by occasional detachments from the militia, or by permanent corps in the pay of the government." There is no doubt as to his preference. "Occasional detachments" are either "impracticable" or "pernicious." His rationale should certainly ring a bell for any reader in the twenty-first century. "The militia would not long, if at all, submit to be dragged from their occupations and families to perform that most disagreeable duty in times of profound peace. And if they could be prevailed upon or compelled to do it, the increased expense of a frequent rotation of service, and the loss of labor and disconcertion of the industrious pursuits of individuals, would form conclusive objections to the scheme." Of course, times of "profound peace" would seem to make such deployments unnecessary. But none of us born since 1941 has lived more than a very few years in which the United States was not involved in one war or another, "hot" or "cold," often requiring extended deployments. Publius has little doubt that we are far better off with a "permanent corps in the pay of the government," that is, a standing army.

One may doubt that we need a "standing army" in order to respond adequately to natural disasters or even threats of domestic violence such as were present in Little Rock, Arkansas, in 1957, when President Eisenhower sent troops from the 82nd Airborne Division to enforce court-ordered desegregation against the attempts of Arkansas Governor Orval

Faubus and his supporters to keep Central High School segregated. National guards were federalized in Alabama and Mississippi in response to local opposition to civil rights advocates. But, of course, the real point of Publius's warnings against rejecting a standing army in favor of citizen militias has far more to do with his belief that "profound peace," however great a blessing, will almost certainly be rare. Interestingly enough, this appeared to be his prognosis even for an America that could still look at the Atlantic and Pacific Oceans as guarantors of perpetual security, at least so long as the United States itself remained undivided. As he noted, the new government of the United States near the turn of the nineteenth century faced myriad threats from American Indians, who recognized that the new nation's success would not benefit them. Today the threats are extraordinarily different, and the great oceans may seem little more useful than "ponds." But the debates about how to constitute an armed force to provide for the "common defence" continue.

## FEDERALIST 25

### More on the Merits of Standing Armies

PUBLIUS SCOFFS AT those who would rely on a citizen militia, for two quite different reasons beyond the inconvenience to militia members forced to uproot themselves from their quotidian lives to be deployed in battle. Most fundamental is his belief that "[w]ar, like most other things, is a science to be acquired and perfected by diligence, by perseverance, by time, and by practice." Reliance on militias, he tells us, is a "doctrine" that came near to "los[ing] us our independence. . . . The facts . . . are too recent to permit us to be the dupes of such a suggestion. The steady operation of war against a regular and disciplined army," like that of the British and their Hessian mercenaries, "can only be successfully conducted by a force of the same kind." Whatever the "valour" of American militiamen, we should have no illusions that they gained us independence. Publius is perhaps too tactful to note that in addition to trained military leaders like George Washington, it was the French who actually defeated the British at the Battle of Yorktown in 1781, which is usually seen as the engagement that decisively ended British attempts to prevent American secession.

There is a reason why the first—and, to this day, only—universities established by the national government are service academies. None other than Thomas Jefferson, notoriously suspicious of a strong national government and thus of many of Publius's arguments, approved the 1802 legislation establishing the United States Military Academy at West Point. Interestingly, it was another vigorous opponent of national governmental power, James K. Polk, who signed the legislation approving the 1845 establishment of the United States Naval Academy at Annapolis. No doubt Publius would rejoice in both, as recognizing the necessity of a cadre of military professionals with systematic training in the "science" of warfare on both land and sea. The importance of protecting America's coastline was signified by the establishment of the Coast Guard Academy in 1876, the last year of the Grant presidency, and the Air Force Academy came along in 1954.

But there is a second reason for supporting not only a professionally trained but a standing army: One simply cannot wait until war breaks out to train military personnel or place them in position to resist attacks. Publius ridicules the proposition that "[w]e must receive the blow, before we could even prepare to return it." He describes opponents of a standing army as in effect advocating that "[w]e must expose our property and liberty to the mercy of foreign invaders, and invite them, by our weakness, to seize the naked and defenseless prey, because we are afraid" of the potential for tyranny ostensibly represented by a standing army. Publius addresses the fear by emphasizing that the armed forces would always be under civilian control, not only of the president as commander in chief, but also of Congress insofar as that body would have absolute discretion over military funding. In addition, the text of the Constitution limits all military budget bills passed by Congress to two years, so that a single Congress cannot assure the funding of the military for the next decade.

But he returns as well to his central theme: The new United States must accept the need to display military power if it wishes to survive in a world of hostile and predatory states. Dismissing his critics as de facto partisans of a "feeble government" that is unlikely "to be respected" by either our adversaries or even "by its own constituents," he returns to one of the guiding tropes of the entire set of essays, which is the inadequacy of "parchment provisions" in the face of the "struggle[s]" generated by "public necessity" to defend ourselves. One must be coldly realistic about the likely nature of those struggles and accept the necessity of a government adequately empowered to meet them. "Wise politicians will be cautious about fettering the government with restrictions" that ultimately "cannot be observed" when the perceived demands of "necessity" override them.

We shall have further occasion, particularly when we come to *Federalist* 40 and 41, to consider that one of Publius's principal messages is the importance of not placing "fetters" on the national government that will serve only as "parchment provisions"—he will later, in *Federalist* 48, refer to "parchment barriers"—against governmental actions that "We the People" will insist the government take in order to fulfill the "principal purposes" set out in *Federalist* 23. Breaking these fetters will not be the acts of power-hungry leaders ignorant of what their oaths of office mean, but of leaders who are responsive to public perceptions of "necessity" or "exigencies."

One might well find these Publian ideas disconcerting. Perhaps readers prefer Thomas Jefferson's statement, written for the Kentucky Resolutions protesting the Alien and Sedition Acts of 1798. "In questions of power," Jefferson wrote, "let no more be heard of confidence in man, but *bind him down from mischief by the chains of the Constitution*" (emphasis added). Might not Publius reply that even chains are made to be broken when circumstances demand it? At the very least, we live in the twenty-first century with the antimonies that were well recognized by those we deem our "founders." Our mistake is to believe that they themselves resolved the tensions instead of simply identifying them. For all of their own "reflection and choice," they scarcely provide unequivocal answers. Once again, we honor them best by engaging in our own anguished reflections—and consequent choices—about the "principal purposes" of our polity and the means we will accept as "necessary" to achieving them.

## FEDERALIST 26

### *In Whom Do We Place Our "Confidence"?*

OPPONENTS OF A STANDING army presented their critiques in the language of liberty: Standing armies would become the tools of reigning leaders, perhaps would-be monarchs. But what was to these critics a bug may be to admirers of a standing army, both then and now, a feature. Consider the words of John A. Nagl, a West Point graduate (and Rhodes Scholar) and combat commander in Iraq before leaving the armed services. Speaking of the members of the modern all-volunteer standing army, he describes "the American public [as] completely willing to let this professional class of volunteers"—which Nagl compares to the Roman "praetorian guard"—be available for service wherever commanded. "This gives the president much greater freedom of action to make decisions in the national interest, with troops who will salute sharply and do what needs to be done," at least according to the commander in chief.[1]

A key part of the British Bill of Rights in 1689, which decisively transformed Great Britain into a *constitutional* and therefore limited monarchy, banned "the raising or keeping a standing army within the kingdom in time of peace, unless it be with consent of Parliament." American armed forces established under the 1787 Constitution would have as their own commander in chief a civilian president who had to face the electorate every four years; more importantly, even the commander in chief depended on the legislature to provide funds, and the two-year maximum duration of all military appropriations bills meant, at least in theory, that the legislature must frequently reevaluate the military's claims on the public fisc.

For Publius, the challenge is to achieve a proper balance between "the energy of government" and "the security of private rights" against those who would oppress us—including, of course, government itself. "[R]estraining the legislative authority" to establish standing armies, he writes, "is one of those refinements, which owe their origin to a zeal for liberty more ardent than enlightened." Proponents of the idea reject both the teachings of political philosophers and the more worldly lessons gained from the Revolution against the British; liberty can be achieved— and maintained—through the use of arms, including, of course, establishing a professional corps skilled in their use.

Publius knows, of course, of the risks attached to standing armies, but he nonetheless cautions that "it is better to hazard the abuse of that confidence [that we place in our leaders] than to embarrass the government and endanger the public safety, by impolitic restrictions on the legislative authority." We should allow legislators, who are either elected directly by the people or, in the case of the original Senate, appointed by state legislators accountable to the people, to delegate to the executive the ability to call upon military resources as deemed necessary for the "common defence" against those who threaten our liberty or attack what the Preamble labels "domestic Tranquility." Even if there is some risk that political leaders will abuse the confidence placed in them, Publius appears to answer that it is a risk worth taking. Surely one must assume that the risk is relatively low precisely because we will be sufficiently skilled at identifying worthy political leaders and can, should that confidence turn out to be misplaced, depose them in time to limit the damage they do. One might wonder how many of us today share this faith in our fellow citizens.

In the twenty-first century, we rarely, if ever, debate the merits of a standing army, including the contemporary version in which it is composed entirely of volunteers. No one need be concerned about being drafted. Approximately 1 percent of the American public serves; far more to the point is that the remaining 99 percent rarely know anyone in service or really care about them, other than by expressing what James Fallows describes as "[o]verblown, limitless praise" of our "heroes," devoid, however, of "the caveats or public skepticism we would apply to other American institutions, especially ones that run on taxpayer money."

In his thoughtful and troubling article, Fallows invokes President Eisenhower's famous "farewell address" warning about the growth of a "military-industrial complex." Eisenhower, the last of our "general-presidents," observed that "[o]ur military organization today bears little relation to that known by any of my predecessors in peacetime, or indeed by the fighting men of World War II or Korea." For better or worse, what had distinguished the United States prior to the period after World War II is that we "had no armaments industry" that depended on selling its handiwork to the national government. We had, by and large, relied on the ability of civilian industry to transform itself, as necessary, into producers of war matériel. Those days are over. "[N]ow we can no longer risk emergency improvisation of national defense; we have been compelled to create a permanent armaments industry of vast proportions," complementing the "defense establishment" consisting of a multimillion-member standing army. "This conjunction of an immense military establishment and a large arms industry is new in the American experience," stated Eisenhower. Its "influence—economic, political, even spiritual—is felt in every city, every State house, every office of the Federal government." It might be an "imperative need," but we should also "comprehend its grave implications."

Thus he issued his famous warning about "the acquisition of unwarranted influence, whether sought or unsought, by the military-industrial complex. The potential for the disastrous rise of misplaced power exists and will persist. We must never let the weight of this combination endanger our liberties or democratic processes. We should take nothing for granted. Only an alert and knowledgeable citizenry can compel the proper meshing of the huge industrial and military machinery of defense with our peaceful methods and goals, so that security and liberty may prosper together."[2]

Can we imagine any candidate for the presidency in the twenty-first century expressing these concerns in such vivid language? Or has it simply become such a conventional aspect of our political system that it goes almost literally unmentioned?

Eisenhower did not express concern about a military coup. The United States has remained remarkably free of any such concerns. Colonel Dunlap's 1992 "forecast" of a military coup in 2012, discussed earlier in the commentary on *Federalist* 8, fortunately remains a dystopian fantasy. But does that constitute an effective response to Eisenhower's warning? One can have a militarized society without overt military leadership. What worried Eisenhower was the extent to which the American economy—and, ultimately, society as a whole—was being warped by military spending. In an era in which the demands for "smaller government" and "austerity" in public spending have become central mantras of the Republican Party (with support from many Democrats as well), spending for "national security" remains near-sacrosanct, with remarkably little true public debate.

Fallows notes that too many contemporary weapons systems—he focuses particularly on the F-35 fighter jet plane—are enormously expensive, with little demonstrated value beyond the provision of jobs to those building the plane. At a time when America's infrastructure—its roads, bridges, and transportation systems—needs significant effort, our major "public works" programs appear often to be building weapons like the F-35. That can be explained in part because contracts for the plane are spread over forty-six of the fifty states and 383 of the 435 congressional districts.

Fallows views the entrenchment of the plane in our defense budget as a triumph of "political engineering," which he defines as "the art of spreading a military project to as many congressional districts as possible, and thus maximizing the number of members of Congress who feel that if they cut off funding," they would be putting their own reelection prospects in danger. It is worth noting that Robert McNamara, as John F. Kennedy's secretary of defense, was a major proponent of such "engineering" as a means of convincing members of Congress of the desirability of building new weapons systems.

Another term for such engineering, of course, is the deliberate creation of "faction," Publius's obsessive concern. Selfless representatives should be willing to finance weapons systems regardless of where they are produced, if they are truly in the public interest, and to vote against them even if they promise to bring sorely needed jobs to one's constituents. But who really believes in such a model of representation, even with regard to the presumed primary goal of safeguarding national security? One can only wonder if Publius, the proponent of a standing army, would be equally supportive of a "military industrial complex," complemented, of course, by such civilian agencies as the CIA or NSA.

It is also worth emphasizing another way that 2015 differs from the 1787 world in which Publius was writing: There were no local police forces at the end of the eighteenth century. They would be created only in the nineteenth century, and it would be the late twentieth century before police forces generally became "professionalized." But surely in 2015 we are well aware of the joint reality of the necessity of local police forces and the fact that they may present their own dangers to liberty. After all, police officers are not only licensed to carry firearms, but they also have the authority to use "deadly force" when they think that public safety requires it. Moreover, as a practical matter, police are rarely disciplined for making mistakes in such judgments. Finally, and perhaps most importantly, public officials are often as unwilling to criticize members of the "thin blue line"—often portrayed as the only force standing between us and anarchy—as they are to question the national military.

One might also note the increasing militarization of local police forces by virtue of "gifts" received from the Department of Defense of war matériel that is no longer needed by the national military. One of the most widely reprinted photographs in 2014 featured an African American in Ferguson, Missouri, who was being stopped by a bevy of local police officers who looked as if they were in fact patrolling Baghdad or some other wartime zone. And many local police departments are busy buying drones for use in surveillance and, perhaps, the application of deadly force in "appropriate" situations.

Given Publius's oft-expressed doubts about local governments and their propensity to fall victim to factional capture, there is good cause to wonder if the fears expressed about the pathologies (as well as the acknowledged benefits) attached to a "standing army" might extend as well to the local equivalents that characterize the modern United States, even if not the eighteenth-century version within which Publius was writing. Even if we are right to have "confidence" in the national military, should that necessarily extend to more local versions of an equally uniformed armed force?

## *Further Reflections on Confidence in the National Government*

IN *FEDERALIST* 27, PUBLIUS addresses perhaps the most fundamental problem, certainly theoretically and often practically, facing any government: Will the citizenry obey the laws or other decrees of the government, and if so, why? At least some of the opposition to standing armies was based on the fear that a recalcitrant public, disinclined to respect the national government and its wishes, could be brought to heel by the force of arms. Publius's response, as befits someone who supports the new Constitution and its greatly empowered national government, is that the great majority will comply with the law voluntarily because "the general government will be better administered than the particular governments." He substantially repeats the arguments set out earlier, especially in *Federalist* 10, that leaders of the extended republic will be "less apt to be tainted by the spirit of faction, and more out of reach of those occasional ill humors or temporary prejudices and propensities, which in smaller societies frequently contaminate the public deliberation, beget injustice and oppression of a part of the community, and engender schemes [that] terminate in general distress, dissatisfaction, and disgust."

It would be illogical to support the new Constitution if one lacked confidence in its capacity to help achieve the "general Welfare," and Publius has no such hesitation. Unless one believes that "the federal government is likely to be administered in such a manner as to render it odious or contemptible to the people, there can be no reasonable foundation" to think the citizenry will resist its demands and thus require the kinds of force represented by a standing army. Yet there is a certain tension in his argument. As someone who was alarmed by the Shays' Rebellion in Massachusetts in 1786–1787, he is well aware of the possibility of popular discontent. (Shays' Rebellion was sparked when creditors, backed by state power, made what debtors perceived as oppressive demands for repayment regardless of the consequences to their individual or collective welfare.) One advantage of the new Union was that armed personnel (including, of course, members of state militias) could be deployed to restore order if needed.

Still, the essence of this quite short essay is that such force would probably not be needed. It is worth attending to Publius's argument at length:

> ... the more the operations of the national authority are intermingled in the ordinary exercise of government, the more the citizens are accustomed to meet with it in the common occurrences of their political life, the more it is familiarized to their sight and to their feelings, the further it enters into those objects which touch the most sensible chords and put in motion the most active springs of the human heart, the greater will be the probability that it will conciliate the respect and attachment of the community. Man is very much a creature of habit. A thing that rarely strikes his senses will generally have but little influence upon his mind. A government continually at a distance and out of sight can hardly be expected to interest the sensations of the people. The inference is, that the authority of the Union, and the affections of the citizens towards it, will be strengthened, rather than weakened, by its extension to what are called matters of internal concern; and will have less occasion to recur to force, in proportion to the familiarity and comprehensiveness of its agency. The more it circulates through those channels and currents in which the passions of mankind naturally flow, the less will it require the aid of the violent and perilous expedients of compulsion.

Once again, we are reading an argument of political sociology and psychology. The more one becomes accustomed to the new government—assuming, of course, that its administration is as competent and benevolent as Publius suggests—the more it will take on the status of a friend whose ministrations are to be embraced rather than feared. To be sure, one must assume that national officials will stay within the boundaries set up by the new Constitution, but as we have already seen, more important than "parchment provisions" is reliance on wise leaders who are motivated to act in the public interest. Publius certainly grants that "an in-judicious exercise of the authorities of the best government, that ever was or even can be instituted," could understandably "provoke and precipitate the people into the wildest excesses." But he is confident that the leaders of the new government will have a suitable "share of prudence" to know their limits and thus create a polity where defiant lawbreakers will be relatively few and easily manageable without the government's having to resort to standing armies. His conclusion is to turn the tables on his adversaries and to ask, even should it be true "that the national rulers would be insen-sible to the motives of public good, or to the obligations of duty," could the Constitution's opponents possibly believe that the "imbecility" created by the Articles of Confederation, the deficiencies of local government, and the rivalries among the separate states would save us?

It is tragically ironic that those who identify themselves as political conservatives and especially attuned to the importance of adhering to the vision of the Framers of the Constitution have in recent years done so much to undercut the political sociology Publius relied on. To be sure, one might argue that the national government has all too frequently proved its ineptitude and deserves the opprobrium visited upon it. But no critique of specific governmental agencies or deficiencies in the enforcement of national programs underlay Ronald Reagan's remark that "The nine most terrifying words in the English language are: 'I'm from the government, and I'm here to help.'"[1] Instead, the comment was designed to convince the public—and, for those already convinced, to reaffirm—that the national government was incapable of genuinely helping them. The reason might be a commitment to malign programs, but even well-intentioned pro-grams would presumably be defeated by inept administration. Far better to minimize the national government—perhaps to agree with conserva-tive leader Grover Norquist that "Our goal is to shrink government to the size where we can drown it in a bathtub"—than to embrace the possibility that Publius might have been correct in advocating a national government empowered to meet whatever "exigencies" face the nation.

Anyone following Norquist's view would presumably take it as a sign of political health that, as the polling data above shows, most of the na-tion has lost confidence in national institutions—other than the military, of course. And, of course, one would not expect political candidates en-amored of this brand of "conservatism"—which might better be described as "anti-governmental radicalism"—to run on platforms of working hard to create a better-functioning national bureaucracy that will generate the kind of support Publius envisioned, especially if that might, for example, require paying administrators truly adequate salaries. Instead, such conservatives dismiss as "chumps" or "losers" anyone with a naive desire to serve the public good through participation in government. Can any political system survive—at least without indeed calling on force of arms to quell popular discontent—a bath in what Oliver Wendell Holmes Jr. once described as the "cynical acid" visited upon us by anti-Publians, however fervently they might profess their admiration for *The Federalist*?

FEDERALIST 28

*The Necessity of Force*

PUBLIUS LEADS OFF *Federalist* 28 by telling his readers that it "cannot be denied" that "the national government may be necessitated to resort to force." He describes "the idea of governing at all times by the simple force of law (which we have been told is the only admissible principle of republican government)" as but "the reveries of those political doctors, whose sagacity disdains the admonitions of experimental instruction." Once again we are directed to "the lessons of . . . experience." That experience includes, however much we might be saddened by it, the almost relentless recourse to arms by tyrants and, more happily, by those resisting tyranny (who would certainly include, both for Publius and for generations of Americans afterward, the brave "patriots" who violently resisted British rule). Alfred Lord Tennyson captured one aspect of what Victorians had learned from experience (including the Darwinian revolution in thought) by referring in *In Memoriam* to "Nature, red in tooth and claw." To this day, it is not pretty to watch, perhaps on the National Geographic cable channel, a lion overtaking a zebra or a gazelle and turning it into dinner. But even as we are immersed in the centenary of the catastrophe that we have labeled World War I, we realize as well the extent to which Woodrow Wilson may have been engaging in a "reverie" when he fantasized not only that American entry into that war would make the world "safe for democracy" but also that the United States and its allies were fighting a "war to end war." Instead, we now know, it served as the foundation stone for an even bloodier World War II, which itself neither secured democracy worldwide nor ended military force as a means of resolving disputes.

Publius occupied an intellectual universe that certainly dismissed as quixotic an exclusive reliance on "the rule of law," at least unless those ruling in the name of the law backed up their demands with the threat of force. Still, he could not possibly have imagined the magnitude of contemporary means of violence—what we have learned to call "weapons of mass destruction." He also presents a picture of the potential standing army—the focus of his attention for many essays now—that is quite different from any modern army. Interestingly, *Federalist* 28 is devoted to the threat of *internal* instability, what Publius almost charmingly calls "commotion" or, more ominously, "insurrection" within a given state. The former might be easily contained by the armed resources available to the state itself, but the latter might require the state to call on its neighbors for aid. Ultimately, he suggests that the best way to assure the availability of such aid is to create a standing army that can supplement inadequate state militias.

Perhaps, though, a state will not be faced with "insurrection" but rather with "usurpation" by its leaders. What then? Publius acknowledges that individuals always retain "the original right of self-defense, which is paramount to all positive forms of government." Interestingly, though, the Constitution drafted in Philadelphia includes no formal acknowledgment of this right (unless one views the Declaration of Independence as somehow part of the Constitution). Compare, for example, the current German constitution, which specifically states that "All Germans shall have the right to resist any person seeking to abolish this constitutional order, should no other remedy be possible." The most threatening such person, obviously, would be someone wielding the legitimacy of public office, but the most basic meaning of the American Revolution is that no one is immune from popular resistance.

Still, the Lockean "appeal to heaven" by an aroused public may prove ineffective if unarmed resisters are facing public officials who are able and willing to call upon the state's own armed force. One might counter that the breakup of the Soviet Empire in 1989–1991 took place in a variety of what came to be called "color revolutions," including, for example, the "Velvet Revolution" in what was then Czechoslovakia. Any full analysis must take into account the possibility, in some times and places, of nonviolent revolution, but it seems foolhardy to view them as typical and to reject Publius's far more dour picture of political life. As Woody Allen reminds us, "The lion and the calf shall lie down together, but the calf won't get much sleep,"[1] at least without the means of violence necessary to fend off an attack.

One response is to advocate that the citizenry itself be armed, the subject of the next essay, but another, as Publius emphasizes here, is to create a national standing army that can, if need be, quell a tyrannical state regime far more easily than a popular resistance movement in which "citizens must rush tumultuously to arms, without concert, without system, without resource, except in their courage and despair," even as "usurpers, clothed with the forms of legal authority, can too often crush the opposition in embryo." But might the cure be worse than the disease? Might not the standing army become the instrument—the "praetorian guard"—of national usurpers?

Against this possibility, Publius offers what some might find a complacent response. States will, after all, have their own militias, which can easily be mobilized against a tyrannical national government. Governments "can readily communicate with each other in the different states; and unite their common forces for the protection of their common liberty." One might describe this as the preferred narrative of the American Revolution itself, where "committees of correspondence" in the various colonies were able to forge the skeleton of a new nation and, upon organizing themselves further as a Congress, appoint George Washington as the commander in chief of the armed resistance. (All this was done without social media!) Once again, the practical threats to liberty are perceived as coming more from the states, subject to the overriding power of the national government, than from the national government, which presumably could not maintain hegemony against united resistance by the states.

In case we are not persuaded by the abstract argument, Publius makes another, more practical point. "For a long time to come, it will not be possible to maintain a large army." Nor, perhaps, will the national standing army have access to means of violence dramatically different from those available to state militias or even to private citizens themselves. Neither of these arguments, of course, has much purchase in the twenty-first century. If one is not worried about a tyrannical national government—and its ability to call upon a standing army in excess of a million persons—one's peace of mind is far more likely to be predicated on confidence in the good faith and ability of national political officials than on a belief that the national government could be defeated in an armed struggle by any realistically plausible alliance of militias.

## FEDERALIST 29

### *"Concerning the Militia"*

E ssays 24–28 all considered the necessity of a standing army. With *Federalist* 29, Publius moves on to the militias, by which he means not the new standing army, which will be created and financed by Congress, but the collective bodies of potentially armed persons arising at the state and local levels. Given Publius's emphasis on training and professionalization, it is not surprising that he puts little stock in militias.

Still, the militias' existence, both in the eighteenth century when Publius was writing and in the twenty-first century when we are reading him, raises both highly theoretical and immensely practical problems. The latter, perhaps, can be underlined by frequent stories about the ease of purchasing and possessing guns in the United States and the violence that results. (As I write these words on May 24, 2014, the day's lead stories include the shooting deaths, the night before, of seven people in a town near Santa Barbara, California, though, to be fair, another story involves the deaths by gunfire of at least three people shot while visiting a Jewish museum in Brussels, Belgium.) One should never forget that anodyne discussions of militias, standing armies, or even, at least in the United States, local police forces inevitably involve the potential for what lawyers call "deadly force," a term that arises with special frequency when police are dealing with alleged criminals, including, in the now-notorious case of Eric Garner, the selling of individual cigarettes on a street corner on Staten Island. The word "alleged" is of special import because, also with some frequency, the victims of such force turn out to be innocent victims of overzealous police. But it is also that at least some uses of state militias and the United States armed forces over our history have been equally problematic, the only difference being that far more lives are lost when the regular army is involved.

Force, including the deadly variety, appears to be an ineradicable part of human society. Cain did not need firearms to slay Abel, and the importance of that particular story, which occurs all too soon after the peopling of the newly created world, is presumably to underline the capacity of human beings to engage in violence against their literal as well as figurative brothers. For better and worse, the most common response to the threats of what the Shadow described as the "evil [that] lurks in the hearts of men" is to threaten violence in return. Ideally, the threat of violence will deter evil acts, but if deterrence fails, then it is vital that armed forces be sufficient in capacity and training to prevail. Presumably all nonpacifists agree with this analysis, even if they disagree on the specific occasions meriting the use of force. But whom should we trust to make such choices?

One deceptively easy answer is, of course, the government itself. The great early-twentieth-century German political sociologist Max Weber defined as one of the central attributes of the state a monopoly over the legitimate use of violence. He did not believe, of course, that any given state could effectively prevent all illegitimate violence. But he did believe that the citizens of a properly organized state would distinguish between legitimate violence, directed by the state against foreign or domestic threats, and criminal violence to which the proper response is repression, ideally through trial and imprisonment, but possibly through the infliction of deadly force by agents of the state.

Consider, though, two central problems that quickly arise with Weber's notion, especially within the specific context of the United States and the constitutional order Publius was writing about. First, Weber assumes that the state is unitary, that is, consisting of only one government to which all other political units are clearly subordinate. A second vital assumption is that the citizenry would automatically trust *any* government with a monopoly on the use of violence.

The first assumption encounters an obvious problem with the United States of America, especially in 1787–1788, when it represented an uneasy coming together of thirteen separate states, each claiming to be "sovereign." By no means could the United States be compared to, say, the United Kingdom. Indeed, a central cause of the American Revolution was the rejection by American patriots of the proposition that they were subject to unfettered legal control by the British Parliament or the British monarch. It is possible that the British Empire could have been saved had London been willing to accept what we would today describe as a "federal" commonwealth, with almost all practical power residing in the constituent countries even as the monarch continues as the symbolic head of state. Perhaps it was too early to expect the British to think their way through to the twentieth-century British Commonwealth of Nations, or perhaps King George and his ministers were simply too stubborn, but for whatever reason, this did not happen. Instead, the colonies seceded from the overreaching empire and established a new nation.

Almost immediately, they faced some of the same quandaries that the colonies had presented to the British. What would be the relation between the new national government, especially the 1787 version designed to replace the patently inadequate structure created by the Articles of Confederation; the states of the Union; and the individual citizens who had rebelled in the name of preserving "republican liberty" against the illegitimate oppression? We will have occasion later in this book to mull over the practical implications of American federalism, but it should be clear that the Constitution, however "consolidationist" it might have been compared to the Articles, contemplated the preservation of the separate state polities and, crucially, their militias. The Constitution explicitly reserves to the states the authority to appoint officers to their militias and to be in charge of their training, even if that training is ostensibly "according to the discipline prescribed by Congress." Publius viewed this appointment power as limiting any legitimate fear that the militias could become a tool of national oppression. Again, his reason is basically sociological. State militia officers would identify far more with their home state, to whose officials they owe their appointment, than with distant national authorities. Because the state officials and state-appointed officers would always have "a preponderating influence over the militia," there could be no legitimate cause for concern even if, as the Constitution authorized, the state militias were called forth "to execute the Laws of the Union, suppress Insurrections and repel Invasions."

Today, most Americans probably inflect *United* more than *States*, partly as the result of the extraordinarily bloody war of 1861–1865 that killed almost 2 percent of the national population; that war is commonly viewed as causing the verb following "United States" to change from the antebellum plural to the modern singular. But even today we have scarcely resolved the question surrounding federalism, which implies the existence of subnational units with at least some degree of legally protected autonomy. At least since the 1990s, the United States Supreme Court has repeatedly recognized continuing elements of "state sovereignty" and, especially when Justice Anthony Kennedy is writing, has recognized as well the duty to honor the "dignity" interests of states. At the very least, this sets up a perhaps irresolvable tension between a national government that would no doubt prefer to possess a monopoly over the use of weapons, and state governments that might have their own reasons, including suspicion of the national government, to maintain their own prerogatives with regard to threatening or inflicting violence. An intriguing case before the Supreme Court in 2012 involved Arizona's desire to use its state police to enforce national immigration law more stringently than was desired by the national government. As I noted earlier, the Court largely ruled against Arizona over the vehement dissent of Justice Scalia, who emphasized Arizona's "sovereignty." But the case underscored the importance of having multiple governments, ostensibly united within a complex political structure, each with its own law-enforcement institutions and the concomitant ability to use force against alleged recalcitrants.

But there is an even deeper problem with Weber's argument, which can arise even in "unitary" states that make no pretense of recognizing autonomous or sovereign units within their borders. Will the citizens of these states trust those ruling the state sufficiently to accept the Weberian monopoly? Or, perhaps thinking of the iconic Minutemen who revolted against King George III, will they imagine that similarly oppressive possibilities in the United States will make it important to have state militias and, quite possibly, to justify as well a right on the part of the general citizenry to "keep and bear Arms"?

The Constitution as understood by Publius did not yet include a Bill of Rights. That would come only in 1791, with the ratification of ten of twelve amendments proposed by the first Congress to the states. The Second Amendment (which, had all twelve been ratified, would have been the Fourth Amendment) famously states, in the version passed by Congress and located at the National Archives, "A well regulated Militia, being necessary to the security of a free State, the right of the people to keep and bear Arms, shall not be infringed." Interestingly, the version ratified by the states as authenticated by Thomas Jefferson, who as secretary of state was charged with indicating when (and how) the new Constitution had been amended, read "A well regulated militia being necessary to the security of a free state, the right of the people to keep and bear arms shall not be infringed." I will leave it to others to decide whether the absence or presence of commas—not to mention the capitalization or non-capitalization of "arms"—changes the text's meaning.

Most twenty-first-century arguments surrounding this amendment concern whether it protects only the right of states to have militias, a right that presumably cannot be limited by the national government (save that such militias, when called into national service, are to be subject to national control), or whether it protects as well the ability of "the people" more generally to "keep and bear Arms." The Supreme Court, in a bitterly divided 5–4 decision, decided in 2008 that the answer was the latter, and in 2010 it limited the ability of states, as well as the national government, to prohibit the possession at least of handguns in the privacy of one's home as a defense against criminal invaders.

Whatever one thinks of these decisions, it should be clear that the most interesting and volatile kind of "self-defense" is that against the oppressive state itself. Most readers are presumably familiar with the bumper sticker that proclaims, "When guns are outlawed, only criminals will have guns." This is patently false. Far more to the point, and far more challenging, is another bumper sticker: "When guns are outlawed, only the state will have guns." This might be false as well, at least as an empirical matter. No American government could entirely eliminate the private possession of guns, any more than Prohibition eliminated the actual possession and use of alcohol. But the theoretical issue cuts much more deeply. Assume for the moment that the state *could* establish a true monopoly on the possession of firearms and the right as well to define their legitimate use. Would we accept that? Or is it part of being "an American," for better or worse, to accept the widespread dispersion, including to the private citizenry, of the means of violence, whatever the attendant costs? Neither public opinion polls nor the actualities of the American legal order leave any doubt that most Americans are willing to accept these costs rather than tolerate a Weberian conception of the state that would legitimize disarming the citizenry.

# PART 5

## *How Does One Pay for the Services Supplied by the Union?*

### *On Taxes and the Taxing Power*

# FEDERALIST 30

## First Death, Now Taxes

IN *FEDERALIST* 23, Publius announced that the first among the "prin-cipal purposes" of any governmental system is to provide for the com-mon defense, which requires organizing and maintaining what Justice Harry Blackmun in a very different context—the legitimacy of capital punishment—described disapprovingly as "the machinery of death."[1] One might well agree with Blackmun about capital punishment, where the presumptive enemy of public order has already been successfully incapac-itated. But the point of the preceding essays is that unless one is a pacifist and agrees with Gandhi and Martin Luther King Jr. that nonviolent re-sistance is the only legitimate mode of opposition to even the most abject evil, one must accept the legitimacy of at least some state-inflicted death and destruction. If one accepts the rhetoric behind the American Revolu-tion, popularly generated violence directed at oppressive states may also be legitimate. As the late Yale Law Professor Robert Cover emphasized, no discussion of law—and of the "rule of law"—should avoid acknowledging the violence that underlies any such rule, whether we focus on the origins of the state or its maintenance.

As the old adage has it, the only certainties are death and taxes. Death, of course, can occur in many ways, most of them having little to do with the state. Taxes, however, make sense only in the context of organized governments. They authorize themselves to collect taxes, and those who refuse to pay may find themselves confronting the coercive force that the state can bring to bear. There is a reason, after all, that one of the first sustained displays of military force following the ratification of the Con-stitution occurred during the Whiskey Rebellion in Pennsylvania, which occurred from 1791 to 1794 as farmers refused to pay the taxes that com-prised a major source of federal revenue. It came to an end only in 1794, when President Washington himself marched at the head of over ten thou-sand state militiamen to confront the resistors.

Still, it takes only the barest familiarity with today's American poli-tics to know that the assignment and enforcement of federal tax burdens remains a volatile issue. Publius, having spent seven essays contemplating the means of violence, follows with an equal number of essays on taxation.

He begins, not surprisingly, by castigating the system of tax collection existing under the Articles of Confederation. The purported national government could only "requisition" desired amounts from the states, and these requests were rarely honored. Publius refers to the "state of decay, approaching nearly to annihilation" attached to the national government's inability to raise adequate revenue. If authorizing a standing army was one of the most important features of the new Constitution, authorizing Congress to tax members of the American political community directly was at least as important. The new country would no longer have to rely on the willingness of state authorities to comply with their requisitions.

"Money," California political leader Jesse Unruh once explained, "is the mother's milk of politics."[2] Even more is it the mother's milk of government institutions. Publius uses the more elegant language of the late eighteenth century to make the same point: "Money is, with propriety, considered as the vital principle of the body politic; as that which sustains its life and motion, and enables it to perform its most essential functions. A *complete power* therefore to procure a regular and adequate supply of [revenue] . . . may be regarded as an indispensable ingredient in every constitution" (emphasis added). To be sure, the "resources of the community" will limit the revenue the government can generate, but prudent political leaders will presumably recognize such limits. Otherwise, we might well ask, "What part of 'complete power' do you not understand?"

Publius emphasizes the stakes of making sure that the new country is to be perceived by its citizenry as providing security and otherwise working toward the "general Welfare," and by the international community as able to lay taxes sufficient to pay its debts. He notes that "in the modern system" (recall that he was writing in 1788), even "nations the most wealthy are obliged to have recourse to large loans." But, he asks, "who would lend to a government that prefaced its overtures for borrowing" by indicating uncertainty about its capacity to generate enough revenues to pay the interest and, eventually, the principal on the debt?

As of December 31, 2013, the Department of the Treasury reported the "external debt" of the United States to be over $16.5 trillion.[3] Presumably any reader of this book is familiar with the various "debt-ceiling crises" provoked by Congress's refusal to authorize increases in the national debt until almost literally the last minute before the United States would have been required to default. One such crisis, in 2011, provoked Standard & Poor's to reduce its rating of U.S. government bonds from AAA to AA. This drastic act was not provoked by fundamental doubts about the American economy's ability to rebound from the near-depression that began in 2008 with the near-collapse of the international banking system, but by concerns about the country's political system. "The downgrade reflects our view," Standard & Poor's explained, "that the effectiveness, stability, and predictability of American policymaking and political institutions have weakened at a time of ongoing fiscal and economic challenges." One can easily hear an echo of Publius's denunciation of the political system facing the United States in 1788. The key difference, of course, is that the "political institutions" being subjected to criticism by Standard & Poor's are those created in Philadelphia, the ones ostensibly designed to create the stability lacking in the system created by the Articles of Confederation.

Infants may survive, and even thrive, without access to their mothers' milk so long as adequate substitutes are available. But there is no substitute for revenues. Without them, polities inevitably decline. If one believes that the present government of the United States has lost its claim to support, then decline is presumably desirable. This is a widespread view. Grover Norquist, earlier cited as hoping to "drown" the national government by starving it of tax revenues, is also famous as the author of "the pledge," the public promise made by almost all Republican candidates for office for at least the past quarter century that they will never, ever vote to raise taxes. George H. W. Bush, in accepting his party's nomination for the White House in 1988, said "Read my lips: no new taxes," and it is widely thought that the major reason he lost his bid for reelection in 1992 was that he broke that pledge. By putting the interests of the country (as he was then) ahead of his own political welfare, Bush destroyed himself politically. Even his own sons have refused publicly to praise their father for doing what both he and most independent analysts believe served the national welfare.

## On the Inutility of Specified Limits

IMAGINE THAT THE Constitution allowed Congress to declare war only if it could guarantee that no more than 10,000 Americans would die. The nation's entry into World War II, the last officially declared war, where it suffered over 291,000 combat deaths, would thus have been unconstitutional if it were shown that this level of casualties was anticipated. Perhaps the Supreme Court would have been required to invalidate the declaration of war and order the troops home upon the 10,001st death.

The Constitution contains no such limitation. For better or worse, it relies exclusively on congressional judgment to do whatever is needed to rebuff threats to the American constitutional order. As much to the point, it would justifiably be regarded as crazy to support amending the Constitution to add such a limitation. Yet it would not be "crazy," at least not in the same way, to adopt a pacifist position that would simply disable the United States from possessing a standing army or even creating an armed force to dispel threats. But if one is not a pacifist, then a constitutional limit on the size of the army makes no sense.

Publius makes a similar argument with regard to the power to tax. Taxes are necessary to provide the benefits of government. "As the duties of superintending the national defense and of securing the public peace against foreign or domestic violence, involve a provision for casualties and dangers, to which no possible limits can be assigned, the power of making that provision ought to know *no other bounds* than the exigencies of the nation and the resources of the community" (emphasis added). So what is the problem?

The fear expressed by some opponents of the Constitution in 1787–1788—and by many opponents of the national government today—is that the national government, through excessive taxation, is in effect "usurping" the powers of the "sovereign" states and, ultimately, the "sovereign" individuals who comprise the public. Thus, according to critics, arises the importance of placing limits on the national taxing power.

Once again, Publius looks to political sociology rather than "parchment" to guard against excess. After all, he notes, the states themselves possess unlimited powers of taxation. Why do those fearful of oppression by the national government not express equal fears about the states? The answer, presumably, is not that state governments are better organized to supply protections that the national government cannot, but that critics of the new Constitution have confidence in state officials because these officials are embedded in the local communities that are the objects of taxing authority. Publius describes this as "a due dependence of those who are to administer [state programs] upon the people," perhaps through frequent elections and other means of accountability. He will ultimately argue that national officials will also be suitably dependent on the people and thus provide the same practical guarantees against usurpation. Our protection ultimately lies in "the prudence and firmness of the people; who, as they will hold the scales in their own hands, it is to be hoped, will always take care to preserve the constitutional equilibrium between the general and the state governments."

The problem, of course, is that there is no agreement on what constitutes the correct "equilibrium" with regard to taxation. It is easy enough to discover that for the fiscal year 2013, there was total governmental revenue of $5.6 trillion, with the national government receiving slightly more than half this amount ($2.8 trillion) and state and local governments splitting the rest ($1.7 trillion and $1.1 trillion, respectively).[1] How does one determine whether this represents a proper division of resources, or whether one or perhaps all governments are overly or insufficiently funded, given the demands now placed on them? We can be certain that elections will continue to feature angry and not always informative debates about the level of taxation. And any given election is more likely to leave the losers angry and preparing for what sometimes seems like political guerilla warfare than that they will accede graciously to the winners and accept the proposition that their views, whether "pro-tax" or "anti-tax," should perhaps prevail.

So how *should* we regard our payments to the Internal Revenue Service and its state and local equivalents? Justice Oliver Wendell Holmes Jr. once famously said, "Taxes are what we pay for a civilized society," a line that appears over the entrance to the IRS building in Washington. But only a "warfare state," perhaps one like ancient Sparta, would confine "civilization" to matters of warfare or even the "common defence." Most of us would find it admirable that the Preamble to the Constitution announces a number of other purposes, every one of which requires purchase, and that Congress is explicitly authorized, in the very first clause of Article I, Section 8 to tax and spend for the "general Welfare."

Only a particular kind of libertarian would identify "the Blessings of Liberty" with the freedom *against* paying taxes, perhaps because one views the state as an affront to, rather than a guarantor of, "civilization." Whatever else may be said about Publius, he clearly was not a libertarian who saw the government's role as limited to providing for the common defense. He consistently adopts a robust notion of government and recognizes the necessity of procuring tax revenues to finance government's legitimate ends. I do not suggest that one ought to adopt a Publian view simply because that was his view. But if one does believe that the Constitution establishes a national government with power commensurate to achieving the ends set out in the text, we still have much to learn from him about the practical entailments of that position.

## FEDERALIST 32

### *Taxation and Constitutional Interpretation*

REMARKABLY FEW OF *The Federalist* essays directly relate to the twenty-first century obsession with "constitutional interpretation," that is, the process of giving meaning to what I call the "Constitution of Conversation." The latter phrase refers to the parts of the Constitution that are decidedly unclear and therefore provoke often acrimonious conversation that in turn generates almost endless litigation, which has the function of continuing the conversation into the foreseeable future. Most of *The Federalist* instead discusses what I call the "Constitution of Settlement"—the parts of the text that, because of their clarity, generate remarkably little conversation among lawyers, law professors, and judges about their meaning. Instead, such discussion as there is involves the *wisdom* of decisions made in Philadelphia, or of the very few amendments that are equally clear in their meaning.

A fine example is the Twentieth Amendment. Its first section establishes that the inauguration of a new president will take place exactly at noon on January 20 following each election year. The second section stipulates that "Congress shall assemble at least once in every year, and such meeting shall begin at noon on the 3d day of January, unless they shall by law appoint a different day"—if, for example, January 3 falls on a Saturday or a Sunday and the previous Congress commands that the next Congress convene instead on the following Monday. Both of these measures effected important changes in the American political system. The first moved inauguration day from March 4 six weeks forward to January 20, recognizing that by the twentieth century—the Twentieth amendment was proposed and ratified in 1933, following Franklin Roosevelt's inauguration on March 4—the hiatus between the first Tuesday in November, when elections are held, and March 4 was simply too long. The world doesn't wait until March 4 to present problems requiring decisions, and lame-duck presidents, some of whom have been repudiated in the election, have lost the political authority attached to the office, even if they retain their technical legal authority. Under the original Constitution, newly elected Congresses were not required to convene for a full year after their election. This meant, among other things, that when Abraham Lincoln became president in 1861, he had no Congress to worry about (or to work with) until, invoking another section of the Constitution, he called it into special session on July 4 of that year. No modern president will have that option. As one might expect, however, there is no litigation involving the "interpretation" of the Twentieth Amendment, because its meaning is crystal clear. Even someone who believes, as I do, that it is past time to move up inauguration day even farther, perhaps even to November 15 (which would, among other things, almost certainly require abolition of the Electoral College), would not dream of filing a lawsuit asking the judiciary to rule that the January 20 date is unconstitutional. That literally makes no sense, even if it makes a great deal of sense to debate the wisdom of sticking to a date established more than eighty years ago.

What makes *Federalist* 32 almost unique is its attention to constitutional interpretation in the context of a particular problem involving the taxation power of the states. Earlier essays in this series have emphasized the basically unlimited powers of taxation possessed by Congress under the new Constitution. And much of the opposition to the Constitution was led by persons afraid of the way this power would affect the survival of states as vibrant "sovereigns" within the complex federal system that characterized the United States. Would Congress, for example, be able to deprive states, as subordinate members of the Union, of their own powers to tax their citizenry and gain the revenues necessary to finance state-level institutions?

Publius tells us unequivocally that states "clearly retain all the rights of sovereignty which they before had and which" are not, under the new Constitution, "*exclusively* delegated to the United States" (emphasis added). Certain powers do meet this condition. For example, only the national government can declare war or enter into treaties. But taxation is certainly not such a power. Both levels of government can raise revenues, subject to specific restraints set out in the Constitution itself. Thus, Article I, Section 9 prohibits the national government from taxing goods "exported from any State," while Article I, Section 10 specifies that congressional approval is necessary before any state can "lay any imposts or duties on Imports or Exports" into or from the United States. (As Publius notes, imposts on exports would seem to be covered by the prohibition in Section 9.) But, Publius argues, adopting a well-known lawyer's tactic, the very specificity of that prohibition on state power is definitive proof that they retain all other traditional powers of taxation. Thus, "as to all other taxes the authority of the States remains undiminished."

Publius admits that this concurrent taxing authority might generate "inconvenience" both for individual taxpayers and for the governments. But such questions of "expediency or inexpediency" would not be legal questions involving the limits of constitutional power. They are "questions of prudence" whose solutions "might require reciprocal forbearances" by leaders of the various governments.

Publius appears to be making a straightforward textual argument: One can ascertain constitutional meaning simply by reading the words set down and engaging in a series of logical operations with regard to the implications of their clear meanings. One might wonder what he would have thought about what is perhaps John Marshall's most important opinion, *McCulloch v. Maryland,* an 1819 case involving the chartering by Congress of the Second Bank of the United States and, crucially for our discussion here, a tax levied against the bank by the state of Maryland. Marshall struck down Maryland's tax, but not on the basis that the state was explicitly prohibited from taxing institutions chartered by the national government. He admitted that "[t]here is no express provision for the case," but he sustained the objection to the tax "on a principle which so entirely pervades the constitution, is so intermixed with the materials which compose it, so interwoven with its web, so blended with its texture, as to be incapable of being separated from it, without rending it into shreds." Maryland's tax was a direct assault on the national government, an attempt to cripple the Bank of the United States. The "power to tax involves the power to destroy," he memorably wrote, and states could not be permitted the legal power to destroy a national institution through taxation. It is worth noting that Marshall's stirring phrase is extraordinarily mischievous; as Publius and Holmes both correctly emphasized, the power to tax is also the power to create and maintain the institutions of governance upon which we depend for our common defense and general welfare.

As I have noted, the practical meaning of recognizing any retained "sovereignty" in the states that comprise the Union continues to haunt our polity. For the contemporary discussion, perhaps the most interesting aspect of Publius's argument in *Federalist 32* is the emphasis he places on text (and, seemingly, text alone) as the method by which to resolve interpretive controversies. Chief Justice Marshall went out of his way in *McCulloch* to note that "the opinions expressed by the authors of [*The Federalist*] have been justly supposed to be entitled to great respect in expounding the Constitution." Still, Marshall cautioned, "in applying their opinions to the cases which may arise in the progress of our government, *a right to judge of their correctness must be retained*" (emphasis added). That is, we must think for ourselves.

As we have just seen, Marshall decisively rejected an exclusive reliance on *text* in favor of *texture*. Any such position, by definition, requires us to recognize the limits of relying on text alone to determine the powers of (and limits on) government, including the powers of "sovereign" states to tax. We will have occasion later to discuss more explicitly the powers held by the Supreme Court, but it should be clear already that *McCulloch*, with its liberation from explicit textual constraints, represents not only an important extension of judicial power, whose ramifications remain altogether controversial almost two hundred years later, but also the explicit rejection of the argument so clearly set out by Publius. "Great respect" in no way entailed supine acceptance.

## FEDERALIST 33

### *The Irrelevance of Text*

THE PREVIOUS ESSAY raises the question of the *sufficiency* of the Constitution's text to provide an understanding of what it does and does not permit. We saw Publius suggesting that states basically had free rein with regard to exercising their "concurrent" power of taxation, save for the explicit limits set forth in the Constitution's text. In *Federalist* 33, Publius raises extraordinarily interesting questions—which, not surprisingly, haunt debates today—about the *necessity* of text to provide authority for governmental action. He focuses on two very important patches of constitutional text. One of them concludes the listing of congressional powers in Article I, Section 8. This is the "Necessary and Proper Clause," which states that "The Congress shall have Power . . . To make all Laws which shall be necessary and proper for carrying into Execution the foregoing Powers, and all other Powers vested by this Constitution in the Government of the United States, or in any Department or Officer thereof." The other is the "Supremacy Clause" of Article VI: "This Constitution, and the Laws of the United States which shall be made in Pursuance thereof; and all Treaties made, or which shall be made, under the Authority of the United States, shall be the supreme Law of the Land; and the Judges in every State shall be bound thereby, any Thing in the Constitution or Laws of any State to the Contrary notwithstanding."

Yet how important are these clauses? Surprisingly, Publius seems to suggest that the answer is "not very." He writes, "[I]t may be affirmed with perfect confidence that the constitutional operation of the intended government would be precisely the same, if these clauses were entirely obliterated. . . . They are only declaratory of a truth which would have resulted by necessary and unavoidable implication from the very act of constituting a federal government, and vesting it with certain specified powers." Were these clauses to be magically erased, it would not matter. They add nothing to what is already set down in the text. Publius calls the Necessary and Proper Clause (sometimes called the "Sweeping Clause") a mere "tautology or redundancy," though it is "at least perfectly harmless."

It happens that this essay's formal subject, like that of the surrounding essays, is the national government's power to tax, which Publius describes as "the most important of the authorities proposed to be conferred upon the Union," but his argument about the irrelevance of the Necessary and Proper and Supremacy Clauses holds for every assignment of power. "What is a power," he asks, "but the ability or faculty of doing a thing? What is the ability to do a thing, but the power of employing the MEANS necessary to its execution? What is a LEGISLATIVE power, but a power of making LAWS? What are the MEANS to execute a LEGISLATIVE power but LAWS? What is the power of laying and collecting taxes, but a LEGISLATIVE POWER, or a power of MAKING LAWS, to lay and collect taxes? What are the proper means of executing such a power, but NECESSARY and PROPER laws?" (capitalization in original). To be sure, laws that are *unnecessary* or *improper* would presumably violate the new Constitution, but that would be so even without the clause. Publius offers a series of examples of laws passed by Congress that would "exceed[] its jurisdiction, and infringe[] upon that of the State," but we do not need the reminder of the clause to know that the Constitution does not award Congress truly unlimited power to do just whatever it wants about whatever it wants. Congress must always be properly motivated to safeguard, for example, the common defense or provide for the general welfare; should it be malign with regard to these ends, that would be another matter entirely.

Similarly, with regard to the Supremacy Clause, it is logic rather than text that establishes the power of the new national government, at least whenever it passes laws that we would acknowledge as deemed necessary by Congress to achieve a proper objective. Again, Publius's capitalization emphasizes how little patience he has for any argument that national supremacy would be in doubt in the absence of this clause. If "individuals" or a "number of political societies" (call them states) "enter into a larger political society" like the one contemplated by the Preamble and set out afterward in the various articles of the new Constitution, "the laws which the latter may enact, pursuant to the powers entrusted to it by its constitution, must necessarily be supreme over those societies, and the individuals of whom they are composed. It would otherwise be a mere treaty, dependent on the good faith of the parties, and not a government, which is only another word for POLITICAL POWER AND SUPREMACY." Again, as with the Necessary and Proper Clause, Publius emphasizes that this is not a license for unrestricted power. "[A]cts of the large society which are NOT PURSUANT to its constitutional powers, but which are invasions of the residuary authorities of the smaller societies, will . . . be merely acts of usurpation, and will deserve to be treated as such."

So now we come to the central issue. Who exactly gets to determine when Congress has acted within the limits that Publius very clearly recognizes, with or without the Necessary and Proper or Supremacy Clauses? The answer is "the national government . . . must judge, in the first instance, of the proper exercise of its powers, and its constituents in the last. If the federal government should overpass the just bounds of its authority and make a tyrannical use of its powers, the people, whose creature it is, must appeal to the standard they have formed, and take such measures to redress the injury done to the Constitution as the exigency may suggest and prudence justify." One way "constituents" can act is to vote the rascals out in the next election, and for their new representatives to use the powers of Congress to repeal the offensive legislation. Another, far more controversial, response was articulated most memorably by Thomas Jefferson in the Kentucky Resolutions of 1798 and then by John C. Calhoun during the aptly named "Nullification Crisis" in 1832, involving South Carolina's attempts to invalidate a tariff passed by Congress. Both suggested that states could "nullify" what they deemed unacceptable overreaching by the national government. Most volatile of all, of course, is the possibility raised by at least one thread of the defense of popular militias and the right to keep and bear arms, which is to emulate the generation of 1776 and engage in armed revolt.

Publius's argument—strikingly to modern readers—makes no mention whatsoever of another possibility: the ability of courts to invalidate acts of Congress that are thought to transgress the Constitution. As we shall see, that theme is elaborated only some five months later, in *Federalist* 78. But that theme is absent here. Instead, Publius makes a far more populist argument, depending on an aroused "people" organized into politically active "constituencies" that will, perhaps like the president, feel themselves under a duty to maintain the boundaries between legitimate and tyrannical government.

A much-discussed topic in the twenty-first century has been "popular constitutionalism," which refers to the ability of "We the People" to be active participants in giving meaning to—and policing the meanings of—the Constitution of Conversation. One central question involves the capacity of ordinary Americans to engage in serious constitutional conversation. How we answer that question structures our response to the topic of the very first *Federalist* and its assumption that ordinary citizens—at least those capable of reading *The Federalist*—can engage in "reflection and choice" about their form of governance. But a second question concerns what *methods* of popular constitutionalism we are prepared to tolerate. It is one thing to suggest that unhappy constituents might vote against those they perceive as defenders of tyranny in the next election. It is quite another to let them engage in what earlier political theorists described (and often defended) as "tumults." In recent years, some members of the Tea Party have been criticized, at least by their opponents, for engaging in tumultuous protest. Such criticisms were also leveled against left-wing protesters during the 1960s and at members of the Occupy movement in 2011–2012. Should we, however, perhaps describe these protests as "Publian moments"?

## FEDERALIST 34

### *Drafting a Constitution with the Long View in Mind*

"CONSTITUTIONS OF CIVIL government," writes Publius, "are not to be framed upon a calculation of existing exigencies; but upon a combination of these, with the probable exigencies of ages, according to the natural and tried course of human affairs." It is altogether sensible, in drafting a budget for a single moment in time, to focus one's attentions on the immediate exigencies, and should they seem not so pressing, to draft a modest budget requiring only modest tax revenues. No one has ever favored the collection of taxes for their own sake. Taxes are *always* means to ends, and the level of taxation at any given time is always a function of the ends deemed pressing and in need of financing. In designing a constitution, however, as in purchasing a long-term insurance policy, one must think of potential "exigencies" and not only those that immediately come to mind. To take a most contemporary example, it is an excellent idea to possess medical insurance even if you are currently healthy. Especially if we are young, we may overestimate the likelihood of good fortune and dismiss the possibility of misfortune. We will want coverage when disaster strikes and will rue the day that we settled for a policy that protects us only against relatively minor diseases.

Near the conclusion of his reflections on the national taxing power, Publius returns to the central point that "the objects that will require a federal provision in respect to revenue . . . are altogether unlimited"—even if we require proper motivation and a desire to remain within the boundary lines that Publius recognizes. And, returning to his earlier theme, in no area is this point more easily demonstrable than providing for the common defense. It would "be the extreme of folly . . . to leave the government intrusted with the care of the national defense, in a state of absolute incapacity to provide for the protection of the community" because of insufficient revenues. It is also folly to assume any long period of international—or possibly domestic—tranquility that can allow permanently reduced budgets. "To judge from the history of mankind . . . the fiery and destructive passions of war, reign in the human breast, with much more powerful sway, than the mild and beneficent sentiments of peace." Thus, "to model our political systems upon speculations of lasting tranquility, [would be] to calculate on the weaker springs of the human character."

One simply cannot escape the extent to which the drums of war provide the background accompaniment to most of Publius's arguments for adoption of the new Constitution. The most fundamental metric against which to measure the new Constitution—or any other constitution—is its adequacy to safeguard the polity against threats. To be sure, one can imagine countries that might plausibly exempt themselves from such concerns. Perhaps New Zealand or Fiji is sufficiently protected by its ocean location against threats of invasion, though even those otherwise idyllic countries are sufficiently rent by internal divisions to make what our Preamble calls "domestic Tranquility" at least on occasion only an aspiration. But their condition is not our own. Our national government must always be concerned about "guarding the community against the ambition or enmity of other nations," and one cannot predict in advance what such protection might cost. Almost all other nations, of course, have similar concerns.

These concerns would arise even were the new United States of America simply a strengthened "Confederation" of independent states that had decided to enter into a mutual security pact against common enemies. Think of NATO, the most enduring of the "entangling alliances" the United States entered into following World War II. Today we may be inclined to dismiss NATO's importance, given the demise of the Soviet Union in the aftermath of the monumental events of 1989. Even if Vladimir Putin might threaten the autonomy of Ukraine, there is no plausible fear that Russia threatens the original members of NATO. But during the height of the Cold War, when it was thought necessary to "deter" the Soviet Union from attacking Western Europe, few were heard to declare that it was just "too expensive" (though one of the arguments for relying on nuclear weapons was that they provided "more bang for the buck"). Those who did protest the costs attached to "containment" usually went on to argue that it was simply not necessary to pay them because more modest responses would be equally effective in achieving our foreign policy objectives. Even today, when we are more likely to focus on ostensible threats posed by Iran or China, the debates are likely to be over what constitutes an effective policy—including the possibility that we must simply learn to tolerate a nuclear-armed Iran—rather than on the economic costs of a given policy.

In his inauguration speech on January 20, 1961, President John F. Kennedy said: "Let every nation know, whether it wishes us well or ill, that we shall pay any price, bear any burden, meet any hardship, support any friend, oppose any foe, in order to assure the survival and the success of liberty." We must ask ourselves whether we still find these words inspiring, or if they now strike us as dangerous and excessive rhetoric. Surely Kennedy knew the number of ways in which we "pay" the "price" of defending liberty; every Memorial Day evokes tributes to those who paid the "ultimate price." But for most of us, the most vivid reminder of the price of government comes each year on April 15, when one must send in one's taxes.

Publius's contemporaries in 1788, when they read about taxes to pay for standing armies, might have thought of such immediate costs as salaries for military personnel and supplying relevant armaments needed to defend vital American interests. But one can be confident that these readers, like Publius himself, were also aware of the nation's obligations to pay pensions to soldiers, especially those injured in the American Revolution. The Continental Congress in 1776 promised pensions to officers and soldiers disabled in the course of military service, and in 1780 the Continental Congress promised that the widows and orphans of officers (though apparently not of ordinary soldiers) who died in service would receive half pay for seven years. These promises built on earlier actions taken by Great Britain and the British North American colonies. Parliament passed legislation during its 1592–1593 session providing relief for soldiers and sailors whose sickness or disability occurred during their time of service. The Plymouth Colony, in what later became Massachusetts, was the first to pass veterans' legislation that was validated by the authorities in London. (They had earlier vetoed legislation passed in the Virginia Colony in 1624.) The Plymouth measure was passed "in 1636 to encourage service in the Pequot War [and] provided for the public maintenance of disabled soldiers. Similar legislation was passed in other colonies throughout the colonial era."[1]

Though these examples may sound like ancient history, they are hardly irrelevant to the costs attached to standing armies today, when American military personnel number more than a million and the United States is, more often than not, involved in wars that put many of them at risk. The good news regarding American involvement in Iraq (twice) and Afghanistan may be how relatively few American soldiers were killed, at least in comparison to the nearly 60,000 who gave their lives in the war in Vietnam. But one explanation for the lower mortality rate is that modern medicine could save many who earlier would have died; they may now need a lifetime of costly medical care. According to Vermont Senator Bernard Sanders, for example, in the years following 2011, the Department of Veterans Affairs gained 1.5 million new patients, 200,000 of whom suffered from traumatic brain injuries or post-traumatic stress disorder.[2] Sanders noted as well that a bill, according to *The New York Times*, "that would have bolstered health and dental care, authorized 27 new clinics and medical facilities, added to veterans education programs, and dealt with veterans who suffered sexual trauma while in the military" could not get a vote in the Senate because of a Republican filibuster. It is no surprise that a major scandal emerged in 2014 concerning the ability of the Department of Veterans Affairs to provide needed care to those whom politicians often call "America's heroes." Talk is cheap, but care is not. There can be little doubt that not only funding the active military but paying for the lifetime treatment that veterans may require will continue to be major issues on the American political agenda. Are we willing to accept the basic Publian insight that paying for the common defense may require taxation limited only by need? It would be comforting to believe that the scandals involving the VA involve nothing more than an inept department's failure to manage the copious resources made available to it by a generous Congress. One suspects that is not really the case.

FEDERALIST 35

## Who Will Allocate the Tax Burdens, and Why Should We Trust Them?

A S WE HAVE SEEN, Publius states several times that the principal—in fact the only—way of making sure that taxes remain fair, whether from the perspective of taxed individuals or of states, is by trusting the prudence of political decision makers. It is only fitting that *Federalist* 35, the penultimate among his seven on taxation, addresses directly why readers worried about creating a strikingly stronger national government should not fear that taxes will be imposed unfairly. As many critics of the Constitution pointed out, there would in fact be relatively few persons serving as "representatives" in the House of Representatives and even fewer in the Senate. How could they really be viewed as "representative"? At the time, the planned 65 members of the House of Representatives were to represent no more than 4 million Americans—many of them slaves who under no plausible theory were meant to be "represented"—plus women who could not, save in New Jersey until 1807, vote, not to mention children below whatever age was established as the time one could vote. Still, this meant that each of the 65 districts would have a voting population of roughly 20,000. Today, each of the 435 members of the House of Representatives notionally serves a proportionate share of a population that is more than seventy-five times that of the United States in 1790. Given the expansion of the electorate, especially through the Fifteenth, Nineteenth, and Twenty-sixth Amendments, the number of voters each member of the House represents is probably closer to 400,000. So the issue of what makes a representative truly representative remains a pressing question that is surely not decided simply by title. We could, after all, have chosen to call them "members of Congress," just as Great Britain and Canada refer to "members of Parliament" or Israel refers to "members of the Knesset."

Publius declares that the "idea of an actual representation of all classes of the people by persons of each class is altogether visionary." John Adams, among others, had written of "mimetic" representation, which, taken to its extreme, *does* mean that the House and Senate would, as President Clinton put it, "look like America." Someone looking around the floor of the House of Representatives would see at least one person who looked like herself and, presumably, could be trusted to convey her point of view to the assembled officials. That, to put it mildly, is not our system. The House and Senate predominantly remain a gathering of middle-aged white males, even if there has been a female Speaker of the House (Nancy Pelosi) and in 2014 a 20 percent female cohort in the Senate. During our entire history, there have been only nine African American senators (one of them, of course, named Barack Obama, who didn't remain in the Senate very long). Most senators in 2015 can accurately be described as millionaires, many of them many times over; however much candidates running for office might like to emphasize their humble backgrounds, not a single member of the current Congress can plausibly be described as a member of the working class. These are only some of the most obvious ways that officialdom differs from the "typical" American. Would this information have surprised, or disappointed, Publius when writing in 1788? More importantly, should it bother us today?

Publius is distinctly unbothered. "Unless it were expressly provided in the Constitution," which of course it is not, "that each different occupation should send one or more members the thing would never take place in practice." But there is no reason to worry, because the various occupational groups are in effect "represented" by the "merchants" who will fill the offices. Though he does not use the term, he could easily be offering a theory of "virtual representation," much beloved of English theorists defending the legitimacy of the House of Commons in an age when no more than 10 percent of commoners played any role in choosing its members. All of them were asked to believe that their interests would be addressed by the (undemocratically) chosen few. According to Publius, the merchant is the "natural patron and friend" of all whose interests depend on a thriving economy. "[H]owever great the confidence they may justly feel in their own good sense, their interests can be more effectively promoted by the merchant than by themselves." Merchants, we are assured, have developed "superior acquirements" linked to the capacity to govern, and in particular to decide what the tax burdens should be.

Of course, not only merchants will be elected to office. One can also look forward to the participation of the "learned professions," who, because "they truly form no distinct interest in society," will merit "the confidence" of all "other parts of the community." Although Publius is too tactful to say so, the leading "learned profession" is surely lawyers, who have never been unwilling to assert their ability to lead.

Finally, there is the "landed interest," and Publius is confident that "in relation to taxes," both the "wealthiest landlord" and the "poorest tenant" will be "perfectly united" in their political wishes. Still, lest we worry that the new Congress will contain too many of the former—given the near-impossibility that any "poor tenants" will be sent there—Publius assures us that "moderate proprietors of land" will tend to "prevail" in both the House and the Senate.

Publius concludes by conceding that "no part of the administration of government" requires such "extensive information and a thorough knowledge of the principles of political economy so much as the business of taxation." In this business, the country will be well served by a Congress dominated by merchants, lawyers, and landowners.

We do not know, of course, what fraction of the population approved of the job Congress was doing before the late twentieth century, when such polls became standard. Given some startling elections in the nineteenth century in which large numbers of incumbents were replaced by their opponents, one can surmise that there were many years when voters did not feel sufficiently "represented" by the incumbents. In the second decade of the twenty-first century, only about one-eighth of the American electorate expressed satisfaction with the Congress or "confidence" that they will be treated fairly by their ostensible "representatives." It is, I dare say, nearly impossible to share Publius's complacent optimism about the quality of America's political leaders, particularly with regard to taxation, and one can wonder about the number of his readers even in 1788 who were altogether reassured by his arguments. In any event, it remains true that decisions about taxation do indeed call for collective political decision making, not the application of some Constitution-given algorithm. Thus we remain at the mercy of the people who are elected to office and of the operation of the institutions they inhabit.

## FEDERALIST 36

### *State and National Officials as Partners or Adversaries*

IN *FEDERALIST* 36, Publius sums up his consideration of the power to tax; appropriately for a summary, he repeats many of his central points, including his reliance on the good sense of public officials at both the state and national levels, to resolve the conflicts that could otherwise arise between state and national governments both in need of revenues. He also notes that the Constitution *does* provide one important constraint on unfair taxation directed against particular regions of the country by requiring that "all Duties, Imposts, and Excises shall be UNIFORM throughout the United States." Congress cannot make it cheaper, for example, to ship goods to Boston than to Charleston. To this extent, the Constitution does more than simply rely on the prudence and good faith of officialdom.

Two additional points are worth noting, one repeating what Publius has said many times before, the other an interesting new point. As to the former, he apparently cannot say often enough that "[t]here may exist certain critical and tempestuous conjunctures of the State," those "common calamities" that call for governmental response and demand assurance of sufficient revenue to pay for it. He refers explicitly to the possibility of a "poll tax," by which he meant *not* a fee charged in order to vote but an assessment laid by the state on each member of the community. Prior to the twentieth century, the last such taxes in Great Britain were imposed by the new monarchs William and Mary immediately after taking office, from 1689 to 1692, and then in 1698. Publius, like most Englishmen, was no friend of the poll tax, but he believed that like all other modes of taxation (other than those explicitly forbidden by the Constitution), it should remain a possibility in case the national government someday needed to use it. Moreover, one advantage of the poll tax, as it was administered in Great Britain, is that it took into account the "rank" of the taxpayers and imposed a greater burden on the higher orders. As Publius writes, "Happy it is when the interest which the government has in the preservation of its own power, coincides with a proper distribution of the public burdens, and tends to guard the least wealthy part of the community from oppression!" While Publius hardly favored "soaking the rich," he clearly did not object to progressive taxation.

At least as interesting, given some decisions of today's Supreme Court, is Publius's emphasis throughout *Federalist* 36 that the national government will be able to call upon state tax officials to help in the collection of national taxes, when necessary, and thus avoid plaguing citizens with "double sets of revenue officers." The national government "will make use of the State officers . . . for collecting" national taxes. Publius here envisions an early form of what might be called "cooperative federalism," in which states are willing, perhaps even forced, to pitch in and help administer what Congress has deemed "necessary and proper" federal policies, including, obviously, the raising of revenue.

The modern Supreme Court has deemed such reliance on state officials to be equivalent to the national government's "commandeering" (even, according to some overheated critics, "kidnapping") state officials for national ends, and therefore, it has ruled, unconstitutional. If the national government wants to administer a national policy, it must do so itself unless a state voluntarily agrees to lend its hand. But, crucially, the national government cannot compel this. Publius does not address the issue of compulsion, perhaps because he presumes that states will be willing to cooperate with decisions reached by the national Congress even if they happen to disagree with the legislation in question. But recall Heather Gerken's and Jessica Bulman-Pozen's emphasis on the importance of what they term "uncooperative federalism." The Supreme Court has granted states a constitutional right to refuse to cooperate. At the very least, this conflicts with Publius's fleeting suggestion in *Federalist* 16 (and the argument he will make later) that the primary role of the judiciary will be to keep states in line. Perhaps, like Marshall in *McCulloch v. Maryland,* the modern Court honors *The Federalist* at least as much in the breach as in the observance of Publius's arguments.

# PART 6

## *To Err Is Human*
## *(and Perfect Clarity Is Chimerical)*

# Human (and Even Divine) Fallibility and Written Constitutions

WERE THE FRAMERS infallible? We already know that their own answer was no. Publius repeatedly urges his readers to learn from experience and *improve* the Constitution. A perfect constitution, by definition, would need no improvement—and certainly no critics—only devotion and ever-faithful adherence. What is wrong with the idea of a perfect constitution is brought home with special force in *Federalist 37*. Its purpose seems to be to elicit the readers' sympathy for the difficulties the delegates in Philadelphia faced in drafting the new Constitution and therefore to excuse the imperfections and lacunae that a careful analyst would surely find. One should not expect perfection from the Framers—or from their Constitution. Fair-minded analysts should not only lack "a disposition to find or to magnify faults" but should be aware "that a faultless plan was not to be expected." We should make allowance for the "fallibility to which the convention, as a body of men, were liable."

Besides acknowledging the inevitability of human error, Publius's readers should also recognize the special difficulties facing the Philadelphians, beginning with the "novelty" of what they were trying to do (though several states had paved the way, at least somewhat, by writing new constitutions in the aftermath of 1776). Publius also notes that the convention featured often-bitter conflicts, for instance between small and large states. (He doesn't dwell in this essay on the conflict between states that relied on slavery and those that did not and were moving toward becoming "free" states.) These conflicts were brought to a provisional end by the adoption of compromises, some of whose language would become the subject of heated dispute.

Publius could well have quoted the adage that "the best is the enemy of the good." He never argued that the Constitution was the best one imaginable. That was scarcely his own view, as he makes clear in *Federalist 62* when discussing the "evil" of equal state representation in the Senate. Rather, the Constitution was good enough, and should be ratified on that basis. As he suggested in *Federalist* 14, it would be up to future generations, understanding its imperfections, to strive to better it through amendment.

The most interesting aspect of *Federalist* 37 relates to the almost tragic dilemma facing anyone trapped within the limits of human understanding. "[A]ll the efforts of the most acute and metaphysical philosophers" have failed to generate an approach to the world or to the languages by which we confront it that allows us to differentiate precisely among the concepts we use to make sense of the world. "The most sagacious and laborious naturalists have never yet succeeded in tracing with certainty the line which separates the district of vegetable life from the neighboring region of unorganized matter, or which marks the termination of the former and the commencement of the animal empire." What, for example, do we make even today of the duck-billed platypus, an ostensible mammal that, nonetheless, reproduces by eggs instead of live birth? Those looking for neat, easily memorizable, dividing lines between mammals and others will be perplexed by the platypus.

If nature presents difficulties of conceptualization and classification, things get much worse when we approach "the institutions of man," such as those that are the subject of the Constitution. Once again, Publius asks for his readers' forbearance. "Experience," the most important of all teachers, "has instructed us that no skill in the science of government has yet been able to discriminate and define, with sufficient certainty, its three great provinces the legislative, executive, and judiciary; or even the privileges and powers of the different legislative branches. Questions daily occur in the course of practice, which prove the obscurity which reins in these subjects, and which puzzle the greatest adepts in political science." Anyone who asserts too confidently what constitutes an "executive" or "legislative" activity should remember the platypus and the puzzles presented by concrete reality.

One might well believe that Publius would sympathize with the thundering assertion with which Oliver Wendell Holmes Jr., almost a century later in 1881, would begin his seminal lectures *The Common Law*: "The life of the law has not been logic; it has been experience." Holmes almost contemptuously dismissed Christopher Columbus Langdell, then dean of the Harvard Law School, as a "theologian" caught up in the mistaken belief that law could be reduced to a series of concepts and propositions by which a professionally trained lawyer could deduce the single right answer to a complex case. Would that life were so simple. But as Publius tells us, it is not.

What came out of Philadelphia, of course, was a text—a document of words. "The use of words," Publius—a good Lockean—reminds us, "is to express ideas." But we must realize that "no language is so copious as to supply words and phrases for every complex idea, or so correct as not to include many" words that are not only vague but also often frustratingly ambiguous, "denoting different ideas." However well motivated an author might be, there is the constant danger—and reality—of "the inaccuracy of the terms" we use to delineate our polity. "And this *unavoidable inaccuracy* must be greater or less, according to the complexity and novelty of the objects defined" (emphasis added). Then comes the essay's most stunning sentence: "When the Almighty himself condescends to address mankind in their own language, his meaning, luminous as it must be, is rendered dim and doubtful by the cloudy medium through which it is communicated." No more devastating dismissal of biblical literalism has ever been penned.

But Publius was not writing an essay on theology. Instead, he was cautioning the people reading the Constitution in 1788 and trying to decide whether to ratify it, that the document was not crystalline in its meanings. It would inevitably be open to future interpretation. How would such interpretation take place?

Consider the following "rules of interpretation" proposed by James Madison in a speech he delivered to the United States House of Representatives (to which he was elected after having been frustrated in his desire to have the Virginia General Assembly name him as one of his state's first senators), explaining why he believed that the bill by which Congress would charter the Bank of the United States was unconstitutional. As it happened, that bill was written—and defended on constitutional grounds—by Alexander Hamilton. That these major founding figures disagreed so strongly on whether Congress, under Article I, Section 8, could charter the bank, suggests not only that the meaning of the Constitution was literally debatable but that there was no consensus, even among the Framers, as to what it meant. Madison offered the following "rules":

[1.] An interpretation that destroys the very characteristic of the Government cannot be just.

[2.] Where the meaning is clear, the consequences, whatever they may be, are to be admitted—where doubtful, it is fairly triable by its consequences.

[3.] In controverted cases, the meaning of the parties to the instrument, if to be collected by reasonable evidence, is a proper guide. Contemporary and concurrent expositions are a reasonable evidence of the meaning of the parties.

[4.] In admitting or rejecting a constructive authority, not only the degree of its incidentality to an express authority is to be regarded, but the degree of its importance also; since on this will depend the probability or improbability of its being left to construction.

An entire book could be written on these four rules and their application. For example, what *is* "the very characteristic of the Government" that purportedly stands before us as a beacon, so that we know that any interpretation that would "destroy" it is illegitimate? One might think the answer is found in the Preamble, which announces *why* the Constitution is being "ordained," and gives as one of its reasons to "establish Justice." But that is not Madison's answer. Instead, he suggests that "[t]he essential characteristic of the [national] Government" is that it is "composed of limited and enumerated powers." As suggested earlier, this seems to conflict with Publius's own arguments that the most essential characteristic is to provide for the common defense. At the very least, this rule tells us that we as interpreters must have our own view as to what the point, the purpose, of the constitutional enterprise really is.

With regard to the second rule, the task is to figure out which parts of the Constitution are truly "clear" and which are not. As a separate inquiry, would we really accept "the consequences, whatever they may be," even with regard to a "clear" textual command? Is it sensible to say "let the text be followed though the heavens fall"? Or do *all* texts, however clear they might be, come with an implicit "escape clause": "except when adherence would lead to the equivalent of the heavens falling"? We have already seen hints of Publius's likely answer in several of the earlier essays, especially *Federalist* 23. As we shall shortly see, this question is at the heart of *Federalists* 40 and 41.

The third rule asks us to divine what some would call "original intent" and what others, especially these days, would call the "original public meaning" of disputed texts. Madison suggests that "reasonable evidence" includes "[c]ontemporary and concurrent expositions" of the Constitution. But, of course, the point of the speech was to attack the view of the Constitution set out by Alexander Hamilton, which could well rely on Publius's own statements for its validity. His rules offer no way to decide between himself and Hamilton, other than reliance on one's opinion of the "consequences" attached to each view.

Finally, Madison reminds us that the Constitution, described by John Marshall as a great "outline," can scarcely be expected to speak clearly to *all* problems that might arise. A lot must be left to later "construction," as events make it necessary to confront problems the Framers might scarcely have anticipated. *Federalist* 37, therefore, may ultimately raise the same "meta-question" as does *Federalist* 14: Do we read them, or any other of *The Federalist* papers, for definitive answers to constitutional conundra? Or perhaps the ultimate message is instead: "Think for yourselves, drawing on your own lessons of experience. We did the best we could do, as inevitably fallible human beings. Now it's up to you."

## FEDERALIST 38

### *The Best as the Enemy of the Good—and the Necessary*

FEDERALISTS 37 AND 38 are perhaps best summarized as entreaties to those who assess the new Constitution not to expect perfection. Publius, fully aware of the objections to what emerged from Philadelphia, lists the critiques with something approaching irony, inasmuch as many of them come from opposite directions. The complaints of large states about the excessive power given small states in the Senate appear alongside the complaints of small states that they will be dominated by the large states in the House of Representatives. His point is that compromises were necessary to achieve any level of agreement in Philadelphia; one might always posit that an even better Constitution was attainable in theory, but the question is whether it was attainable in practice.

Even if we were to discount the political elements that demanded messy and frustrating compromises, there is the practical reality that those designing the Constitution were doing something unprecedented.

Mistakes were inevitable. "Is it an unreasonable conjecture," Publius asks, "that the errors which may be contained in the plan of the convention are such as have resulted rather from the defect of antecedent experience on this complicated and difficult subject, than from a want of accuracy or care in the investigation of it?" Even the best-motivated, most virtuous decision makers will display the all-too-human propensity toward error precisely because their knowledge is necessarily limited. Publius constantly reminds us of the importance of learning from experience, but that only suggests that the future will inevitably bring its own challenges to our perhaps overly confident beliefs about decisions we have made in the past. The "errors" of which he speaks "will not be ascertained until an actual trial shall have pointed them out." A mature person will not expect perfection, but she might expect that one will always be ready to reassess the status quo in light of new, often unexpected circumstances.

Publius underscores this point by emphasizing that "[i]t is not necessary that [the new constitution] should be perfect; it is sufficient" that it is better than what it seeks to replace. "No man," he suggests, "would refuse to quit a shattered and tottering habitation for a firm and commodious building, because the latter had not a porch to it; or because some of the rooms might be a little larger or smaller, or the ceiling a little higher or lower than his fancy would have planned them." The correct basis of comparison is not an idealized notion of "the right" constitution, but the existing system under the Articles of Confederation. Even Goldilocks would have been satisfied with porridge that was too hot or too cold, if baby bear's bowl were unavailable and she was sufficiently hungry. To be sure, if she had not been that hungry—if the American government established under the Articles of Confederation were not an "imbecility," but instead was working tolerably well to achieve the general public happiness and establish the United States within the concert of nations, then it would be perfectly reasonable to reject the new possibility as imperfect. But for Publius, the central lesson of experience actually before Americans in 1788 was the inadequacy of the existing order.

Publius notes that the Congress established by the Articles in effect recognized the limitations placed upon it by making several decisions that went well beyond its limited mandate. The maintenance of the Union has in effect already required that Congress "assume" powers not clearly granted to it. Describing the Articles as only a "lifeless mass" of authority, Publius notes that the Congress has already exercised "an excrescent power, which tends to realize all the dangers that can be apprehended from a defective constitution." It has repeatedly engaged in actions "without the least color of constitutional authority. Yet no blame has been whispered; no alarm has been sounded." Why? Because sober leaders realize that it would be foolish to stay within the boundaries of the Articles if the public good requires more energetic action. "The public interest, the necessity of the case," he concludes, "imposed upon them the task of overleaping their constitutional limits." This very fact offers "an alarming proof of the danger resulting from a government which does not possess regular powers commensurate to its objects. A dissolution or usurpation is the dreadful dilemma to which it is continually exposed."

Publius clearly does not blame the members of the existing Congress for preferring "[t]he public interest" and "the necessity of the case" over any purported duty to remain within "constitutional limits." *That* may be the most important of the "lessons of . . . experience" on which he draws. We shall return to such arguments when we come to *Federalists* 40 and 41. As with so much else in *The Federalist,* we must constantly ask ourselves whether the arguments apply only to the brand-new nation in the late eighteenth century, or whether they state enduring truths that must structure our own conversations and actions in the present time, as frightening as some of the implications may be.

## FEDERALIST 39

### *Federalism, "Compact," and the Specter of Secession*

POLITICAL THEORISTS speak of "essentially contested concepts," by which they mean terms that, despite having no uniform definition, nonetheless enjoy a great deal of cachet, not only among political theorists but, more importantly, among the public at large. Today, for example, no American political leader rejects the normative importance of "democracy," either within the United States or abroad. Yet beyond the bare requirement of holding elections, few pause to define which of the many conflicting notions of "democracy" they actually accept or reject. *Federalist* 39 is an essay about two "contested concepts," both extremely important within the debate over ratification.

The first concerned how to define a "republic" or "republican form" of government. Did the Philadelphians design such a government? The text of the Constitution guaranteed to all states the maintenance of a "Republican Form of Government," but the quality of that promise depends, of course, on what the term means. Publius begins by noting its protean character: The very different governments of Holland, Poland, Venice, and Great Britain all called themselves "republican." Any definition that allows this, he contends, is "inaccurate." What, then, constitutes a "republic"? The answer is deceptively simple: It is "a government which derives all its powers directly or indirectly from the great body of the people, and is administered by persons holding their office during pleasure, for a limited period, or during good behavior." The word "all" is crucial; whatever one thinks of the republican bona fides of Britain's House of Commons, for example, it is clear that neither the members of the eighteenth-century House of Lords nor the monarch held their offices for a limited period at the pleasure of the people. One might argue, given the turbulent history of Great Britain in the seventeenth century, that the Restoration of the aristocracy and monarchy and the supplanting of James II with the new kingship of William of Orange, brought to the United Kingdom from Holland, signified a certain kind of "consent of the governed." But the meaning of the American Revolution was presumably that such consent had to be less metaphorical and more instantiated in elections.

Still, a "republic" need not be anything close to a modern "democracy," if by the latter term one means that all primary political leaders are popularly elected. That is why Publius emphasizes the people's indirect choice. Senators under the Constitution were chosen by state legislators, just as presidents were selected by electors. It sufficed, at least for Publius, that the state legislators and electors were themselves chosen by voters even if the electorate was shut out of directly choosing either senators or presidents. Obviously, "We the People" ultimately rejected the "indirect election" of senators by ratifying the Seventeenth Amendment in 1913, which established direct popular election of senators, though widespread calls for similar repudiation of the Electoral College in favor of direct election have been rejected. Moreover, when Publius was writing in January 1788, it was no doubt widely believed that once George Washington left office, the House of Representatives would frequently have to pick the president from among the top five candidates after none achieved the support of a majority of the electors. As we shall see later, even though the number was rejected by the Twelfth Amendment in favor of the top three candidates, the specter of a president chosen by the House, on a one-state/one-vote basis, still hangs over us.

The second essentially contested concept at the heart of *Federalist* 39 is federalism itself. As noted earlier, opponents of the new Constitution, such as Patrick Henry, accused its supporters of advocating a national government with such "consolidated" powers that states became merely hollow shells bereft of their once-robust powers. Pleading guilty to this charge would have doomed the prospects for ratification, just as, even in the twenty-first century, no mainstream politician (or even Supreme Court justice) can admit that Henry was correct—and that we are, as a country, better off for our consolidation.

How does Publius fend off Henry's (and others') accusation that supporters of the Constitution reject federalism? He begins by looking at a provision that is unknown to most Americans today, Article VII of the Constitution. This sets out the procedure by which the new Constitution will take on legal life, since, after all, coming out of Philadelphia it was only a lifeless *proposal.* Only if the terms of Article VII were met would it become the country's supreme law. Article VII required the approval of nine states, in conventions that had been elected by the people, who alone supplied the republican bona fides of the new order. One can speak of "the act of the people" but at the same time note that these were the people of "so many independent States, *not* . . . one aggregate nation" (emphasis added). The Preamble speaks of the Constitution as being ordained by "We the People of the United States," but it does not tell us how to inflect the title of our country. Some suggested that the new country take on a new name, such as Columbia; they were obviously rejected, in favor of retaining a name that in no way resolved the question of the Union's ultimate nature. Consider, for example, the United Nations, which no one would confuse with a "world government," or, more to the point, a united international "nation." Save in the minds of certain utopian dreamers, it is a collection of sovereign states that have come together for certain limited purposes and that may freely exit should they lose patience with the international organization. (Thus the call among some political conservatives for America to leave the United Nations.) The same is true of the European Union, whose basic constitution-like treaty includes a specific provision allowing the withdrawal of a member country.

One can see in *Federalist* 39 the origins of the argument that Madison and Jefferson would articulate with far greater force in the Virginia and Kentucky Resolutions of 1798, which set out the so-called "Compact Theory" of union. Under this formulation, the Constitution was a compact by which "We the People" of Virginia chose to enter into a union with "We the People" of all other specific states whose people made the same choice. This is the meaning of ratification. As Publius correctly insists, Article VII did not require a "decision of a MAJORITY of the people of the Union." One could easily assume that if nine states ratified the Constitution, a majority of the population would have voted in favor, but this is not necessary. The real point is that the nine represented a supermajority of the states themselves. Even those nine states could not force membership on a state whose people voted against it. This is why, when George Washington took the oath of office in April 1789, there were only eleven states in the Union. Rhode Island and North Carolina remained holdouts.

Compact Theory raised many questions. The most important, both conceptually and practically, was whether it allowed secession by a state whose people concluded that the Union was not living up to its promise. Madison was still alive in 1830 to take umbrage at suggestions that his Compact Theory supported the secessionists' arguments, made most notably by South Carolina's John C. Calhoun. But as with all essentially contested theories, their authors have little control over how their arguments are used once they enter the marketplace of ideas. It may be of interest that the author resists the manner in which someone else uses his or her argument; but unless the interpreter makes a true logical error, one simply cannot say that it is "wrong" merely because the original author rejected it. Intellectual history is rife with persons who were aghast at the uses made of their ideas.

"Federalism" can mean many things. But surely one possible meaning is that the original entity that chose to enter into union retains an option to exit. Lincoln offered a mocking response to defenders of secession: "In their view, the Union, as a family relation, would not be anything like a regular marriage at all, but only as a sort of free-love arrangement to be maintained on what that sect calls passionate attraction."[1] This comment drew a laugh from Lincoln's audience, but it is scarcely a laughing matter.

After all, consider a sentence that appeared in the penultimate paragraph of the penultimate draft of the Declaration of Independence, in which Thomas Jefferson noted that British misconduct served to generate "the last stab to agonizing affection," so that "manly spirit bids us to renounce forever these unfeeling brethren."[2] The affection necessary to maintain political unity, especially in a federal political system that can be understood only against the background of *dissensus* and the potential for "disaffection," can never be taken for granted. We *were* a "house divided," as Publius well knew, and it was the perhaps dubious premise of the 1787 Constitution that it was building a house that would be able to stand.

This question is posed most directly by the tall statue that today dominates the grounds of the Texas state capitol, dedicated to those who died fighting for the Confederacy between 1861 and 1865. Those who placed the monument on the capitol grounds in 1901 also provided, on one side of the monument, this message: "DIED FOR STATE RIGHTS GUARANTEED UNDER THE CONSTITUTION. THE PEOPLE OF THE SOUTH, ANIMATED BY THE SPIRIT OF 1776, TO PRESERVE THEIR RIGHTS, WITHDREW FROM THE FEDERAL COMPACT IN 1861. THE NORTH RESORTED TO COERCION. THE SOUTH, AGAINST OVERWHELMING NUMBERS AND RESOURCES, FOUGHT UNTIL EXHAUSTED."

Texas Governor Rick Perry made news in 2010 when he granted a measure of respectability to the threat of seceding from the Union should the national government not stop what Perry regarded as illegitimate interference in the prerogative of states to govern themselves. Two years later, several hundred thousand Americans—over one hundred thousand in Texas alone—made more news when they signed a petition addressed to the White House, asking in effect to be allowed to secede from a union they thought was in terminal decline because it had reelected President Obama. One can obviously doubt whether any real threat of secession exists in the United States today. But we may still ask whether a modern secessionist movement would necessarily be un-American or anti-constitutional, or instead would be an intellectually admissible version of the essentially contested concepts of federalism and republican government.

# PART 7

## *On the Limits of the "Rule of Law"*

# FEDERALIST 40

## *Exigency and Fidelity to Law*

THE CENTRAL THEME of *Federalist* 40, an extraordinarily interesting essay, appears in the very first sentence: "whether the convention were authorized to frame and propose this mixed Constitution." It was not remotely clear that the delegates who convened in Philadelphia had been faithful either to the mandate given them by Congress, which was only to propose "revisions" of the Articles of Confederation or far more seriously, to the Articles themselves. Under Article XIII, amendments could be adopted only by the consent of the state legislatures of each and every state within the "perpetual Union." Yet Article VII of the proposed new Constitution stated that "The Ratification of the Conventions of nine States, shall be sufficient for the Establishment of this Constitution between the States so ratifying the Same." New Hampshire, the ninth state to register its approval, did so on June 21, 1788.

Ironically, inasmuch as *The Federalist* was primarily directed to the delegates to the New York convention meeting in Albany, it was irrelevant. When these delegates voted on July 26, they faced a very different reality from that existing six weeks earlier, when their ratification might have been legally necessary to bring the Constitution into being. By July 26, there was no such necessity. One can easily find this a somewhat fanciful analysis, for like the tenth state, Virginia, which ratified on June 25, 1788, it was certainly politically necessary that New York agree with the Constitution. Had either Virginia or New York refused to ratify, it is hard to imagine that many people would have thought it didn't matter or that the Union could have lasted very long without these states. Yet it clearly was not crucial that neither North Carolina nor Rhode Island had ratified the Constitution when George Washington took the oath of office on April 30, 1789, as the first president under the new government. Both states eventually did: North Carolina on November 21, 1789, and Rhode Island on May 29, 1790. Interestingly, the vote in Rhode Island, even under the extreme circumstances of being the sole remaining holdout (and, according to some, facing a possible invasion from Massachusetts or Connecticut), was only 34–32. We will never know what would have happened had two delegates changed their minds and voted against ratification.

What makes the *Federalist* 40 of continuing interest is Publius's defense of the delegates' indifference to the restraints imposed by Article XIII. Front and center in his defense is that these delegates "were deeply and unanimously impressed with the crisis" facing the country because of the manifest deficiencies of the Articles, and were convinced "that such a reform as they have proposed was absolutely necessary to effect the purposes of their appointment," which was to resolve the crisis. If this could have been accomplished within the boundaries of the Articles, they would have done it. But it was far better to confront the crisis and reach a resolution than to insist on thoughtless fidelity to a provision of the Articles that itself helped to cripple the country by making amendment nearly impossible.

Now we come to the heart of the matter: What do we expect from political leaders, such as those present in Philadelphia, when confronted with ostensible crises? Publius's guiding rule is deceptively simple: "[I]n all great changes of established governments, forms ought to give way to substance." He condemns "a rigid adherence" to "forms," inasmuch as that "would render nominal and nugatory the transcendent and precious right of the people to 'abolish or alter their governments as to them shall seem most likely to effect their safety and happiness.'" He is obviously evoking the Declaration of Independence, which gives consent of the governed priority over the "forms" of "established governments." How are such revolutionary transformations achieved? Here, too, Publius supplies an answer: Because "it is impossible for the people spontaneously and universally to move in concert towards their object; . . . it is therefore essential that such changes be instituted by some INFORMAL AND UNAUTHORIZED PROPOSITIONS, made by some patriotic and respectable citizen or number of citizens."

"INFORMAL AND UNAUTHORIZED PROPOSITIONS" means rejecting legal form in favor of doing what the situation demands. Publius praises those who brought about the American Revolution for having "no little ill-timed scruples, no zeal for adhering to ordinary forms." To evoke Ecclesiastes once more, if there is a time for legal fidelity, there is also a time for placing the law to one side and doing what is necessary to overcome a crisis. The delegates are saved from condemnation not only by the goodness of their motives but by the fact that their proposals were "to be submitted TO THE PEOPLE THEMSELVES"—or, more accurately, to conventions elected by a relatively wide (for the time) franchise of the people. Should "the people" themselves approve the new Constitution, this would "blot out antecedent errors and irregularities."

Publius concludes *Federalist* 40 by stating that even if the delegates "had violated both their powers and their obligations, in proposing a Constitution, this ought nevertheless to be embraced, if it be calculated to accomplish the views and happiness of the people of America." The message appears to be that the United States, at least in its origin, should be viewed less as a "rule of law" regime than as one in which the people, under presumptively patriotic leaders, are always free to determine that the law must be bent and subordinated when this is necessary to achieve a great national purpose.

The question, as with all of *The Federalist* essays sounding the same theme, is whether we can restrict this message to the particular crises or "exigencies" of 1787–1788, when the essays were written and published, or whether Publius's denunciation of "ill-timed scruples" and the need to accept the leadership of "patriotic" leaders has purchase in the twenty-first century. It takes little effort to think of presidents, all of them undoubtedly patriotic, who pushed various envelopes of legal constraints. Abraham Lincoln, notably, is more easily described as the "Savior of the Union" or the "Great Emancipator" than as a paragon of legal fidelity. One of Lincoln's best-known lines, after all, is his question to critics of his unilateral suspension of habeas corpus, deemed unconstitutional by Chief Justice Roger Brooke Taney (and many others, then and now): "[A]re all the laws, but one, to go unexecuted, and the government itself go to pieces, lest that one be violated?" All of America's presidents since Franklin Roosevelt might well have offered the same question at one or another point in their presidencies.

The United States is always faced with adversaries, both internal and external, who themselves are less than paragons of legal fidelity. Is the Constitution ultimately to be dismissed as mere "parchment," easily ignored, whenever such adversaries generate a crisis that must be met? Is the "constitutional order" different from a single aspect of that order, the written Constitution? And if there is a conflict, is not Publius justifying the subordination of the latter to the former?

## Existential Dangers and Legal Fidelity

*F*EDERALIST 41 OFFERS a "General View of the Powers Conferred by
The Constitution." Many powers that were discussed in 1788 remain
obviously relevant in the twenty-first century. But Publius's most interesting, and perhaps ominous, remarks involve creating a government that
can provide "[s]ecurity against foreign danger," which he plausibly describes as "one of the primitive objects of civil society." It is hard to recommend adoption or maintenance of a constitutional system that does not
provide such security.

Safeguarding security may require war. Thus it is no surprise that the
Constitution explicitly gives Congress the power of declaring war. One can
argue whether this power is exclusive to Congress or whether the president, as commander in chief, can do so on his own, but there is no serious
argument about the necessity of contemplating war to protect the United
States. War involves armed forces, which the Constitution authorizes the
national government to "raise and support."

Then we come to a central question: Are there limits on what the
national government can do to preserve security? "[W]as it necessary,"
Publius asks, "to give an INDEFINITE POWER of raising TROOPS, as well as
providing fleets; and of maintaining both in PEACE, as well as in war?" He
believes the answer is "obvious." How could one limit "the force necessary
for defense" unless one could also "limit the force of offense? If a federal
Constitution could chain the ambition or set bounds to the exertions of
all other nations, then indeed might it prudently chain the discretion of
its own government, and set bounds to the exertions for its own safety."
But that, obviously, is a fantasy. Publius's vision of the international system is thoroughly Hobbesian; the United States is part of an international
system of rapacious states whose actions against potential adversaries
are limited only by circumstances, not by any genuine legal constraints.
"How," he asks, "could a readiness for war in time of peace be safely prohibited, unless we could prohibit, in like manner, the preparations and
establishments of every hostile nation?"

It is futile to think that law or morality would (or should) limit "readiness for war," or even more, the actual conduct of any war deemed legiti-

mate. "The means of security can only be regulated by the means and the danger of attack. They will, in fact, be ever determined by these rules, and *by no others. It is in vain to oppose Constitutional barriers to the impulse of self-preservation. It is worse than in vain; because it plants in the Constitution itself necessary usurpations of power, every precedent of which is a germ of unnecessary and multiplied repetitions*" (emphasis added). Thus even "the most pacific nations" will be obliged to "maintain[] constantly a disciplined army, ready for the service of ambition or revenge" when it faces an armed enemy.

Would that we could view *Federalist* 41 as simply a relic, of interest only to historians of the period and raising no questions today. That is, obviously, not the case. September 11, 2001, is only the most recent example of a watershed moment that, in the minds of many, "changed everything." From the very beginning, the United States has been faced with possible "existential moments" that, many proclaim, call for the suspension of ordinary norms. Søren Kierkegaard famously referred to "the teleological suspension of the ethical." What this means, basically, is that end (the *telos*) will always justify the means, including the suspension of what otherwise would be disciplining rules. Publius, like Hobbes, suggests that the most obvious end is "self-preservation," and that those with governmental power will inevitably believe they are justified in doing whatever it takes to prevail.

For examples, one need look no farther than the rationales offered for the use of torture by the Bush administration and the rendition of suspected terrorists to countries that undoubtedly used torture in their interrogations. One can also point to the Obama administration, not because there is evidence that that administration engaged in identical practices, but because of President Obama's systematic refusal to hold anyone accountable for arguably illegal acts done as part of the "global war on terror." It is especially telling that this de facto mercy shown torturers and other miscreants has not been matched with regard to the treatment of those who have embarrassed the administration by leaking information of questionable national security policies. With regard to the latter, the administration has not only prosecuted but also insisted on jail sentences for their breach of the classification system.

Whether or not the Obama administration agrees with the arguments made by John Yoo, who as a lawyer for the Office of Legal Counsel within the Justice Department argued that the president in effect had the inherent power to order torture and violate any other legal rule standing in the way of national defense, it clearly seems to agree that Yoo was a dedicated patriot motivated to protect the country. Indeed, the theme of "patriotism" suffused the initial statements by the White House following the publication of a devastating report by the Senate Intelligence Committee detailing the misconduct and mendacity of the CIA. The president resolutely refused to take any position on the report (including whether the behavior described in fact counted as "torture"). One does not have to believe that "patriotism is the last refuge of the scoundrel" in order to recognize that it can serve as the excuse for horrendous actions. Thus, in effect, proper motivation and "purity of heart"—at least with regard to torturers, though not leakers—triumph over the almost irrelevant detail that the United States had signed the United Nations Convention Against Torture and Other Cruel, Inhuman or Degrading Treatment or Punishment, Article 2 of which explicitly provides that "No exceptional circumstances whatsoever, whether a state of war or a threat of war, internal political instability or any other public emergency, may be invoked as a justification of torture." Is this just another "parchment provision," to be disregarded whenever one believes, however debatably, that national survival is at stake?

I noted earlier that the American Bar Association is in the habit of exporting copies of *The Federalist* to constitution drafters around the world. Perhaps one should wonder how carefully the ABA has itself read *The Federalist* and, therefore, exactly what messages about constitutions and constitutionalism they believe it sends to readers in the twenty-first century. Of no essay is this more true than *Federalist* 41, which appears to put the "rule of law" in its place, so to speak, which is distinctly subordinate to beliefs by "patriotic" ruling elites that the "preservation" of the polity is at stake, requiring desperate measures that may well be "illegal."

# PART 8

*National and State Prerogatives
(and Maintenance of a
Federal Political Order)*

# Who Should Control Naturalization
## (and Immigration)?

T HE GENERAL THEME of *Federalist* 42 is the desirability of giving the centralized national government decision-making capacity on a host of issues, including the conduct of foreign policy and regulation of interstate and foreign commerce. For twenty-first-century readers, Publius's most interesting comments may involve the importance of assigning to Congress the power to establish "an uniform Rule of Naturalization." Although each state would retain the power to declare whether a particular alien X was a citizen of that state, that decision would have no consequences for any other state. For X to become a citizen of the United States, recognized in all states alike, would take compliance with national legislation. This is no small matter, then or now, inasmuch as states have always differed significantly on their hospitality to outsiders, while the new Constitution provides that "the Citizens of each State shall be entitled to all Privileges and Immunities of Citizens in the several States," including having the right to travel from one state to another. Without being very specific, Publius adverts to the possibility that "certain descriptions of aliens" might "render[] themselves obnoxious" in some states even while other states prove more accepting. (It takes no great imagination to imagine that these "descriptions" might involve race or religion.) "What would have been the consequence," Publius asks in what he surely believes is a rhetorical question, "if such persons, by residence or otherwise, had acquired the character of citizens under the laws of another State, and then asserted their rights as such, both to residence and citizenship, within the State proscribing them?" Thus only the national government definitively says who is welcome to join the American political community and who is not.

The Naturalization Act of 1790, one of the first pieces of legislation passed under the new Constitution, declared that only "free white persons" were eligible to become citizens, a limitation that remained part of American law until after the Civil War, when black aliens (as differentiated

from freed slaves whose citizenship was recognized by the Fourteenth
Amendment) were made eligible for naturalization. Asians did not become generally eligible for naturalized citizenship until 1954, though the
ban against Chinese was lifted in 1943, no doubt because we were allied
with China against Japan.

Aliens of Japanese origin remained ineligible for citizenship until
1954. During World War II, some 120,000 Japanese resident aliens and
Japanese American native-born citizens were removed from the West
Coast and detained in concentration camps in a policy upheld by a divided
Supreme Court in 1944. There were Japanese-American citizens only because Section 1 of the Fourteenth Amendment gave birthright citizenship
to anyone born within the territory of the United States (though this was
interpreted not to apply to American Indians born on reservations, who
did not get birthright citizenship status until 1924). Obviously, the Fourteenth Amendment arrives in the Constitution some eighty years after
Publius was writing, and it is interesting that he makes no reference to
one of the significant lacunae in the original Constitution: the failure to
provide any definition of "natural born Citizen" and therefore eligibility
to become president of the United States. Does this mean anyone born
within the United States? As a political matter, the answer must be no, or
else all slaves born in the United States would automatically be citizens. It
was unthinkable that that could be the case. To be a slave was emphatically
not to be a citizen. Indeed, Chief Justice Taney wrote in the infamous *Dred
Scott* case in 1857 that neither slaves nor anyone descended from slaves—
which, in effect, meant every "Negro" in the antebellum United States—
could be a citizen. Blacks (and not only slaves) had no rights that whites
were "bound to respect." Taney did concede that particular states could,
if they wished, grant citizenship rights, including even the right to vote,
to their native black populations. But such a decision by a state bound no
other state, for the reasons set out by Publius with regard to alien naturalization. It would take a war to resolve this definitional question through
the addition of the Fourteenth Amendment.

Surely Publius realized that the status of those born within the United
States and the naturalization of aliens raised profoundly important questions for the new nation, but he also clearly believed that the less said
about this the better. His reticence is placed into especially interesting
relief by his almost bizarre praise of the new Constitution for specifying

the national power "of appointing and receiving 'other public ministers and consuls'" in addition to ambassadors. One can be confident that few readers today, including professors of constitutional law, ponder the importance of this clause. Publius, on the other hand, after noting that the Articles of Confederation refer only to "ambassadors," suggests that this "comprehends the highest grade only of public ministers, and excludes the grades which the United States will be most likely to prefer, where foreign embassies may be necessary. And under no latitude of construction will the term [ambassador] comprehend consuls." He commends the drafters in Philadelphia for their precision in correcting this deficiency in the Articles. Perhaps this is one of the "lesser instances in which the convention have improved on the model before them. But the most minute provisions become important when they tend to obviate the necessity or the pretext for gradual and unobserved *usurpations* of power" (emphasis added).

As we have seen, Publius argues that under the limitations of the Articles, Congress has been "forced by the defects of the Confederation, into violations of their chartered authorities," which one might easily argue violates the central purpose of a constitution. One can only wonder, of course, whether the absence of the "Public Ministers and Consuls Clause" in the Constitution would really have prevented Congress from arguing that the Necessary and Proper Clause allowed treating "ambassadors" as representing the entire category of foreign representatives (and representatives sent by the United States to foreign countries), especially if one adds to the argument the "exigencies" that might follow from the kind of literalist interpretation he suggests. Still, at least with regard to appointing or receiving "consuls," there is no need to engage in fancy interpretation. One can simply point to the Constitution's text and end the discussion. But a reader, both then and now, might still be excused for wondering how truly important the clause is and wonder why equal attention was not paid to limning the definitions of citizenship. There is an easy explanation, which simply reminds us of the fact that constitutions are always drafted in "real political time," with concomitant attention to those issues that are best left unmentioned. To pay attention to their ramifications would run the risk of exposing fault lines that might lead to the unraveling of the whole enterprise of constitutional formation. Let sleeping dogs lie—at least until they awaken and turn out to be wolves that threaten the maintenance of an existing constitutional order, as happened in 1861.

FEDERALIST 43

## Controlling Internal Insurrections

OF ALL OF THE ESSAYS making up *The Federalist*, essay 43 may be the most meandering. Publius covers a lot of territory, often simply quoting the text of the Constitution and making a relatively perfunctory comment about its purpose. A modern reader will not find much of it riveting. There *is* a potentially interesting discussion of what it might mean to guarantee states a republican form of government, but few readers who are not political theorists are likely to find it very compelling, simply because the language of "republican government" has largely dropped out of our general vocabulary. One of the reasons is that the Supreme Court has resolutely refused to treat the "Guarantee Clause" as "justiciable," which means, almost by definition, that there is no body of case law developing the concept and wrestling with its complexities.

Of more contemporary relevance are Publius's musings about the actualities of responding to potential violence within a particular state. One thing that the "Republican Form of Government Clause" does is license the federal government, at least on the state government's "application," to intervene with armed force to protect the existing (presumptively republican) government. Publius offers the prospect that an internal insurrection might be led by noncitizens. "Nothing can be more chimerical," he suggests, "than to imagine that in a trial of actual force, victory may be calculated by the rules which prevail in a census of the inhabitants, or which determine the event of an election!" Wars are not elections. We might wish to substitute ballots for bullets, but those who lose out in a system that relies exclusively on ballots—perhaps because they are excluded from voting—may well prefer bullets.

It is possible, Publius reminds us, "that the minority of CITIZENS may become a majority of PERSONS, by the accession of alien residents, of a casual concourse of adventurers, or of those whom the constitution of the State has not admitted to the rights of suffrage." He goes on ostentatiously to "take no notice of an unhappy species of population abounding in some of the States, who, during the calm of regular government, are sunk below the level of men; but who, in the tempestuous scenes of civil violence, may emerge into the human character, and give a superiority of strength to any party with which they may associate themselves." Publius, in other words, always had to take into account the possibility of slave insurrections, particularly in states like South Carolina, where slaves were a majority. It is, of course, one of the dreadful anomalies of not only American political thought but of American history that a socioeconomic system built on the ownership of human beings was seen as compatible with the prerequisites of a republican form of government. One ordinarily thinks of the Constitution's recognition of slavery in the context of protecting the international slave trade until 1808; guaranteeing slave states the return of fugitive slaves who had fled to so-called "free states"; and perhaps most importantly, the three-fifths compromise, by which slave states were in effect guaranteed enhanced representation in the House of Representatives (and, therefore, also the Electoral College). But the Guarantee Clause was, in some eyes, yet another sop to slave states inasmuch as their governments could call on the armed assistance of the national government to suppress any slave uprisings.

Publius exclaimed about the potential benefits of the Guarantee Clause: "In cases where it may be doubtful on which side justice lies," he writes, "what better umpires could be desired by two violent factions, flying to arms, and tearing a State to pieces, than the representatives of confederate States, not heated by the local flame? To the impartiality of judges, they would unite the affection of friends." But, of course, the national government could not be impartial if it was bound to support the plea by the established state government to reinforce the status quo by suppressing any insurrectionists. In any event, Publius writes, "Happy would it be if such a remedy for its infirmities could be enjoyed by all free governments; if a project equally effectual could be established for the universal peace of mankind!" That is, one advantage of a federal regime is precisely that each constituent state would have the United States Army (and other states' militias) as backups in case certain natives got restless.

But what if the entire society was riven by insurrection? Here, Publius is less reassuring. "[N]o possible constitution can provide a cure" if an insurrection arises "pervading all the states, and comprising a superiority of the entire force." Instead, one must take solace in the fact that the federal Constitution "diminishes the risk" of such a "calamity."

Also of interest to some twenty-first-century readers, especially if, like myself, they are critics of the Constitution who believe significant amendments are necessary in order to construct a system of government suitable for twenty-first-century realities, is Publius's discussion of Article V, the "Amendment Clause." He addresses "[t]wo questions of a very delicate nature," both arising as implications of Article VII, which stated that the new Constitution would become valid, thus supplanting the Articles of Confederation and the government established under its provisions, with the ratification of conventions in *nine* states (against the unanimous consent required by the Articles). What justified the willful setting aside of the Articles' terms? One possibility is that the Articles of Confederation should be viewed more as a treaty among sovereign states than an amalgamation of those states into a genuinely *United* States of America. If so, then a principle of treaty law, good to this day, is that breach of treaty obligations by one signatory in effect frees other signatories from their duties to comply. "[A] breach, committed by either of the parties, absolves the others; and authorizes them, if they please, to pronounce the compact violated and void." Yale Professor Akhil Reed Amar, emphasizing this aspect of Publius's argument, has asserted that it is simply mistaken to believe that the Framers of the Constitution "violated" the terms of the Articles. They had already lost their legal force through multiple breaches, including the failure by various parties to supply the tax revenues "requisitioned" from them. Yet Publius only broaches this possibility; he does not wholeheartedly adopt it.

Instead, he enthusiastically adverts to "the absolute necessity of the case; to the great principle of self-preservation; to the transcendent law of nature and of nature's God"—this, incidentally, may be the only reference to God in any of the 85 essays—"which declares that the safety and happiness of society are the objects at which all political institutions aim, and to which all *such institutions must be sacrificed*" (emphasis added). By now, of course, we should be used to such arguments; they were at the heart of *Federalist*s 40 and 41. Their repetition underscores the fact that there was nothing remotely inadvertent about such appeals. And equally obvious, appeals to "absolute necessity" are hardly absent in our own time. If anything, the integration of the United States into the world "community," and the multiple tensions provoked by living within that decidedly uneasy conglomeration, only multiply the occasions for suggesting that threats to "self-preservation" warrant the sacrifice of institutional niceties, including, perhaps, the duty of fidelity of adhering to the rules for amendment set down in the 1787 Constitution insofar as they make it nearly impossible to respond adequately to "exigencies" of our own time.

## FEDERALIST 44

## *Confidence, Money, and Debt*

*F*EDERALIST 43 CONCLUDES the discussion of the affirmative powers granted to the new national government. In *Federalist* 44, Publius turns to the "Restrictions on the Authority of the Several States." Many of these, he notes, are simply carried over from the Articles of Confederation, such as the Articles' ban on entering into any treaty with a foreign country without Congress's consent. The Constitution eliminates the possibility of congressional permission, presumably out of a belief that states should be discouraged from even contemplating conducting their own foreign policies. But how, precisely, can one prevent states (or even entities like New York City) from creating policies that certainly implicate America's foreign interests?

Interestingly, we have seen in our own times the interest of some states in creating international environmental understandings in face of Congress's seeming unwillingness to move on such issues. Thus the governors of California, Washington State, and Oregon in 2013 entered into an agreement with British Columbia regarding the adoption of "cap-and-trade" laws as a means of reducing carbon pollution.[1] As the Governor of Washington put it, "While the process in Washington, D.C., is strangled by climate deniers, there is no denying the fact that the West Coast is rip-roaring and ready to go." Earlier, in 2006, California Governor Arnold Schwarzenegger had met with British Prime Minister Tony Blair to discuss an environmental agreement. As is often pointed out, if California were an independent country, it would have one of the top ten economies in the world, and there is good reason to wonder why it should be held prisoner to a national government that is increasingly incapable of making timely decisions on such crucial issues as climate change. Of course, "agreements" are not necessarily "treaties," and there is probably no effective legal enforcement should one of the parties renege. But that is true of many international treaties. They rely more on each nation's moral obligation to keep its promises and the desire to avoid reputational damage than on the likelihood of enforcement by courts or by force of arms.

What may be most interesting for a modern reader in the litany of forbidden conduct involves the realm of monetary policy. In the Constitution, immediately following the prohibition of independent treaties, alliances, or confederations with foreign countries, comes the banning of "coin[ing] Money; emit[ting] Bills of Credit; [or] mak[ing] any Thing but gold and silver Coin a Tender in Payment of Debts." It has been an item of contention, at least since Charles Beard wrote his 1913 *An Economic Interpretation of the Constitution of the United States,* to what extent this line was drafted by those far more sympathetic to the interests of creditors (like themselves) than of debtors, who were the primary victims of economic developments following the end of the Revolutionary War. There is general agreement that Beard overstated his argument, but it is impossible to understand this clause outside the context of the 1786 Shays' Rebellion in Massachusetts, led by disgruntled farmers who were forced to pay their onerous debts in hard-to-find (and therefore expensive) "specie" of gold or silver rather than state-issued paper money. Some states, notably Rhode Island, were more debtor-friendly, much to the dismay of those in Philadelphia.

It is one thing to adopt a free-trade zone and to prohibit states from taxing any goods imported from foreign countries or other states. It is quite another thing to adopt a single-currency zone. One of the central sagas of the European Union is the transition of nineteen of its members from their own national currency to the transnational euro. As the economist Paul Krugman has insisted, that decision to move toward a common currency, effectuated between 1999 and 2002 (when currencies like the French franc, the German mark, or the Italian lira were formally retired and made worthless), has had grave consequences for countries like Greece, Spain, and Portugal. Their inability to devalue their currency in the face of large fiscal imbalances and trade deficits made the "Great Recession" that began in 2008 far more severe than it might otherwise have been. No longer, for example, can they make their exports cheaper and their imports more expensive, or use inflation to help people pay off debts denominated in their national currency. Instead, all goods are denominated in euros, and all monetary policy decisions are made by central bankers, not by treasury officials in Athens, Madrid, or Lisbon. Yet unlike the U.S. federal government, the European Central Bank does not make any of these nations' welfare or pension payments; the national governments are forced to pay these from their own treasuries, in euros, or risk massive social unrest.

Publius is an unabashed admirer of this aspect of the Constitution. Prohibiting bills of credit, he asserts,

> must give pleasure to every citizen, in proportion to his love of justice and his knowledge of the true springs of public prosperity. The loss which America has sustained since the peace, from the pestilent effects of paper money on the necessary confidence between man and man, on the necessary confidence in the public councils, on the industry and morals of the people, and on the character of republican government, constitutes an enormous debt against the States chargeable with this unadvised measure, which must long remain unsatisfied; or rather an accumulation of guilt, which can be expiated no otherwise than by a voluntary sacrifice on the altar of justice, of the power which has been the instrument of it.

To allow the states autonomy in such matters would inevitably mean that "the intercourse among them would be impeded" and, ultimately, that "animosities" would "be kindled among the States themselves," not to mention the potential harm to our foreign relations if "the Union be discredited and embroiled by the indiscretion of a single member." This analysis, incidentally, is meant to apply to an additional clause of Section 10, which prohibits states, seeming absolutely, from "impairing the Obligation" of existing contracts by, for example, passing debt-relief legislation that makes compliance with contracts less onerous.

There are two ways to read these passages. One is as part of Publius's general critique of state autonomy, given the propensity of selfish factions to capture state government, in presumed contrast to the new national structures the Constitution will establish. Thus it may be important that Article I, Section 9, which sets out certain limits on national power, does not include an analogue to the "Contracts Clause." Moreover, Congress is explicitly granted the power, in Article I, Section 8, to pass "uniform Laws on the subject of Bankruptcies." Given that the essence of bankruptcy is liberation from preexisting contractual obligations and granting the bankrupt a "fresh start" free of prior debt, it seems clear that the Constitution was not written by people who believed in the absolute sanctity of contracts, come what may. Rather, the question is who is trusted to set the terms by which one can be relieved of these encumbrances. The answer, unequivocally, is the national government.

But one can also read Publius as offering a far more general denunciation, in the name of universal norms of justice, of the "pestilent effects" of paper money. Paper money was adopted as "legal tender" only during the Civil War, and the Supreme Court, in a bitterly contested 5–3 1870 decision (overturned a year later when President Grant successfully named two new justices to the Court to replace retirees), declared that it was unconstitutional for the national government to make anything other than specie the legal satisfaction for debts. Even after paper currency became common, it was backed up by the promise of the United States treasurer or the Federal Reserve System to redeem any currency in gold. Franklin D. Roosevelt famously took the United States off the gold standard in 1933. The Supreme Court, in yet another 5–4 decision in 1935, decided in effect that this action was probably unconstitutional but, crucially and decisively, that no one had "standing" to challenge it in a court of law, so it stood. It is unclear whether the justices knew that Roosevelt apparently had already drafted a presidential statement, on the expectation that the Court would order the United States to return to the gold standard and be prepared to give an ounce of gold for every thirty-five dollars of currency proffered to it, announcing his refusal to comply. To this day, one can find adherents of returning to the gold standard, though most economists agree with John Maynard Keynes, who was bitterly critical of what he saw as Britain's irrational and fetishistic commitment in the 1920s and 1930s to keeping the pound tied to gold. He welcomed FDR's decision, and today no country backs up its currency with a promise to redeem it for a certain amount of specie.

Still, even if one does not advocate a return to the gold standard, one must recognize that the basis of any contemporary monetary system is trust in the willingness of strangers (including the state) to accept otherwise worthless pieces of paper (or bits of computer code) in return for tangible goods like food, clothing, shelter, medical treatment, university tuition, or any of the limitless array of goods and services that money can buy. Publius is absolutely right to speak of the "necessary confidence between man and man." Without this confidence, it is all too easy to imagine Hobbes's state of nature (which seems unhypothetical in many parts of the world), where waking hours are spent in constant anxiety.

An increasingly pressing subject of debate in the contemporary United States is the amount of unfunded debt of various levels of government, including, crucially, pensions owed to retired public servants. The bankruptcy of Detroit in 2013 was generated in significant measure by unfunded liability for pensions, and public employees were forced to accept significant cuts in the amount of money they were counting on for survival during their old age. As of 2013, at least three states, Illinois, Connecticut, and Kentucky, held in reserve less than 50 percent of the money they were obligated to pay their retirees.[2] A February 2015 report on the particular problems facing Illinois has suggested that "state retirement systems will need $131 billion to cover benefits, but there's only $46 billion in the bank."[3] The *Chicago Tribune* reported on February 27, 2015, that Moody's Investors Service had downgraded Chicago's debt to just above "junk-bond" level because of its own unfunded obligations of approximately $20 billion of pension benefits and an additional $8.3 billion of bond-related debt.[4]

There is also the separate issue of the United States debt, which as of March 2015 stood at $18.1 trillion. This figure may be meaningless by itself. What one really wants to know is the strength of the overall economy and the probability that future economic growth, in part the result of debt-purchased investment, will permit the country to cover its obligations. Still, should the United States be faced with "insurmountable" difficulties in meeting its obligations, it has one weapon in its arsenal that Illinois lacks. Both, of course, can simply default and face whatever (likely disastrous) consequences ensue. But only the United States, by printing a vast amount of new dollars, can simply make the "real value" of its debt go down.

There can be little doubt that adjustment to new economic realities following the Great Recession, the development of a more globalized economy, and the decline in unskilled jobs will require many sacrifices from the citizenry. Harold Lasswell many years ago defined politics as "who gets what," a definition that Publius would certainly have appreciated. Perhaps the central question facing the modern United States is whether "We the People" have any more confidence in the United States government than Publius had in the states to maintain monetary policies and practices sufficient to engender loyalty among the citizenry.

## FEDERALIST 45

# *Evaluating the Constitutional Order*

ONE WAY OF READING *Federalist* 45 is as part of Publius's continuing assault on the notion that states are truly important. Near the beginning of the essay, he asks yet another set of rhetorical questions: Do his contemporary readers—or we, reading him nearly 230 years later—agree that the Union, including the enhanced powers of the national government, will

> be essential to the security of the people of America against foreign danger; if it be essential to their security against contentions and wars among the different States; if it be essential to guard them against those violent and oppressive factions which embitter the blessings of liberty, and against those military establishments which must gradually poison its very fountain[?] [I]f, in a word, the Union be essential to the happiness of the people of America, is it not preposterous, to urge as an objection to a government, without which the objects of the Union cannot be attained, that such a government may derogate from the importance of the governments of the individual States? Was, then, the American Revolution effected, was the American Confederacy formed, was the precious blood of thousands spilt, and the hard-earned substance of millions lavished, not that the people of America should enjoy peace, liberty, and safety, but that the government of the individual States, that particular municipal establishments, might enjoy a certain extent of power, and be arrayed with certain dignities and attributes of sovereignty?

If we haven't already gotten the point, Publius compares those who prefer maintaining state prerogatives as against the new country envisioned by the Constitution's supporters to those who adhere to "the impious doctrine in the Old World, that the people were made for kings, not kings for the people." Renunciation of such a pernicious doctrine was the central meaning of the American Revolution, especially as enunciated by Thomas Paine. But, asks Publius, "Is the same doctrine to be revived in the New, in another shape that the solid happiness of the people is to be sacrificed to the views of political institutions of a different form?" What follows are, according to political theorist Sotorios Barber, perhaps the key sentences in all of *The Federalist*.

It is too early for politicians to presume on our forgetting that *the public good, the real welfare of the great body of the people, is the supreme object to be pursued;* and that no form of government whatever has any other value than as it may be fitted for the attainment of this object. Were the plan of the convention adverse to the public happiness, my voice would be, Reject the plan. Were the Union itself inconsistent with the public happiness, it would be, Abolish the Union. In like manner, as far as the sovereignty of the States cannot be reconciled to the happiness of the people, the voice of every good citizen must be, Let the former be sacrificed to the latter. (emphasis added)

The goal of the Constitution, then, is crystal clear, proclaims Publius. It is the "public good" and "real welfare" of the people. If one prefers more elevated language, there is always the Preamble to remind one of the great purposes of the constitutional enterprise. Whatever is not conducive to this end, Publius suggests, should be rejected. There is no sentimentality here. Going back to the theme of the very first *Federalist,* we should engage in cold "reflection" on the adequacy of the framework of government and, should it be found inadequate to achieve "real welfare" and provide us with requisite "happiness," we should abolish it. Strong words indeed!

Perhaps Publius would have been content to end the essay there had he not been faced with the obvious political problem. The wavering delegates in New York and Virginia were likely to reject his paean to Union and to think far more of states and the protection of state autonomy. What follows, therefore, are assurances that "state governments may be regarded as constituent and essential parts of the federal government." Publius notes, for example, that senators will be "elected absolutely and exclusively by the state legislatures." But, of course, this is only to establish that, for better or worse, the Constitution did indeed maintain some important state prerogatives that might limit the national government's own efforts. These assurances do not in the least support the argument that we are in fact better off with such prerogatives. That would be true if and only if we believed that, all things considered, a powerful role for states would enhance our prospects of achieving the general welfare and maintaining public happiness. But everything Publius has written denies this.

One can say the same of his assurance (whether sincerely believed or not) that "[t]he powers delegated by the proposed Constitution to the federal government are few and defined." But given that one of these "few and defined" powers is that of taxing and spending for the general welfare, which he has assured us earlier will largely be defined by Congress subject only to electoral constraints, one can be skeptical that Publius would ever reject as "unconstitutional" any national measures that he thought were conducive to these great ends. As he argues so eloquently at the outset, why would we? Wouldn't we be absurdly sacrificing the ends set out in the Preamble for a fetishistic piety toward what later generations would call "states' rights"?

I do not need to spell out the many ways in which these questions are not of merely historical import. One need think only of the myriad of Supreme Court decisions or the spate of contemporary political discourse issuing from the political right that has substantially taken over the Republican Party. Anyone who defends the national government today risks being portrayed as a dangerous "liberal" who has betrayed the authoritative vision of American constitutionalism articulated by Publius. It is immensely foolish to try to say what U.S. political party Publius would identify with; indeed, he might well identify both major parties as captives of particular "factions" inimical to the common good or general welfare. And it is ever more foolish to predict his views on the specifics of any public policy.

Yet it is not foolish to ask what standards of assessment Publius might ask us to adopt. We can predict with complete confidence that "what serves the interest of our own group" or "helps our political party win the election" would not count. Even more to the point is that he would have to reject as well *either* "whatever enhances the power of the national government" *or* "whatever maintains or enhances state prerogatives." One always has to ask what the relationship is between any of these powers or prerogatives and the public good.

However, perhaps what distinguishes us from Publius is that we, unlike him, no longer believe in the existence of a genuine "public good" or "general welfare." They are, many sophisticated (and not so sophisticated) thinkers would tell us, ideological obfuscations meant to disguise assertions of private good or selective welfare. A cynic would do this quite self-consciously, whereas a more naive person might genuinely believe that what serves his own interest also, as if by magic, serves the public interest. Either way, the conclusion is the same.

I do not want to deny the power of such arguments, which go back to Plato (though he placed them in the mouths of sophists and cynics).

The point is that in *Federalist* 45, Publius asks the most basic questions one can imagine about politics. It has been very easy to view Publius as our contemporary with regard to many of the concerns he has expressed. Whether we can view him as a contemporary with regard to his optimism, first about the ability to discern a specific public interest and then to place in office leaders whom we can trust to have and to act on such abilities, may be doubted.

## FEDERALIST 46

## *The Political Sociology of Federalism (Part II)*

O N JANUARY 29, 1788, Publius continued comparing what he called "The Influence of the State and Federal Governments." What is especially interesting about *Federalist* 46 is his argument as to why those who are suspicious of a greatly empowered national government should relax and realize that states have nothing to worry about. He makes his argument not by careful exegesis of the Constitution's text, but by offering what might be called a "social psychological" account of Americans, which he believes should reassure strong proponents of state power. We saw the precursor of this argument in *Federalist* 17.

He begins by asking "whether the federal government or the State governments will have the advantage with regard *to the predilection and support of the people*" (emphasis added). The answer, he says, is that the nod will clearly go to "State governments" (note his capitalization, itself a clever rhetorical move): It is "beyond doubt that the first and most natural attachment of the people will be to the governments of their respective States." Consider, in this context, the career of John Jay, appointed the first chief Justice of the United States by George Washington in 1789. In 1792 he ran for governor of New York and lost on what might be called a legal technicality of New York's election law. He was more successful in 1795, after which he resigned from the Court. Implored by John Adams to accept reappointment as chief justice in 1801, he rejected the offer, not least because he had no desire to resume the task of "riding circuit." (Members of the Court were then required to travel throughout the country hearing cases.) Indeed, during the debates about the Constitution, some participants worried that bright and ambitious individuals would prefer to remain at home, as it were, within their states, rather than journey to the new national capital. Publius in effect suggests that the difficulty of getting first-rate people to serve at the national level should reassure anti-federalists. The greatest vindication of Publius's argument, ironically, would come in 1861, when the country's leading general, Robert E. Lee, dramatically proved that his primary identity was "Virginian" rather than "American."

Moreover, Publius argues, the people themselves will place greater reliance on their state identities, in part because the issues they consider most important will almost certainly be addressed at the local rather than the national level (as was arguably the case for the first century after ratification). As a result, "the people will be more familiarly and minutely conversant" with state rather than national politics. They are also far more likely to have "ties of personal acquaintance and friendship, and of family and party attachments" with local officials. Even if there was "transient enthusiasm" for national leaders during and just after the intense days of revolution, that would fade. What Warren Harding would later call "normalcy" would return, and national loyalties and identifications would take a distinctly subordinate role.

Even those who choose to become national-level officials will carry with them "prepossessions" that "will generally be favorable to the States." It "will rarely happen," Publius asserts, "that the members of the State governments will carry into the public councils a bias in favor of the general government. A local spirit will infallibly prevail much more in the members of Congress, than a national spirit will prevail in the legislatures of the particular States."

But wait, there's more. Publius offers yet another argument for the priority of states within the new Union: the ability of states to resist what they regard as "an unwarrantable measure" imposed by the psychologically remote national government. "The disquietude of the people; their repugnance and, perhaps, refusal to co-operate with the officers of the Union" would likely generate opposition to perceived national overreaching by state legislators and governors. All of these, taken together, "would form, in a large State, very serious impediments; and where the sentiments of several adjoining States happened to be in unison, would present obstructions which the federal government would hardly be willing to encounter."

These sociological, psychological, and political realities make it "madness" to believe the national government could ever behave in an extreme fashion. It would, in effect, be in the same position as the British government when faced with the united opposition of the colonies, and we know how that turned out!

"The only refuge left," Publius asserts, "for those who prophesy the downfall of the State governments is the visionary supposition that the federal government may previously accumulate a military force for the projects of ambition." This too he denies, in part because the standing army available to the national government would be limited to a maximum of twenty-five to thirty thousand soldiers (in a country of nearly 4 million). "To these would be opposed a militia amounting to near half a million of citizens with arms in their hands, officered by men chosen from among themselves, fighting for their common liberties, and united and conducted by governments possessing their affections and confidence." In addition, Americans "possess over the people of almost every other nation . . . the advantage of being armed." And "the existence of subordinate governments, to which the people are attached, and by which the militia officers are appointed, forms a barrier against the enterprises of ambition, more insurmountable than any which a simple government of any form can admit of."

As with Publius's other essays, one can ask how accurate this really was. Many significant leaders would leave successful careers in state politics to serve the national government. Two of the three cabinet officials in George Washington's first term were former governors of Virginia, Edmund Randolph and Thomas Jefferson. The third was Alexander Hamilton, who was certainly a presence in New York politics, though he never occupied the high offices of his colleagues. James Madison, following brief and distinctly unhappy service in the Virginia House of Delegates (where he lost all remaining faith in the capacity of localist legislators), served at the national level as representative, secretary of state, and then president. But such historical inquiries are not the point of these commentaries. Rather, the question is whether we today, when imagining our own identities and those of our fellow Americans, give the same priority to state identity and state governments as Publius describes.

Surely some people—and given the size of the United States today, they undoubtedly number in the millions—would fit Publius's description. But just as surely, most would not. One of the mythic symbols of America is the covered wagon taking individuals, families, and, in some cases, entire communities from one state to another, perhaps across the country. Some sought greater economic opportunities; others, like the Mormons, sought to construct a state according to their own theology. The point is that one could scarcely understand even earlier Americans as "stay-at-homes" brimming with local loyalties. The "Virginia Dynasty" of Washington, Jefferson, Madison, and Monroe; or the Massachusetts twosome of John Adams and his son John Quincy, were strongly identified with their states; but they were succeeded by individuals who had often moved around. Lincoln was born in Kentucky and raised in Indiana but elected from Illinois; Woodrow Wilson, a native Virginian, went to the White House from service as governor of New Jersey. Illinois-born Ronald Reagan went, as did so many Americans, to California to achieve fame, fortune, and political office; his vice president and successor moved from Connecticut (where his father had served as United States senator) to Texas. Bill Clinton may have returned to Arkansas to begin his rise to the top; his presidential library may be in Little Rock, but he himself now lives in New York, which, of course, his wife represented in the Senate. Whatever explains Barack Obama's rise to the top, it is not his deep roots in Hawaii.

Moreover, we can ask what Publius would make of the increasingly standard career path for legislators: several terms in the House or Senate, followed by retirement to Washington's K Street, where they triple their salaries by taking jobs lobbying their former colleagues. Neither Trent Lott nor Tom Daschle, respectively the former Republican and Democratic majority leaders of the Senate, chose to return to his home state when his service ended—Lott because he resigned from the Senate, Daschle because he was narrowly defeated. Both stayed in Washington as lobbyists.

So what? If one doubts the states' capacity to function effectively as governments and looks instead to a strong national government, then one should approve the demise of this Publian vision and applaud the triumph of a more cosmopolitan (or at least national) sensibility. But what if one actually believes the country would benefit from strong state governments? Is protection for such governments likely to be found within the four corners of the Constitution, or within the hopes and expectations of the Framers? Or was Publius basically correct, that the only effective protection must lie in what a much later generation would call the "hearts and minds" of the people?

We could do worse than consider a song written in 1919, on the return of American soldiers from America's first serious military venture abroad, tellingly titled "How Ya Gonna Keep 'Em Down on the Farm (After They've Seen Paree)?" Can American federalism as a truly vibrant system of governance survive the transformations of consciousness that occur when local representatives experience life in Paris, New York, or even Washington? Is there any reason to believe that "American exceptionalism" somehow inoculates honest locals against the virus of cosmopolitanism?

## FEDERALIST 47

## *Is "Separation of Powers" a Helpful Maxim?*

*F*EDERALIST 47 IS SURELY one of the better known of the eighty-five essays, largely because it, together with *Federalist* 51, offers the fullest explication of a term dear to the hearts of Americans: "separation of powers." Analytically, one can easily distinguish the creation of new law from the execution of the law; and both of these from the interpretation of laws to resolve ambiguities in meaning. The question is whether these different activities should be assigned to different persons or departments. There is no logical necessity to do so, but it is often argued that these three roles should not be entrusted to the same individuals but distributed into separate institutions that we have learned to label the "legislature," "executive," and "judiciary." The question that arose during the debate over ratification, and to which Publius responds in this essay, is whether the three branches of government are sufficiently separate to comply with what he describes as the "political maxim, that the legislative, executive, and judiciary departments ought to be separate and distinct."

Ever the clever rhetorician, Publius agrees that this maxim has great "intrinsic value," not least because it "is stamped with the authority of . . . enlightened patrons of liberty." He offers his own paraphrase: "The accumulation of *all* powers, legislative, executive, and judiciary, in the same hands, whether of one, a few, or many, and whether hereditary, self-appointed, or elective, may justly be pronounced the very definition of tyranny" (emphasis added). A great deal of work is done by the word "all," for its function in the rest of his argument is to assert—altogether cogently,

I might add—that although the system of government instantiated in the Constitution features *some* important overlaps of political powers and functions, it does not threaten to become tyrannical precisely because the blending is only partial.

It is useful to contrast the United States Constitution with the text of the Massachusetts constitution of 1780, drafted in substantial measure by John Adams: "In the government of this Commonwealth, the legislative department shall never exercise the executive and judicial powers, or either of them: The executive shall never exercise the legislative and judicial powers, or either of them: The judicial shall never exercise the legislative and executive powers, or either of them: to the end it may be a government of laws, and not of men." Similar language can be found in the constitutions of Maryland, Virginia, North Carolina, and Georgia. All seemingly require extensive formal definition of what distinguishes "the legislative, executive, and judicial powers" in order to prevent any branch from exercising even an iota of the powers assigned elsewhere. But Publius tells us that such fastidious separation is a mistake that is fortunately absent from the United States Constitution.

Although the United States Constitution, at the beginnings of Articles I, II, and III, refers to the three powers by name, it contains nothing comparable to the specific language of the Massachusetts text, and it is crystal clear that there is indeed overlap. Not once does the Constitution include the term "separation of powers." Instead, as the political scientist Richard Neustadt put it, the American political system features "separated institutions sharing powers." There can be no doubt that Publius would agree. He is critical of the oft-cited Montesquieu for failing to recognize that the (unwritten) British constitution that he was ostensibly explicating "by no means totally separate[d]" and rendered "distinct from each other" the institutions performing these analytically distinguishable functions. The easiest example involves the veto power, whether we think of English kings (who stopped exercising any such power in 1709) or, more to the point, American presidents or state governors. John Adams praised the veto power as in effect creating a *tricameral* legislative system. Though that is probably the most obvious violation of an overly fastidious (and wooden) interpretation of the Massachusetts formulation, there are many others. Judges are appointed by presidents and confirmed by senators, who also have the power to remove both judges and presidents from office upon convicting them of the impeachable offenses asserted by the House of Representatives. Publius emphasizes that neither Montesquieu nor any other reliable adviser could possibly mean that the great departments of government "ought to have no partial agency in, or no CONTROL over the acts of each other."

The maxim of "separation of powers" is often seen as synonymous with another guiding maxim of American political thought, "checks and balances," but in fact the two ideas are at war with each other. Checking Congress, for example, requires that the president be able to think and act precisely like Congress: to assess the value of legislation and then support it by signing it, or attempt to negate it by issuing a veto. Publius points out that the executive's power to "put a negative on every law" is not the same as the power to "make a law," which is surely true, just as Congress can "fire" presidents or judges by impeaching them, but cannot name their replacements.

Publius acknowledges the language of the Massachusetts constitution, but he notes as well that that constitution, in its assignment of various explicit powers, also includes "a partial mixture of powers," the most prominent being the gubernatorial veto. Reviewing all of the state constitutions drafted in the aftermath of the American Revolution (thereby excluding Rhode Island and Connecticut), he notes similar mixtures in all of them. He commends the New Hampshire constitution of 1784 for its nuanced requirement "that the legislative, executive, and judiciary powers ought to be kept as separate from, and independent of, each other AS THE NATURE OF A FREE GOVERNMENT WILL ADMIT; OR AS IS CONSISTENT WITH THAT CHAIN OF CONNECTION THAT BINDS THE WHOLE FABRIC OF THE CONSTITUTION IN ONE INDISSOLUBLE BOND OF UNITY AND AMITY."

What all this adds up to, with regard to political controversies of 1788 and the twenty-first century, is that we should be suspicious of catch phrases, including "separation of powers." They may stifle badly needed rethinking of conventional wisdom instead of providing a useful framework for analysis that sloganeers (including, on occasion, the United States Supreme Court) suggest. The United States government, like all governments, has always been remarkably complex, and Publius tells us we must evaluate it for its ability to create and maintain a "whole fabric" that permits all of us to achieve the aspirations set out in the Preamble. To rely instead on simple maxims is to betray our own capacity for "reflection and choice" about what we mean by self-governance.

## FEDERALIST 48

### *"Parchment Barriers"*

I n *FEDERALIST* 48, PUBLIUS continues his discussion of how to create the necessary separation of powers without also accepting a completely untenable theory of hermetically sealed boundaries. Again he begins his central argument by asking a cleverly worded question: "Will it be sufficient to mark, with precision, the boundaries of these departments, in the constitution of the government, and to trust to these parchment barriers against the encroaching spirit of power?" The answer is no, for two quite different reasons, both of continuing importance.

The first reason was more than hinted at in *Federalist 37*, dealing with the inevitable indeterminacies attached to almost all human language. We delude ourselves if we believe it is possible to "mark with precision the boundaries" of the legislature, executive, and judiciary—a task that has grown almost infinitely more difficult since 1788 with the development of the "administrative state." That state includes multiple agencies, notionally located within the executive branch but often having far more independence than formal departments, whose secretaries serve at the pleasure of the president in a way that the heads of the Securities and Exchange Commission, Federal Communications Commission, and Federal Reserve do not. These administrative agencies regularly create fundamentally new laws, in the form of regulations that give flesh to sometimes wildly open-ended legislation passed by Congress, a task that may also involve controversial "interpretations" of the legislation; they also have the primary responsibility for enforcing their own regulations, though, to be sure, many controversies end up in ordinary judicial litigation.

Most "parchment barriers" invite conversation rather than end it. Perhaps this is not true with regard, say, to the number of senators each state is awarded, but it is surely the case with the parts of the Constitution that come before courts or serve as the subjects of barroom arguments or newspaper editorials. Even if we admire Justice Hugo Black's insistence that the First Amendment command that "Congress shall make no law" abridging freedom of speech meant *no law,* one cannot possibly understand American constitutional law as it has developed by believing that such literal interpretation describes our operating legal system. A major theme of many of the previous essays is that effective responses to exigencies must take precedence over what Publius in *Federalist* 40 criticized as "rigid adherence" to mere "forms."

But the difficulty of giving solid meaning to vague or ambiguous language is not the only problem with "parchment barriers." Publius suggests as well that even if we *could* engage in precise boundary marking, both our political challenges and, perhaps more importantly, the ambition of those called upon to interpret the barriers will make them highly permeable. Much of *Federalist* 48 is devoted to instances of legislative overreach in both Virginia and Pennsylvania. There is good reason, Publius argues, to believe that legislatures will tend to transcend constitutional limits, especially if their constituents support these efforts. How does one protect against such overreach in state governments, Publius writes, when "the executive department had not been innocent of frequent breaches of the constitution"?

One answer, for those of us with experience of twenty-first-century American government, is to rely on the judiciary to police the boundaries, to be the umpire willing to call fouls on institutional actors who step out of line. But it is worth repeating that *The Federalist* contains a stunning paucity of references to judges playing such a role (though we will find a strong defense of the judiciary in *Federalist* 78). Publius is concerned with the design of institutional structures that will work naturally, as it were, by relying on the ordinary dispositions of ambitious politicians to limit the possibility or costs of overreach.

Our choice is either to accept the legalization of constitutional boundaries or rely on the political process itself, and the almost endless conflict this entails, to safeguard against tyrannical government. To accept legalization is also to accept the power of judges. Perhaps there is a good reason for doing that, at least on occasion, but it is obvious that choosing de facto rule by the judiciary—and rejecting the priority of politics—has significant implications for the meaning of "republican" (or "democratic") government. It also invites precisely what Publius criticizes, the creation of unnuanced slogans of "separation of powers" that not only deny the realities of our political system but, more importantly, deprive us of the needed flexibility to confront our pressing challenges.

# PART 9

## *Veneration versus Reflection*

# FEDERALIST 49

## *"Veneration" versus "Reflection and Choice"*

ONE POSSIBLE RESPONSE to institutional overreach is that "We the People," exercising the right suggested by Article V of the Constitution, may call a new constitutional convention to rectify matters. The *Federalist* 49 is interesting in part because in arguing against this option it offers a direct critique of Thomas Jefferson. In his *Notes on the State of Virginia*, Jefferson endorsed frequent conventions in order to assess how well the Constitution was working and, if advisable, to propose revisions. But that critique is primarily only of historical interest. What gives this essay its continuing relevance is Publius's insistence on the importance of "veneration" for sustaining the project of American constitutionalism. Jefferson derided those who would view the Constitution as similar to the "ark of the covenant," impervious to change (and, presumably, improvement). Recall Publius's emphasis on "reflection and choice" in *Federalist* 1. One can see this as evidence that whatever their intense differences, most of the leading founders shared an Enlightenment sensibility that emphasized the importance of learning from experience and resisting claims based simply on adherence to tradition. We certainly wrestle with the same tensions in the twenty-first century.

As Publius frames it, the discussion is whether there ought to be "recurrence to the people" or whether, in effect, "We the People" who "ordain" the Constitution may speak directly only once, and thereafter refrain from challenging the ratified Constitution or attempting to "ordain" anything drastically new. The heart of his argument comes in the following sentence: "[E]very appeal to the people would carry an implication of some defect in the government[;] frequent appeals would, in a great measure, deprive the government of that veneration which time bestows on every thing, and without which perhaps the wisest and freest governments would not possess the requisite stability."

Government in general is like a political leader who, asked to think of any mistake he or she made in office, replies that nothing comes to mind. After all, to admit error is to risk losing one's authority, which was defined

many years ago by political theorist Carl J. Friedrich as precisely the placing of confidence by an audience in the ability of an individual or institution to make wise judgments, even (or especially) if one might not be able
to understand the reasoning behind the judgment in question. It is difficult, in a world that respects expertise, to imagine eliminating such literal
authoritarianism, but it is also obviously important that one not lightly
give up one's intellectual self-reliance.

A reality of American constitutional history, of course, is that within
three years of *Federalist* 49, ten new amendments were added to the Constitution (out of twelve that were proposed in 1789), and Publius knew
that many delegates to the state ratification conventions, both supporters
and opponents of the proposed constitution, were suggesting that it be
tweaked.

So perhaps Publius simply "overspoke" in 1788, especially since he
may have been trying to head off the suggestion, made by a number of
New York delegates, that a new convention be called as soon as possible.
Or perhaps one has to place the initial amendments in some special category, not least because they did not come through a second convention
but through what we now regard as the "standard" operation of Article V,
which is proposal by Congress and ratification by state legislatures, with
hardly a word heard from the people directly. (One can compare the national ratification process, incidentally, with those in forty-nine of the fifty
states, where constitutional amendments *must* be ratified by a vote of the
general electorate.)

One might also think that perhaps Publius was addressing the kind
of political psychology necessary in the first generation or so of a new
constitutional order. The young nation will need time to grow up, and in
the early years it will be especially important for the populace to learn to
venerate what are, after all, brand-new institutions. Perhaps they need
to venerate the leaders selected to preside over those structures; this was
one of the arguments by which members of the Federalist Party defended
the Sedition Act of 1798, which made it a criminal offense to cast the
president of the United States into disrepute. Madison vociferously opposed the act and contributed mightily to a libertarian reading of the First
Amendment.

But can it be the case that the time for "veneration" in fact never
passes? To answer this question may require assessing the moral and in-

tellectual quality of "the people themselves"—or ourselves. "In a nation of philosophers," Publius wrote, one might expect that "[a] reverence for the laws would be sufficiently inculcated by the voice of an enlightened reason." He doesn't mention that the philosophers might conclude that the laws were in fact bad laws, not worthy of obedience, but let that pass. More important is that "a nation of philosophers is as little to be expected as the philosophical race of kings wished for by Plato." In the world as it is, with people as they are, even "the most rational government will not find it a superfluous advantage to have the prejudices of the community on its side." The Preamble speaks of the importance of protecting "domestic Tranquility." Doing so might require trying to prevent "the public passions" that "a frequent reference of constitutional questions to the decision of the whole society" might engender. Just think of the public disorder that some would link to the rise of the Tea Party or Occupy movements. Publius seems to suggest that we were extraordinarily lucky to survive the initial constitutional convention, and it would be pressing our luck to try the experiment again. What he fears more than anything is that "[t]he PASSIONS, therefore, not the REASON, of the public would sit in judgment" (capitalization in original).

It would be absurd to dismiss such fears. But we also ought to realize that submitting to them calls not only the wisdom of a new convention into account but also, more seriously, the very possibility of democratic decision making, at least if democracy is assumed to have much to do with government "by the people" and not only "for the people." Any vision of "democratic" government, including the kind that the United States now claims to support around the world, requires a degree of faith in "public reason." One need not dismiss the role that passions play in political judgment—Hume, after all, called reason the "slave of the passions"—but one can nonetheless believe that there exists sufficient public virtue that the base passions can be tamed or otherwise disciplined, because of our commitment to a "passion for justice." When Martin Luther King Jr. described himself as a "drum major for justice," his listeners certainly didn't picture a detached scholar in his study, poring over books. Our abstract commitments take life only when joined with passion. To commit oneself to subdue passion—or to venerate what has been handed down because of lack of confidence in one's own capacity, or the collective capacity of one's fellow citizens—is to accept a desiccated notion of citizenship, and ultimately of life itself.

## FEDERALIST 50

# *Maintaining Constitutional Fidelity*

STONE TABLETS OR pieces of paper, whether one calls them the Ten Commandments or the Constitution of the United States, are not self-enforcing. Some religious fundamentalists jibe that contemporary secularists, if they think of the former at all, view them as the "Ten Suggestions." "Parchment barriers" are thus equivalent to rules that are made to be broken whenever one finds it convenient to do so. For Publius, as for us today, one central concern is how one assures that the presumptive commands of the Constitution are translated into actual behavior.

Will the threat of future constitutional conventions, or of discrete constitutional amendments, be enough to channel legislative behavior? Publius believes not. "Is it to be imagined that a legislative assembly, consisting of a hundred or two hundred members, eagerly bent on some favorite object, and breaking through the restraints of the Constitution in pursuit of it, would be arrested in their career, by considerations drawn from a censorial revision of their conduct at the future distance of ten, fifteen, or twenty years?" Moreover, "the abuses would often have completed their mischievous effects before the remedial provision would be applied." There is also the danger that any deviations from constitutional propriety would, by the time of a convention, "have taken deep root, and would not easily be extirpated."

What about a special body that would meet at stated intervals to assess the degree to which public officials were faithfully following their constitutional obligations? Publius discusses the Council of Censors established by the Pennsylvania constitution of 1776, which was required to meet every seven years to make just such an assessment. As the historian J. R. Pole notes in his excellent edition of *The Federalist*, this "was an old republican precept which can be found in Machiavelli." But Publius was dubious, partly for the reasons given above. Indeed, contemporary political scientists are rightly skeptical that legislators, when deciding how to vote, take into account the possibility that the Supreme Court will someday strike down a law as unconstitutional. The present gratification of voting for a piece of legislation, especially if one thinks it will please voters or campaign contributors, easily outweigh the anticipated costs of seeing the law struck down years later. The late Pennsylvania Senator Arlen Specter, as chair of the Senate Judiciary Committee in 2006, voted for what *The Washington Post* described as "landmark changes to the nation's system of interrogating and prosecuting terrorism suspects" even after telling reporters the bill was "patently unconstitutional on its face" because military detainees would be denied the right of habeas corpus. He justified his vote by saying the Supreme Court "will clean it up" by invalidating the habeas corpus provisions. One might also believe that Specter, who had not yet dramatically crossed the aisle to become a Democrat after many years in the Senate as a Republican, was concerned that angry Republicans might take away his chairmanship if he voted against what the Bush administration was describing as legislation vital to protect American national security. Democratic Senator Patrick Leahy of Vermont, meanwhile, said the bill showed that America was losing its "moral compass."[1] Whatever explained Specter's vote, he was hardly a paragon of constitutional fidelity. Publius might have been dismayed, but surely not surprised.

But there is a second reason why Publius thought the Pennsylvania Council of Censors could not maintain a spirit of constitutional fealty. He describes the council as split "into two fixed and violent parties" to the extent "that unfortunately PASSION, not REASON, must have presided over their decisions" (capitalization in original). The proof of the triumph of partisan passion was not that the council was often divided. After all, "[w]hen men exercise their reason coolly and freely, on a variety of distinct questions, they inevitably fall into different opinions, on some of them." One would expect differences of opinion. The key, for Publius, was that "[i]n *all* questions, however unimportant in themselves or unconnected with each other, the same names, stand invariably contrasted on the opposite columns" (emphasis added). Every issue, small or large, came down to a party-line vote.

We see the same partisanship today and call it "polarization." Political scientists note, for example, that for the first time in our history, no Republican in either the House or the Senate is to the left of any Democrat; and obviously, no Democrat is to the right of any Republican. The consequence is an unprecedented number of party-line votes. Recall from *Federalist* 10 the conjunction of Publius's deep antagonism toward agents of "faction" with his rueful recognition that the aspects of human nature that result in factions and parties cannot be eliminated. He repeats the point here: "[A]n extinction of parties necessarily implies either a universal alarm for the public safety, or an absolute extinction of liberty." Publius would likely be extraordinarily skeptical of contemporary calls to temper the passions of partisanship. One might be forgiven, when reading him, for believing that the project of republican government is basically hopeless. There are many reasons to believe it is desirable, but very few to believe it is really sustainable. In some ways, the entire remainder of *The Federalist* is devoted to overcoming these worries, and the great question, from our vantage point, is whether we should in fact be comforted.

# PART 10

## *Institutional Design*

### *The Legislature*

# Designing Institutions for Devils (Who Organize Themselves into Political Parties)

Mᴏꜱᴛ ᴀɴᴀʟʏꜱᴛꜱ ᴄᴏɴꜱɪᴅᴇʀ *Federalist* 51 to be Publius's most im-portant discussion of the merits of separation of powers. If an American today has read only a few of *The Federalist* essays, the short list almost surely includes 51. Not that it begins by saying anything truly new. As in *Federalist* 47, Publius displays great skepticism about the "strong" notion of separationism set out in documents like the Massachusetts con-stitution. Once again we read that separation of powers is important, even "essential to the preservation of liberty," but only to "a certain extent" or as much "as possible." Good constitutional design is a matter of prudence and pragmatism, not the rigid application of abstract theoretical concepts. *Federalist* 48 warned us, in addition, of the danger of relying on "parch-ment barriers" to safeguard liberty against institutional encroachments. So what is to be done? Or, to quote the opening sentence, "To what expedi-ent then shall we finally resort for maintaining in practice the necessary partition of power among the several departments, as laid down in the Constitution?"

By now we know that the answer is not to count on the judiciary to enforce highly legalized notions of constitutional limitations. The Publian answer, which as much as anything accounts for *The Federalist*'s continu-ing prominence among those interested in constitutional design, is that one must "so contrive the interior structure of the government, as that its several constituent parts may, by their mutual relations, be the means of keeping each other in their proper places." We are moving fully into the land of checks and balances, where one relies on a complex relationship *among* the distinctly but not completely separate bodies to keep each other in line. But as always, Publius rejects abstract theory in favor of prudence. Thus, for example, one way to protect institutions from one another would be to deprive them of any role in selecting each other's members. But of course this is not the case. Every federal judge is nominated by the chief executive and confirmed by a majority of the Senate. Although presidents are elected independently of the Congress, it is Congress that was given the power to break deadlocks in the Electoral College when no candidate has received a majority of the electoral votes. This famously occurred in the elections of 1800 and 1824, when Thomas Jefferson and John Quincy Adams, respectively, were in effect chosen by the House of Representatives. With the switch of a small percentage of the overall popular vote in a number of states, it could have easily happened again in 1948, 1968, and 2000. When Publius writes that "the members of each department should be as little dependent as possible on those of the others," it should be clear that the words "as possible" are doing a lot of work.

So the key argument—the one that accounts for this essay's lasting fame—is found in the following paragraph, almost all of which could be italicized for emphasis:

> But the great security against a gradual concentration of the several powers in the same department, consists in giving to those who administer each department the necessary constitutional means and personal motives to resist encroachments of the others. The provision for defense must in this, as in all other cases, be made commensurate to the danger of attack. Ambition must be made to counteract ambition. The interest of the man must be connected with the constitutional rights of the place. It may be a reflection on human nature, that such devices should be necessary to control the abuses of government. But what is government itself, but the greatest of all reflections on human nature? If men were angels, no government would be necessary. If angels were to govern men, neither external nor internal controls on government would be necessary. In framing a government which is to be administered by men over men, the great difficulty lies in this: you must first enable the government to control the governed; and in the next place oblige it to control itself.

There is no evidence that Publius read Immanuel Kant, and the basically empiricist, prudential (some would say Anglo-American) style of thought instantiated in *The Federalist* seems to differ fundamentally from Kant's formidably abstract and conceptual philosophy. But consider this statement from Kant's 1795 essay *Perpetual Peace* (in the "First Supplement"),[1] surely the most utopian of ideals: "The problem of organizing a state, however hard it may seem, can be solved *even for a race of devils*, if only they are intelligent" (emphasis added). Who more than devils would realize that people are not angels, and that any workable government for humanity must take this fundamental reality into account? Yet as Kant suggests, they are "intelligent" enough to know that the multitude of devilish beings require "universal laws for their preservation," even as they realize that each of them "is secretly inclined to exempt himself from them." The solution is "to establish a constitution in such a way that, although their private intentions conflict, they check each other, with the result that their public conduct is the same as if they had no such intentions." A 2008 article in the *Swiss Political Science Review* examining the sources of Kant's essay suggested that he had probably read at least some of *The Federalist*, including 51.[2] Perhaps Kant overemphasized Publius's dour view of human nature and paid insufficient attention to those passages throughout *The Federalist* that suggest the capacity, at least on the part of well-chosen leaders, for "virtue" and commitment to the "public good" as well as a sheer self-centeredness. But it is also true that Publius and Kant, whatever their differences, evoked similar images and rested arguably fanciful hopes on the ability of "reflection and choice"—even if performed by devils—to design institutions that would provide acceptable governance.

The key is to make use of "opposite and rival interests," even in the absence of "better motives." Crucially, the interests that most concern Publius are institutional ones. One must aim "to divide and arrange the several offices" of government "in such a manner as that each may be a check on the other; that the private interest of every individual, may be a sentinel over the public rights. These inventions of prudence" will safeguard liberty and provide for a republican form of government. To the extent that government will be successful in the new state operating under the American Constitution, one might paraphrase Mae West and say that "goodness has nothing to do with it." Instead, the artful design of institutions must play devilish passions against one another.

The new Constitution, Publius tells us, is artfully designed in several ways. Because of the fear of what a runaway legislature might be able to do if left unconstrained, Congress is divided into two separate houses that are elected in fundamentally different ways—or were, before the Seventeenth Amendment mandated popular election of senators. But even bicameralism is not sufficient, so we have as well a presidential veto that in effect makes the legislature tricameral. Moreover, the vertical division of power between national and state governments provides additional safeguards.

Publius returns to the argument most strongly set out in *Federalist* 10, about the necessity to fragment public opinion and thus power. Even if a republican government must ultimately be "derived from and dependent on the society, the society itself will be broken into so many parts, interests, and classes of citizens, that the rights of individuals, or of the minority, will be in little danger from interested combinations of the majority. . . . In the extended republic of the United States, and among the great variety of interests, parties, and sects which it embraces, a coalition of a majority of the whole society could seldom take place on any other principles than those of justice and the general good. . . ." The Publian anxiety seems to be resolved much as Kantian devils would do it, if called upon to use their intelligence to create a workable government.

So can we see *The Federalist* ultimately as a comedy, providing a happy ending that should reassure us today as much as it reassured at least some readers in 1787–1788? Alas, the answer is probably no. One thing we understand today that they did not is the overwhelming importance of political parties and their consequent role in governance. Richard Pildes and Daryl Levinson (no relation), in a famous article in the 2006 *Harvard Law Review* entitled "Separation of Parties, Not Powers,"[3] pointed out that whatever Publius might have hoped, the "ambition" of governmental officials is "attached" far less to the particular institutions in which they serve and far more to their party loyalty and their desire for reelection. Although on occasion one can see the Publian model in operation, as when Democratic members of the Senate insisted, very much against the wishes of the Democratic President Obama, on release of a report detailing the use of torture by the Central Intelligence Agency during the Bush administration, those have become far more the exception than the rule.

Recall Senator Specter, who was, albeit reluctantly, altogether willing to betray his oath of office and undermine the Senate's ability to stand up to executive overreaching, in order to remain in good standing with his Republican colleagues and thus retain his position as chair of the Senate Judiciary Committee. It should be obvious that one of the functions political parties serve is to overcome significant aspects of the fragmentation of the "extended republic" by creating national institutions that are designed, for better and worse, to bring people together under a common banner.

But the reality of partisan motivation goes far deeper. Senate Republican leader Mitch McConnell is (in)famous for declaring in 2010 that his primary legislative goal was to ensure that Barack Obama became a one-term president. That he failed is beside the point. Rather, McConnell made the altogether rational calculation that the best strategy for achieving this aim was for Senate Republicans to do whatever they could to deny Obama any achievements on which he could run in 2012. I have argued, for example, that the late Massachusetts Senator Edward M. Kennedy paved the way for George W. Bush's successful reelection campaign in 2004 by cooperating with him to pass the No Child Left Behind Act in 2002 and then a prescription-drug bill in 2004. Neither bill stood a chance of passage without Kennedy's ability to round up Democratic votes, and they allowed Bush to campaign as a successful domestic-policy president in addition to his record as commander in chief in what he termed the "global war on terror." One can hardly blame McConnell for not wishing to emulate Kennedy. Perhaps a more angelic McConnell would have behaved in a more bipartisan manner, but the point, as Publius clearly recognized, is that it is foolish to rely on a high measure of public virtue.

The practical question facing us today is whether the Publian system of ambition countering ambition has yielded endless gridlock and ineffective government, regardless of which party notionally wins a given election cycle. As Pildes and Levinson point out, the United States Constitution says absolutely nothing about political parties and the implications of the fact that we divided ourselves by party. Yet partisan division followed remarkably soon after the new government was established and George Washington was elected as the first president. In modern parlance, Secretary of State Thomas Jefferson and Treasury Secretary Alexander Hamilton could be described as a "team of rivals," whether or not Washington realized it when he appointed them. In 1800 Vice President Jefferson ran a bitter (and ultimately successful) campaign to succeed the man under whom he ostensibly served, President John Adams. The country came close to civil war after an Electoral College tie vote between Jefferson and his running mate, Aaron Burr, when the Federalist House of Representatives was tempted to deny Jefferson the presidency. The governors of Pennsylvania and Virginia threatened to send their state militias to the new capital of Washington, D.C., if the Federalists did not agree to the election of a man many of them viewed as the devil. In those days the winner of the Electoral College vote became president, and the candidate who got the second most votes became vice president; this is how Jefferson became Adams's vice president despite their being of opposite parties. In the aftermath of the 1800 election, the nation passed the Twelfth Amendment, which provided that the president and vice president be elected in separate votes. This amendment is the Constitution's only hint that political parties are an important institution of American governance.

One can only wonder what Publius would have made of the Democratic and Republican parties today and the extent to which personal ambitions are linked to party success. There is a reason, after all, that Barack Obama did not want to spend one more day in the Senate than he had to. He had no desire to be a genuine "legislator," which requires spending years developing the particular skill sets attached to putting together successful legislative programs. The awful truth is that it is not clear that the modern Congress includes many members with such skill sets, not least because their electoral "bases," whose votes in primaries are particularly crucial for political survival, may define manifestation of those skills as an unacceptable willingness to compromise (or "appease") political adversaries.

One does not have to reject the Publian-Kantian argument about the importance of artful institutional design in order to doubt particular decisions made in Philadelphia and vigorously defended by Publius. But we should recognize that political parties deserve a level of attention that Publius certainly never gave them.

## FEDERALIST 52

### *Suffrage and Representation*

HAVING INFORMED US that the salvation of our republican political order lies in sound institutional design, Publius now gives extensive consideration to the specific institutions created by the Framers. He turns his attention first to the House of Representatives, the subject of the next seven essays. The first article, *Federalist* 52, focuses on what made the House distinct in the original Constitution: It was the only branch of the national government directly elected by the people themselves. Senators were to be chosen by state legislators, and presidents by the complex mechanism of the Electoral College.

As Publius wrote, "The definition of the right of suffrage is very justly regarded as a fundamental article of republican government." A reader would be excused if she expected that Publius would then define the "republican" notion of suffrage, but he does not. As the Constitution informs us, representatives are to be chosen by the "electors of the most numerous branch of the state legislature." What this means, of course, is that the right to vote for national officials is entirely derived from one's right to vote in state elections. More to the point, there is no notion at all that states must agree on the standards for voting. Women, for example, could vote in New Jersey until 1807; a number of states, including North Carolina until 1835, allowed free blacks to vote. Most states in 1788 had property restrictions on voting. All of these presumably complied with Publius's criteria for "republican government." After commenting that a uniform rule "would probably have been as dissatisfactory to some of the states as it would have been difficult to the convention," Publius immediately goes on to suggest that "[t]he provision made by the convention appears therefore, to be the best that lay within their option." One might well read a sigh of resignation in this: The delegates in Philadelphia had to submit to the political realities before them. "The perfect," goes the old saying, "is the enemy of the good," and Publius had seemingly learned that it was fruitless to hope for perfection in Philadelphia. A "good enough" Constitution would have to do, even if, almost by definition, it lay open to attacks from a variety of directions.

The Constitution's reliance on states to set the terms of suffrage has been under sustained attack at least since 1870. That was the year the Fifteenth Amendment prohibited barring anyone from voting because of his race. The pronoun is used advisedly: A number of early feminists, including Susan B. Anthony, opposed the amendment because they thought it reinforced the legitimacy of states' continuing to bar women from voting. Some even opposed the Fourteenth Amendment, inasmuch as Section 2 of that amendment indicated, in what became a true example of a "parchment barrier," that states would lose representatives in Congress if they denied the vote to African American *males*. This implied that denying suffrage to women was, as a constitutional matter, just fine, as was affirmed by the United States Supreme Court in an 1875 decision rejecting the argument of Virginia Minor, a Missouri feminist, that the amendment allowed her to vote. Of course, the Nineteenth Amendment, requiring that states grant the vote to women, was added to the Constitution in 1920. The Twenty-fourth Amendment, added in 1964, eliminated the use of a poll tax as a requirement for voting for federal officials, and the Voting Rights Act of 1965 extended that prohibition to state elections as well. Finally, the Twenty-sixth Amendment, in 1971, lowered the national voting age from what was then the standard age of twenty-one to eighteen. States have also been restrained in their ability to restrict the right to vote by Supreme Court decisions interpreting the "Equal Protection Clause" of the Fourteenth Amendment and, at least as importantly, by the Voting Rights Act of 1965, one of the great accomplishments of the civil rights revolution.

All of these constitutional and statutory changes being granted, a cursory glance at the news (in any medium) reveals that eligibility to vote remains an extraordinarily volatile political issue. States within the United States are among the most punitive in the world, for example, in depriving convicted felons of the right to vote. Literally millions of Americans, a disproportionate percentage of whom are African American males, are excluded from suffrage. To be sure, some states are far less punitive, but this only underscores the significance of leaving decisions about suffrage up to states rather than having a single national rule. Similarly, the twenty-first century has seen the rise of requirements for various forms of identification in order to vote. These are defended by proponents as a way of preventing voter fraud and attacked by opponents as an ill-disguised method of voter suppression, inasmuch as those lacking the requisite identification are likely to be poor members of minority groups. Much of the debate is carried on in terms reminiscent of *Federalist* 10, in which opponents of various restrictions describe the state governments as having been captured by "factions" intent on doing whatever they can to remain in power.

If the Constitution, as a practical matter, says nothing illuminating about who can vote, it does explicitly set out the eligibility requirements for election to the House of Representatives. A representative must be at least twenty-five years old, a resident of the state from which he (or now she) is elected, a citizen of the United States for at least seven years, and not concurrently occupying an "office" in the United States. This last re-

quirement is the most important in terms of the Publian system of separation of powers, for it forbids a member of Congress from simultaneously serving, say, as a member of the president's cabinet or as an active
member of the regular armed forces. Several twentieth-century would-be
reformers, thinking we were not well served by this limitation, suggested
that we would have benefitted if, for example, the chair of the House or
Senate Committee on Agriculture could simultaneously serve as the secretary of agriculture, precisely because the legislature could benefit from
the insights that executive-branch service could bring. But this would also
lessen the identification with only one branch that Publius relied on in
*Federalist* 51 to keep each branch ultimately in line with constitutional
ideals.

Not that the remaining limitations fail to raise important questions.
Why should the Constitution deprive us of the opportunity to vote for
an unusually precocious youngster who might well bring a different perspective to vital issues, ranging from how we finance higher education to
treatment of young veterans wounded in America's frequent wars? States
generally are more generous in allowing young people to run. One might
well believe that national representatives ought, as a general matter, to
have some significant life experience; we should ask, though, if the Constitution should deprive individual voters of making their own decisions
about young candidates. Similarly, in a country roiled by debates about
immigration, both legal and illegal, it is not at all fanciful to believe that
someone only recently naturalized as a citizen (which requires, save for
those serving in the military, at least five years of well-behaved residence
in the United States) might be thought by potential voters to be an effective representative. Again, decisions made in 1787 deprive the electorate of that choice. One might regard both of these provisions as creating
"second-class citizens," inasmuch as they discriminate against young or
recently naturalized citizens. But Publius, accentuating the positive, accurately notes that except for "these reasonable limitations, the door of this
part of the federal government is open to merit of every description . . .
without regard to poverty or wealth, or to any particular profession of
religious faith." Even if a state can constitutionally restrict the right to
vote—or could until the twentieth century—by taking wealth into account,
it cannot prevent a poor person from running for the House and, if successful, taking the seat.

## FEDERALIST 53

# *For How Long Should Representatives Serve?*

*F*EDERALIST 53 CONTINUES the previous essay's discussion about the length of a term in the House of Representatives, which the Constitution sets at two years. "[I]t is particularly essential," Publius had written in *Federalist* 52, that the House of Representatives "should have an immediate dependence on, and an intimate sympathy with, the people." This requires "[f]requent elections." How frequent is not to be decided by reference to abstract theory but by reference to how other polities have handled the question. Publius notes that in Great Britain elections to the House of Commons were held only every seven years. In *Federalist* 53, however, he directly confronts the common American slogan "where annual elections end, tyranny begins." In 1788, Connecticut and Rhode Island conducted elections every six months, and ten of the remaining eleven states had annual elections, save for South Carolina, which held elections biennially. He remarks laconically that "it would not be easy to show that Connecticut or Rhode Island is better governed, or enjoys a greater share of rational liberty, than South Carolina" (not mentioning that at the time, South Carolina was probably more dependent on slavery than any other state). This raises an extraordinarily important question, important not only to Publius's argument in 1788, but also to anyone in the twenty-first century trying to assess the operation of political institutions or, perhaps, design a new constitution in one of the many countries embarking on constitutional reform. That question involves the *empirical* basis of our judgments. To what extent do frequent elections—or for that matter any other aspect of a constitutional system, including the separation of powers—result in better democratic performance?

In any event, Publius's task is to discredit the adage about annual elections and instead to defend the convention's decision to grant representatives a two-year term before they have to face the voters again. Interestingly, he also defends entrenching this decision in the Constitution itself rather than leaving it up to future Congresses to decide through ordinary legislation how long their terms should be. That was deemed too dangerous, as illustrated in Great Britain itself when the members of Parliament effectively extended their term by four years simply by changing the time between elections from every three years to every seven. One might view this as a variant of the "ambition" that Publius described as all-important in *Federalist* 51, except that it is obviously a kind of ambition we do not want to encourage. Thus the term of office is fixed in the Constitution. Still, that does not tell us what the ideal term is. Why two years instead of one, or three?

"The period of service," Publius argues, "ought . . . to bear some proportion to the extent of practical knowledge requisite to the due performance of the service." He goes on to suggest, altogether plausibly, that national representatives need a greater degree of "practical knowledge" than do their state counterparts. Not only will the former be representing far more people, but they will also be called upon to make decisions about the national interest of what is quite literally an "extended republic." Publius writes dismissively of the "small compass" of states, in contrast to the "great theatre of the United States." For instance, members of the House, even if not asked to ratify treaties, must still develop a knowledge about foreign affairs that few state officials must have.

The difference, one might suggest, is equivalent to the difference between learning the lines of a relatively simple one-act play and preparing for a role in a Shakespearean drama. The latter demands a far greater skill set. One might hope that elected representatives would possess the requisite skills before acquiring office in the first place, but all of us know that even the most talented persons almost always require a learning period in any new job. Few can really "hit the ground running"; most need to feel their way. Thus "the business of federal legislation must continue so far to exceed both in novelty and difficulty, the legislative business of a single state as to justify the longer period of service assigned to those who are to transact it."

It is, I think, impossible to disagree with Publius here. But what about even longer terms of office? It seems impossible to deny that the scope of knowledge required of an effective national official is vastly greater now than at the end of the eighteenth century, if for no other reason than that, for better or (as some believe) worse, the national government's reach is so much more extensive than it was in past decades. Eighteenth-century legislators did not have to learn the basic science behind climate change and try to figure out politically acceptable solutions to the problem. Nor did anyone imagine in 1788 that Congress would concern itself with the health care of more than 300 million Americans.

In the modern world, the United States almost certainly holds elections more frequently than any other major country; every member of the House, upon taking her oath of office in January, knows that she will have to defend her seat no later than twenty-two months later. This means that campaigning, including the raising of increasingly vast sums of money, is in effect a full-time job (on top of the more important full-time job of being a conscientious legislator). The result is that the modern House of Representatives, when in session at all, meets basically from Tuesday through Thursday, with the other days being left free, save in exceptional circumstances, for the representatives to return to their districts.

Fewer and fewer representatives even bother to "live" in Washington, in the sense of moving their families to our national capital and sending their children to school there. Instead, some live in dormlike (or fraternity-like) apartments, often with other representatives, almost always from their own party. All of this contributes to a well-recognized phenomenon: Members of the modern House rarely have time genuinely to interact with one another socially or to partake in the Washington dinner-party scene, where they might meet a wider range of people. Analysts of Congress who have vehemently criticized the House for its rabid partisanship—more pronounced than at any time at least since the run-up to the Civil War—lay at least part of the blame on the two-year electoral cycles and the pressures of fund-raising. Partisanship is particularly bad among representatives who fear being "primaried." For most members of the House, challenges from within their party are the biggest threat to reelection, given that an increasing number of districts are safely Republican or Democratic, making the November elections relatively meaningless in at least 80 percent of the 435 districts.

Some of the deficiencies of the modern House could be cured without constitutional amendment, even if it is hard to imagine both sides' agreeing to do so. (Congress could, for example, repeal legislation going back to 1842 requiring that elections be held in single-member districts. Multimember districts elected on a proportional representation basis would go a long way to alleviating the consequences of political gerrymandering.) But to the extent that the two-year term makes its own contribution to the dysfunction of the modern House, it would obviously take a constitutional amendment to fix the problem. Some reformers have suggested moving to four-year terms, with representatives elected at the same time as the president. This would presumably make the elections more truly "national" in terms of the issues likely to be debated and the motivations of the voters. Others approve the notion of four-year terms but would stagger the elections so that half the House would be up for reelection every two years. This would permit the electorate to register its opinion more often than once every four years. The key question, though, is whether there is sufficient dissatisfaction with biennial elections to place reform on the national agenda. Even if one is persuaded that two-year terms were the right decision for 1788, does it follow that we are well served by them today? Are all other major countries around the world mistaken in electing their representatives for terms longer than two years?

## FEDERALIST 54

### Who Counts as Worthy of Representation, and for How Much?

HOW DO WE DETERMINE the number of representatives each state gets? However small its population, each state is entitled to at least one representative, which means that, as a practical matter, very small states will get greater representation than they would if we simply divided the entire country into districts of equal population. Thus, in the modern United States, Wyoming, with roughly 585,000 total population, gets one full representative even though the division of the entire population—currently around 320 million and growing—by the 435 representatives would yield a district of approximately 736,000 persons. (This presupposes that each district should be equal in population, which the Supreme Court in 1964 declared was constitutionally required.)

What the Court did not do was to explain exactly who should count as part of the population and why. Consider, for starters, very young children and aliens, whether fully legalized residents or undocumented. It is clear that infants and aliens both have genuine interests, which could, at least in theory, be represented in Congress. But it is also clear that neither of these groups, nor many others besides, will in fact be allowed to vote. Thus the number of eligible voters, let alone the number of actual voters, may differ dramatically among districts that are close to equal in population. So how does one decide "who should count" when determining the number of representatives each state should receive?

*Federalist* 54 discusses this issue in the context of the most wrenching aspect of American history, the institution of chattel slavery and the legal ownership of one set of human beings by another. Slaves were not regarded as "persons" within the political community. Children were (and still are) expected to become full participants as they grew older, and women were said to be "virtually represented" by the husbands, fathers, and brothers, who were ostensibly concerned to protect their interests. But since slaves enjoyed neither benefit, why should states receive the benefit of having them counted as part of the basis of representation? Would it not make as much sense to count trees or cattle, both of which are important, but neither of which has any possible political agency?

Publius relates the discussion to other debates about the basis of taxable wealth, where slaves *were* part of the property on which landowners might have to pay taxes. Crucially, though, the computation for slaves, unlike that for other forms of property, included only three-fifths of their presumptive value. Moreover, Publius wrestles with the root moral dilemma of anyone considering slavery (and slaves). Are slaves persons, with a person's claims to natural rights or justice, or are they merely items of property? The answer Publius gives is a ringing "both." Had the law not enslaved "negroes," then, says Publius, they would undoubtedly be entitled to "an equal share of representation with the other inhabitants." But since most *are* enslaved by operation of law, an "equal share" is unthinkable.

As he often does, Publius directs our attention to the political realities underlying these apparently abstract debates. "Could it be reasonably expected, that the Southern States would concur in a system, which considered their slaves in some degree as men, when burdens [of taxation] were to be imposed, but refused to consider them in the same light, when advantages [such as receiving seats in the House of Representatives] were to be conferred?" Moreover, is it not incongruous that those who "reproach the Southern States with the barbarous policy of considering as property a part of their human brethren" should then argue that these people should not be counted in the number of "persons" who form the basis for representation?

Publius adverts to the sheer happenstance that the basis of representation will ever actually correlate with the actual number of voters, given each state's freedom to choose its own suffrage rules. All of this is the prelude to his justification of the Three-fifths Compromise, by which the basis of representation is the total of all free persons (including women and children) plus three-fifths of the total number of slaves in any given state. For example, if a given state has 100,000 free persons and 100,000 slaves, its representation in Congress would be based on a "population" of 160,000, the total of 100,000+3/5 (100,000).

Publius concludes by saying that the reasons for the "Three-fifths Clause" comprise "the reasoning which an advocate for the Southern interests might employ on the subject." These arguments, he admits, "may appear to be a little strained." But surely the explanation has more to do with the need to keep the slave states in the Union. There is no "principled" defense of the Three-fifths Compromise other than that union was sufficiently important as to justify the price paid. The question, both in Publius's time and in the twenty-first century, is whether these two premises are correct. Was it in fact necessary to agree to the Three-fifths Compromise to gain the acquiescence of Virginia, South Carolina, and other leading slave states? But if it was necessary, one must go on to assert that gaining the Constitution was important enough to justify what William Lloyd Garrison described as a "covenant with death and an agreement with hell."[1]

It may be utopian to deny that pacts with the devil are ever necessary. I presume that most of us support, as a historical matter, the alliance with Stalin's Soviet Union in order to defeat the even greater evil of Hitler's Germany. More recently, the United States (like all countries) has collaborated with distinctly unsavory individuals and regimes to achieve foreign policy objectives that its leaders regarded as essential to national security or other important national goals. Machiavelli's great insight, supported by social and political theorists ranging from Max Weber to Michael Walzer, is that political leaders must sometimes put their states' legitimate interests ahead of what private morality structuring the everyday life of ordinary people might teach. One does evil not for the pleasure of transgressing or for private advantage, but to serve the interests of a legitimate and admirable state.

Whether or not to "compromise" has become one of the great issues of twenty-first-century American politics. Candidates for office regularly trumpet their refusal ever to compromise what they assert to be fundamental interests or values, and I suspect that all of us have admired at least one such candidate. But a complex and heterogeneous polity composed entirely of stiff-necked moralists unwilling to make what Israeli philosopher Avishai Margalit calls "rotten compromises"[2]—and no compromise was more rotten than the one Publius defends here—is unlikely to agree on a constitution in the first place or maintain it long afterward. That turned out to be the story of American constitutionalism as well, which crashed into flames—and over 750,000 deaths—in 1861–1865 over the polity's inability to engage in yet further compromises involving the extension of slavery into the American territories gained during the nineteenth century.

Or one can easily look outside the United States at the many countries facing their own choices between stability and justice when designing new constitutional forms. Modern countries designing new constitutions are likely to be invaded by NGOs (non-governmental organizations), all advocating their commitments with great and often-justified eloquence. But the facts on the ground might not support making great—or perhaps even any—efforts to achieve these commitments and might, indeed, require quite rotten compromises placing significant hurdles to their realization. Think only of the rights of women or religious minorities, for starters. As a practical matter, to what degree should the United States insist that a given constitution being drafted elsewhere not subordinate the demands of justice to the exigencies presented by a concrete political situation? The 1787 Constitution scarcely serves as such a model, and Publius was more than willing to defend the necessity to compromise. He teaches many different lessons, and one of them is the potentially limited domain of abstract justice when faced with "exigency."

### FEDERALIST 55

## *Does Size Matter, and If Not, What Does?*

As Publius continues his long consideration of the House of Representatives, he turns in *Federalist* 55 to the very important question of its optimal size. It should be clear by now that an important influence on my own thought has been the teaching of that great theorist Goldilocks with regard to the constant quest for the "just right" level between whatever we define as too cold or too hot. One can easily imagine a too-large representative body: Just think of the National People's Congress of the People's Republic of China, which in 2013 had 2,987 members. Even if we know nothing else about the Chinese government, we can be confident that a body this large could not possibly support genuine debates among its members. Perhaps we cannot pinpoint precisely when a legislative body becomes too large to be taken truly seriously, but wherever that boundary is, the NPC has crossed it. Similarly, a national legislature consisting of, say, only 6 members would strike many of us as too small to capture the diversity of opinion needed in a "representative" body. Even the roughly 80,000 people of Andorra are represented in a national council of 28 members, while the parliament of the approximately 320,000 inhabitants of Iceland, which may be the world's oldest, currently has 63 members. The smallest American state, Wyoming, has a 60-member house of representatives, which means that each member in 2013 represented approximately 9,600 persons. California, with nearly seventy times Wyoming's population, has only 80 members in its assembly, with each representing approximately 475,000 persons. (Its senate has only 40 members, which means that each of California's senate districts is larger than each of its 53 congressional districts.) The largest legislative house by far is New Hampshire's, where each of the 400 members represents approximately 3,300 persons; the smallest is Alaska's, where 40 members each represent approximately 18,300 Alaskans.[1] The city councils of even America's largest cities, meanwhile, are remarkably smaller. Los Angeles has a city council of 15 members, while the larger Los Angeles County is governed by a 5-member board of supervisors. New York City, with a population larger than all but 11 states, has a 51-member city council. One may question how important these differences in size actually are, but it is hard to believe that size does not matter at all.

Publius surveys the states as of 1788 and easily demonstrates the same kinds of variance. Delaware, at that time the smallest state, had a larger house consisting of 21 representatives (it has 41 today), while Massachusetts was like contemporary New Hampshire, having between 300 and 400 representatives. Similarly sized states, not surprisingly, varied significantly. New York and South Carolina then had roughly similar populations, but the Empire State had "little more than one third of the number of representatives," even though it was (and is) far larger in territory. Publius concludes that "nothing can be more fallacious than to found our political calculations on arithmetical principles. Sixty or seventy men may be more properly trusted with a given degree of power than six or seven. But it does not follow that six or seven hundred would be proportionably a better depositary. And if we carry on the supposition to six or seven thousand, the whole reasoning ought to be reversed." Beyond a certain number, we risk "the confusion and intemperance of a multitude" where "passion never fails to wrest the scepter from reason." Then follows one of the most famous sentences in all *The Federalist:* "Had every Athenian citizen been a Socrates, every Athenian assembly would still have been a mob."

These observations still do not provide concrete guidance as to the right size of the House of Representatives. According to the Constitution drafted in Philadelphia, the first House of Representatives would contain 65 members, drawn from 13 states with a total of about 4 million people. But one of the Constitution's more important requirements is that a national census be taken every ten years, with the first one to be conducted in 1790, at which time the membership of the House can be "augmented" so that there is 1 representative for every 30,000 people. Future censuses would presumably reveal continuing population growth and the need for further augmentation. By the end of fifty years, Publius estimates, should the ratio of representatives to constituents be kept at 1 per 30,000, the House would have 400 members, "which I presume will put an end to all fears arising from the smallness of the body." Concerns about the eventual size of the House led Congress in 1789 to submit, as the original "first amendment," a provision that "there shall be one Representative for every thirty thousand, until the number shall amount to one hundred." (What we call the "First Amendment" was initially the third among the twelve amendments submitted to the states for ratification.) When the number of one hundred was reached, the apportionment "shall be so regulated by Congress, that there shall be not less than one hundred Representatives, nor less than one Representative for every forty thousand persons, until the number of Representatives shall amount to two hundred; after which the proportion shall be so regulated by Congress, that there shall not be less than two hundred Representatives, nor more than one Representative for every fifty thousand persons." This amendment failed to receive the approval of the requisite number of states, so the number of representatives and the sizes of the populations they represent are left entirely to Congress. One can only wonder what Publius would have thought about the present size of the House, reached as early as 1913 following the "filling out" of the continental United States with the admission of Arizona and New Mexico as states, or about the fact that the number of representatives has not changed in the century since then. If each representative were notionally responsible for "only" 250,000 persons, we would require in 2015 a House of over 1,275 members.

Still, Publius's immediate problem is to assuage the concerns of the Constitution's opponents, who believe that the initial allocation of 65 members is too small. His response is to assert that those elected to office will be sufficiently virtuous, without any disposition "to form and pursue a scheme of tyranny or treachery." Ultimately, he takes refuge in declamation:

> As there is a degree of depravity in mankind which requires a certain degree of circumspection and distrust, so there are other qualities in human nature which justify a certain portion of esteem and confidence. Republican government presupposes the existence of these qualities in a higher degree than any other form. Were the pictures which have been drawn by the political jealousy of some among us faithful likenesses of the human character, the inference would be, that there is not sufficient virtue among men for self-government; and that nothing less than the chains of despotism can restrain them from destroying and devouring one another.

What should we infer from this, especially if we, whether at home or abroad, are looking to Publius for wisdom about our twenty-first-century polity? Are numbers irrelevant, because the character of representatives is our ultimate safeguard (which presumably means we should spend most of our time and energy on trying to assure the election of virtuous officials)? Or are they relevant only at a margin of "way too small" or "way too large," with a wide range of "just right" in between?

We also need a sense of *why* numbers might matter. If we are concerned about the range of views and perspectives held by representatives—think of contemporary debates about the values of "diversity"—then presumably higher numbers are better, at least until we reach the limit of effective debate. But we might also be concerned about the total workload engendered by the legislative agenda, and whether there are enough representatives to accomplish their tasks in a way that serves the public.

University of Virginia political scientist Larry Sabato, for example, laments that we have not "hired" any additional representatives since 1913, though we did "hire" four new senators with the admission of Alaska and Hawaii in 1958 and 1959. It is not only that the population of the United States in 1910 was still short of 100 million, versus our present population (on St. Patrick's Day in March 2015) of more than 320.5 million;[2] at least as important is the obvious fact that members of the contemporary House deal with a range of problems that would have been thought incredible a century ago.

To be sure, businesses do not have to hire new employees in order to increase production, *if productivity increases.* But that surely does not describe, nor is it plausible to think that it ever could really describe, legislatures, whose business is to engage in "reflection and choice" about an ever wider range of problems, including, if thought necessary, the production of new legislation that serves the general welfare and increases the prospect of public happiness. As a matter of fact, current Congresses are widely described as the "least productive" in modern history, at least as measured by the sheer number of laws passed (independent of assessment of their actual quality). This, of course, may be a function of the partisan gridlock discussed earlier. But even if a single party were in firm control of both houses of Congress, one might still be concerned about the ability of the present membership of Congress to spend enough time on the issues that require suitable reflection prior to choice.

It is also inconceivable that legislators a century ago could have imagined the pressures to raise campaign funds that today envelop the working lives of most members of Congress. According to Harvard Professor Lawrence Lessig, the typical member of Congress now spends—and is strongly advised by party elders to spend—30–70 percent of every day raising money. Lessig suggests this is one explanation for why the typical representative spends ever less time participating in committee hearings, which are designed, in theory, to bring to Washington informed witnesses who can truly educate representatives, partly by offering different views on ways to important problems. But even if this scandalous consequence of our method of financing political campaigns were magically eliminated, a conscientious legislator would be like the proverbial donkey unable to choose between a delicious carrot and a succulent apple. There is so much to do and so little time.

Some political scientists have suggested that polities tend toward a legislative size that is roughly the cube root of their overall population. The cube root of 320 million is approximately 684, which means that the present House of Representatives should grow by about 50 percent. What are the arguments against this? That the taxpayers would have to cover the extra salaries as well as collateral expenses, such as office space, computer equipment, and the payment of a necessary staff? Such an argument requires us to believe that we are sufficiently well served by the present 435. That is obviously possible, but one wonders how one would demonstrate that we were equally well served by 435 throughout the past century (and counting). One might argue that 684 is too large to maintain a semblance of debate, yet the House of Commons in Great Britain currently has 650 "constituencies," each of which elects a single member, meaning that there is approximately 1 member for every 98,000 persons, given the 2013 population of 64.1 million people. Anyone who has ever enjoyed watching "question time," when the prime minister tackles barbed questions from the opposition, knows that debate seems alive and well in that country. Still, Parliament plays a far less determinative role than Congress, in that its job, with rare exceptions, is more or less to rubber-stamp the proposals of "the government" that Parliament itself selected (and can bring down through a vote of no confidence).

Perhaps this discussion of numbers is irrelevant, and it is enough to rely on the republican character—note the small "r"—of those who inhabit the House of Representatives. But contemporary polling data suggests that we do not in fact possess great confidence in our representatives, and one can only wonder about the consequences for the project of self-government.

## FEDERALIST 56

### *"Local Knowledge" and Representation*

IN *FEDERALIST* 56, Publius continues to defend the size of the original House by addressing the complaint "that it will be too small to possess a due knowledge of the interests of its constituents." Here, perhaps more than in any other essay in *The Federalist* corpus, we can feel the distance between 1788 and the twenty-first century. Publius's defense lies in the premise that Congress will have relatively little to concern itself about, and for those few matters, sixty-five representatives will be ample. After all, he blithely informs us, "[a]n ignorance of a variety of minute and particular objects, which do not lie within the compass of legislation, is consistent with every attribute necessary to a due performance of the legislative trust." The "objects of federal legislation" that are "of most importance," requiring the most "local knowledge," he tells us, are "commerce, taxation, and the militia." In all cases, a "sufficient degree" of knowledge will be possessed "by a very few intelligent men diffusively elected within the state."

But Publius offers a fascinating reason why the number of legislators will suffice. Members of the House will most likely "have been members, and *may even at the very time be members, of the State legislature,* where all the local information and interests of the State are assembled, and from whence they may easily be conveyed by a very few hands into the legislature of the United States" (emphasis added). The Constitution clearly bars any national "officer" from serving simultaneously in the Congress, but it is indifferent to, perhaps even welcomes, simultaneous service as a representative and as a state legislator, governor, or judge.

This makes sense not only from the Publian perspective—at least in this essay, which expresses more confidence in state legislators than we have seen elsewhere—but also with regard to Publius's assumption that Congress would meet relatively rarely because it would have so little to do. Although Congress was required to convene at least once a year, it may be that it was envisioned as likely to meet no longer than, say, the biennial session of the Texas legislature, which by the state constitution is limited to 140 days. We are likely to think of serving in Congress as a full-time job, which begins the first week in January and extends through Christmas, even if one counts the weeks-long recesses that ostensibly allow representatives and senators to check the pulses of their constituents.

Some states appear to bar state public officials from holding simultaneous national office; many bar the simultaneous holding of *state* offices. But it is not clear whether any of these state provisions apply to being a member of the national Congress, given that there is a strong (and somewhat technical) legal argument that "offices" under the Constitution are those filled by executive appointment (including judges); that is clearly not true of legislators, presidents, or, most of the time, vice presidents.

The exception is a vice president selected in accordance with the Twenty-fifth Amendment, when a vacancy has arisen; the president nominates the new vice president, who must be confirmed by a majority of both houses of Congress. Save for the requirement of approval by the House of Representatives rather than the Senate, one might compare Vice Presidents Gerald Ford and then Nelson Rockefeller, the only beneficiaries of the amendment, to federal judges, who go through the identical nomination and confirmation procedure. In any event, it is probably overdetermined that no member of the Congress in many decades has also served as a state official. Louisiana's flamboyant Huey P. Long did serve as his state's governor and simultaneously as a United States senator in the 1930s, but his career—or the more general "exceptionalism" of Louisiana politics—may be explanation enough why it hasn't happened since.

It is safe to say that few people today, including professors of constitutional law, are aware that their state officials may run for the House or Senate without giving up their state offices (or, presumably, salaries). Some might even argue that the bar on simultaneous representation has become a part of the "unwritten Constitution." We do frequently see candidates for the vice presidency who simultaneously run for reelection to the House (Paul Ryan in 2012) or Senate (Joseph Lieberman in 2000) as a de facto insurance policy in case the party ticket fails, even if election to the vice presidency would likely require resigning their legislative seats.[1] We have no way of knowing whether Publius would have been gratified that these developments have rendered *Federalist* 56 nearly irrelevant.

## FEDERALIST 57

## *Does "Representation" Mean "Mirroring"?*

PUBLIUS'S CENTRAL TOPIC continues to be the House of Representatives, and now he must forestall the accusation that representatives will tend to "be taken from that class of citizens which will have least sympathy with the mass of the people" and that they will work for "the aggrandizement of the few." The fear is that the Constitution sets out a recipe for government by oligarchy. Not surprisingly, Publius has no sympathy at all for this argument, though twenty-first-century readers aware of the net worth of most representatives, not to mention knowing how modern campaigns are financed, may have their doubts about the relative presence (or even practical impact) of the 99 percent as against the 1 percent in contemporary congresses.

What is most visible in this essay is another swing of the pendulum between two Publian positions. One might be described as the "realist" (or "cynical") Publius, suspicious of people's motives, dismissive of "parchment barriers," and concerned to construct a complex network of institutions capable of setting the ambitions of selfish individuals against one another in a way that will serve the public interest. The French philosopher Bernard de Mandeville, in his *Fable of the Bees,* was the first to suggest that the correct arrangement of "private vices" could serve the "public interest." There are overtones of this in Adam Smith's famous notion of the "invisible hand" of the marketplace, where the actions of a myriad of individuals driven only by the quest for private gain nonetheless generates goods and services that satisfy public wants at reasonable prices.

The other side of Publius is instantiated in his definition of the "aim of every political constitution." These aims are, first, obtaining "for rulers men who possess most wisdom to discern, and most virtue to pursue, the common good of the society; and in the next place, to take the most effectual precautions for keeping them virtuous whilst they continue to hold their public trust." In other words, we need virtuous officials to run institutions designed for the un-virtuous. So how does the House of Representatives, at least as designed in Philadelphia (and more importantly, as defended by Publius), meet these criteria?

Publius first emphasizes that those choosing representatives will be "[n]ot the rich, more than the poor; not the learned, more than the ignorant; not the haughty heirs of distinguished names, more than the humble sons of obscurity and unpropitious fortune." We know from earlier essays how important it is that elections to the House will be frequent, giving the electorate ample ability to discipline wayward representatives. These officials, presumably desiring reelection, will try to preserve "the favor" of the electorate and therefore work against any "innovations . . . subversive of the authority of the people." There are at least two glaring problems with this argument.

The first is that the states control who can vote, and they may well favor the rich over the poor through property qualifications or poll taxes.

The second and perhaps more fundamental problem is that Publius trusts especially the "ignorant" and "humble" to choose representatives with the wisdom and virtue to "pursue the common good" instead of, say, the particular interests of the voters placing them in office (or those financing their runs for office). Although, as I noted in the introduction to this book, it is not my aim to discern whether Publius presents a fully worked out and coherent philosophy of politics, it is hard not to notice that there are tensions among some of the arguments presented in various essays. But so what? After all, that most American of all philosophers, Ralph Waldo Emerson, cautioned us that "A foolish consistency is the hobgoblin of little minds," and that "With consistency a great soul has simply nothing to do." Presumably we wish to develop capacious minds and great souls like those of Emerson himself. Or we might take after that most American of all poets, Walt Whitman, and proclaim "Do I contradict myself? Very well, then I contradict myself, I am large, I contain multitudes." The point is not even that "to err is human," but that to recognize the pull of different, indeed, contradictory arguments without jumping decisively one way or another is to be fully mature. One might turn, then, to the quintessential American novelist F. Scott Fitzgerald, who famously wrote in *The Crack-Up* (1936) that "the test of a first-rate intelligence is the ability to hold two opposing ideas in mind at the same time, and still retain the ability to function." One can hardly doubt that Publius, by any criteria, possessed a first-rate intelligence.

Still, one had to wonder then, and perhaps even more now, whether a "faithful discharge" of the electorate's "trust" that their representative will fight doggedly for their factional, selfish interests should reassure us as to the likely work-product of the House of Representatives. It would, of course, be a different matter if we could trust the public to be as selflessly republican in disposition as Publius seems to suggest. But that view, as already suggested, seems to be in stark contrast to many of his other comments.

Publius adheres to what has been his principal themes, at least since *Federalist* 47: the importance of clever institutional design and the creation of incentives designed to tilt representatives away from miscreance. We have already seen, though, that the resort to frequent elections almost completely begs the question, since their effectiveness depends on the wisdom of the electorate (or of that portion of the public that is allowed to vote). Publius suggests that another valuable safeguard against "oppressive measures" is that representatives "can make no law which will not have its full operation on themselves and their friends, as well as on the great mass of the society." But this assertion, too, does not hold up to empirical examination, especially if one looks, for example, at the tax code. Representatives spend much of their time figuring out ways to reward their political friends and punish their adversaries. Very little legislation applies literally to "everyone." Most of it slices and dices the population into discrete entities and allocates benefits or burdens accordingly. It *matters* whether one is, say, a grower of soybeans, a patent holder, or an investor who can claim "capital gains" instead of "ordinary income." Even if, in theory, anyone is eligible to become a hedge-fund manager or, for that matter, a capital murderer, most of us realize that inhabiting either role is extremely unlikely, and we can look at the statute books and predict quite easily who the actual beneficiaries (or victims) will turn out to be.

A Gallup Poll in 2014 on "trust in government"[1] indicates a remarkable drop in the number of Americans who believe they can trust the national government to do what is right most of the time. From a perhaps artificially high percentage of Americans who in the aftermath of September 11, 2001, indicated either a "great deal" or a "fair amount" of confidence in the national government, the total percentage plummeted to 43 percent in 2014, with only 9 percent indicating a high level of confidence. As of September 2014, only 3 percent indicated a "great deal" of trust in Congress, though an additional 25 percent acknowledged a "fair amount" of trust. Data compiled by the American National Election Studies at the University of Michigan show that with the exception of 2002, not since 1968 have a majority of Americans believed that the government is "run for the benefit of all" instead of a "few big interests."[2] This particular data set goes only through 2008, the beginning of the Great Recession, but it is hard to believe that popular trust in government has improved since then. Certainly that is not the message sent by either the Tea Party or Occupy movements, or by most candidates for national office, who in effect run against entrenched interests in Washington no matter how long they themselves have served there. A 2015 book by Tulane Law School Professor Stephen Griffin, *Broken Trust: Dysfunctional Government and Constitutional Reform,* delineates the costs for effective government of such pervasive mistrust: Why, after all, would Americans support controversial initiatives if they have no regard for the political leaders supporting them or do not believe that the Executive Branch will do an effective job in enforcing them after passage? Thus the Gallup Poll discussed above found that only 14 percent in September 2014 indicated great trust in the executive branch, though another 29 percent had a "fair amount" of such trust; 28 percent had "none at all."

Publius appears to manifest far greater trust in potential representatives. "[W]hat is to restrain the House of Representatives," he asks, "from making legal discriminations in favor of themselves and a particular class of the society?" His answer is that he trusts "the genius of the whole system; the nature of just and constitutional laws; and above all, the vigilant and manly spirit which actuates the people of America, a spirit which nourishes freedom, and in return is nourished by it." Should "this spirit . . . ever be so far debased as to tolerate a law not obligatory on the legislature, as well as on the people, the people will be prepared to tolerate any thing but liberty."

What do we in the twenty-first century think when reading this? Does it speak to us, and if so, do we read it as an inspiration or as a de facto jeremiad about our own debased politics? Is the correct response to say that Publius fundamentally misunderstood either the nature of republican government or what was necessary to maintain it, or perhaps that we today no longer care about maintaining a republican form of government, that "the genius" of *our* system today is very different because too many of our fellow citizens have other visions of politics in mind?

## FEDERALIST 58

### Does the "Iron Law of Oligarchy" Apply to the House of Representatives?

FEDERALIST 58, THE LAST OF Publius's seven essays devoted to the House of Representatives, largely repeats his earlier discussion of the "augmentation" of the House by a regular increase in the number of members from the original sixty-five. Most of the essay is taken up by a tedious discussion of the relative ability of large states, where the population is growing and thus creating an incentive for reapportionment of congressional seats, to protect themselves against small or population-stable states that would try to forestall any such action.

Publius does have some interesting warnings against bringing in large numbers of new representatives. We see the pendulum swing once more as he becomes skeptical about the benefits of involving too many people in the ostensible project of self-governance. Publius often adopts the stance of a political scientist, and here he offers the "observation" that "in all legislative assemblies the greater the number composing them may be, the fewer will be the men who will in fact direct their proceedings." The German political sociologist Robert Michels, in his 1911 book on political parties, coined the term "iron law of oligarchy" to suggest that in any sizable organization (like a political party), leadership will invariably be concentrated in relatively few hands. Moreover, Michels suggested, these leaders will increasingly distance themselves in important ways from the larger groups that presumably placed them in power. Not only may they begin making considerably higher salaries than ordinary members of their constituencies, they may also begin hobnobbing with other leaders and begin developing quite different perspectives about the relative role of leaders and constituents. Economists often refer to the "principal-agent" problem, in which the principals who hire agents to serve *their* interests may nonetheless be disserved by the agents who, perhaps as Publius would easily predict, would be less selfless than the principals would prefer. This is especially likely to be the case if in fact it is difficult for the principals to monitor their agents or otherwise easily hold them accountable.

But Publius also suggests that "the more numerous an assembly may be, of whatever characters composed, the greater is known to be the ascendency of passion over reason." This, of course, simply repeats his earlier comment about the Athenian assembly invariably turning into a mob. Reason is fragile and easily overcome by those with passion. Even if one assumes a constant ratio of "passionate" to "reasonable" people in assemblies of different sizes, it is obviously true that the larger the group, the greater the absolute number of people whose passion dominates their reason. Perhaps we assume that even a relatively small number of people can, through the force of their personalities, defeat less-passionate devotees of reason in a legislative battle. This might be true, but a modern political scientist would ask not only how one may confidently distinguish between the passionate and the reasonable, but also how one would demonstrate the greater probability that the former would enjoy undue influence in the legislative chamber.

Publius goes on to assert that "the larger the number, the greater will be the proportion of members of limited information and of weak capacities" who will be especially susceptible to the blandishments of skilled rhetoricians. But he presents nothing to justify his astounding proposition that larger size will generate not only a larger number but a greater proportion of problematic members. Presumably the argument is that the electorate will find it harder to winnow out the good from the bad candidates. But this calls into doubt the value of electoral accountability that he has earlier offered as a defense of the House of Representatives.

Publius summarizes his argument by stating that "the more multitudinous a representative assembly may be rendered, the more it will partake of the infirmities incident to collective meetings of the people. Ignorance will be the dupe of cunning, and passion the slave of sophistry and declamation." It is, he suggests, a gigantic intellectual error to believe that a larger representative assembly will be conducive to self-government or will "strengthen the barrier against the government of a few." Having more members may lead to the "countenance of the government" becoming "more democratic, but the soul that animates it will be more oligarchic. The machine will be enlarged, but the fewer, and often the more secret, will be the springs by which its motions are directed." Perhaps we should conclude that Publius's uncertainty about the "just right" size of the legislature has been resolved, at least to the extent that the burden of proof is placed on the person who wants to increase the size of the body. So to proposals such as Sabato's, which would increase the size of the House or the Senate, Publius seems predisposed to say that augmentation would probably make things worse, and we should be satisfied with the status quo.

In some ways the most interesting part of the essay, especially for a twenty-first-century reader, is the very end, where Publius addresses the objection to allowing a bare majority of the House to constitute a quorum and thus license the passage of legislation. This allows, for example, 26 percent of the membership to pass legislation should only 50 percent of the total membership be present for the vote. Publius concedes that there might on occasion be advantages to requiring a supermajority quorum. "It might have been an additional shield to some particular interests, and another obstacle generally to hasty and partial measures. But," he says, "these considerations are outweighed by the inconveniences in the opposite scale.

"In all cases where justice or the general good might require new laws to be passed, or active measures to be pursued, the fundamental principle of free government would be reversed. It would be no longer the majority that would rule: the power would be transferred to the minority. Were the defensive privilege limited to particular cases, an interested minority might take advantage of it to screen themselves from equitable sacrifices to the general weal, or, in particular emergencies, to extort unreasonable indulgences." Those opposed to specific legislation could, for example, simply refuse to constitute the supermajority that is now necessary to produce the quorum, thus giving a minority of the assembly the ability to block votes or, at least, "to extort unreasonable indulgences" as the price of cooperation. This, of course, is the consequence of the filibuster in the Senate.

It is also possible, as observers of Texas and Wisconsin politics can attest, that minorities who are aware that they will lose, should a vote be taken, but who have enough votes to block a quorum, may simply engage in "the baneful practice of secessions; a practice which has shown itself even in States where a majority only is required; a practice subversive of all the principles of order and regular government; a practice which leads more directly to public convulsions, and the ruin of popular governments, than any other which has yet been displayed among us." The "secession" being denounced here is not a state's leaving the Union but, as happened in Texas, members of the minority party, in that case Democrats, fleeing to New Mexico and Oklahoma en masse in order to make it impossible for the Texas senate to conduct its business under the two-thirds quorum requirement. Given the existence of such a requirement, perhaps one should not be critical of minorities who take advantage of the "rules laid down" to block what they may rightly believe is pernicious legislation. My own political sympathies were surely with the Texas Democrats, who tried to paralyze the Texas legislature, and with the Wisconsin Democrats, who likewise attempted to prevent the Wisconsin legislature from passing anti-union legislation. But does this provide adequate support for a *general* rule giving the minority a de facto veto over legislation in the House? Or must any small-"d" democrat agree with Publius that we are better off, all things considered, with majority rule than with the potentially perverse consequences of supermajoritarian government?

# PART 11

## *Who Should Be in Charge of Elections?*

# FEDERALIST 59

## *The Death of State Autonomy?*

To its opponents, the new Constitution created a frightening potential for overreach by the newly empowered national government. This meant, in a zero-sum political world, less power for state governments. Some of the fears expressed might strike a twenty-first-century (or eighteenth-century) reader as exaggerated; others seem altogether prescient and, indeed, still define contemporary cleavages in American politics. The next three essays, published between February 22 and 26, 1788, all concern one fear in particular. What, precisely, did Article I, Section 4, mean when it said, "The Times, Places and Manner of holding Elections for Senators and Representatives, shall be prescribed in each State by the Legislature thereof; but the Congress may at any time by Law make or alter such Regulations. . . ."? The first clause seems to reaffirm state autonomy, but clause two is another matter. Does Congress's power to "alter" all "such Regulations" in effect leave states at the tender mercies of the House and Senate (together with the president's decision whether to sign any relevant legislation) with regard to the basic mechanisms of choosing national legislators? And if it does, so what?

Years ago, when I first read some of the "anti-federalist" critiques of the Constitution and came to the almost frenzied worries expressed about congressional power under this clause, I tended to dismiss them as paranoid and, therefore, of relatively little analytic interest. More recent developments have changed my mind, not least because I would welcome greater congressional activity under the "Elections Clause," which has rarely stirred Congress's interest. It does raise important questions about the relative state and national roles in maintaining a "Republican Form of Government," whatever that might mean in the twenty-first century, and for that reason Publius's arguments take on a special significance.

Near the beginning of *Federalist* 59 Publius offers the following proposition, capitalized in the original: "EVERY GOVERNMENT OUGHT TO CONTAIN IN ITSELF THE MEANS OF ITS OWN PRESERVATION." The Philadelphia

Convention was wise, he tells us, in refusing to place control of elections entirely in the hands of either the state or national governments. Instead, the default rule is that states will be trusted to manage elections for national office. But the Framers "have reserved to the national authority a right to interpose, whenever extraordinary circumstances might render that interposition necessary to its safety." To do otherwise would "leave the existence of the Union entirely at [the] mercy" of state governments. Publius too sounds more than a bit paranoid when he suggests that a state could simply refuse to conduct elections. Yet, he writes, the very "possibility of the thing, without an equivalent for the risk, is an unanswerable objection." If critics of the proposed new Constitution assert the possibility of abuses of power by the national government, "it is as fair to presume them on the part of the State governments." And given that the Constitution itself is the strongest possible evidence that the Articles of Confederation had to be supplanted by a new arrangement that significantly increased the power of the national government in order to assure a "more perfect Union," it is "consonant to the rules of a just theory, to trust the Union with the care of its own existence."

Publius suggests that a provision "empowering the United States to regulate [all] elections for the particular States" would have undoubtedly been viewed "as an unwarrantable transposition of power, and as a premeditated engine for the destruction of the State governments." But the Elections Clause is not that sweeping. It applies only to elections for the exceedingly few popularly chosen national officials and is the equivalent of a "lifeline," to be activated only in extraordinary conditions where a state's outright refusal to conduct elections for congressional seats threatens the Union's existence. If that is the sole reason the clause exists, then it is no surprise that it has played such an insignificant part in our constitutional history.

One might think Publius had said all that is necessary, or even all that *can* be said. But he hasn't, and that fact testifies to the effectiveness with which opponents were able to set the terms of debate. Perhaps one should think of the "death panels" debate surrounding the Patient Protection and Affordable Care Act of 2010 (often labeled as "Obamacare"), with which opponents got remarkable traction from the completely spurious claim that the act would create panels of physicians that would in effect decide whether elderly patients would live or die. Those making such claims, notably including former Alaska Governor Sarah Palin, were relying on provisions in the proposed legislation (ultimately dropped, alas) that encouraged physicians to discuss "end of life" medical care with their patients, including such questions as whether extraordinary medical measures should be used to maintain life. Obviously, these discussions touch many raw nerves, and Obamacare opponents played very effectively on the anxieties attached to thinking about one's inevitable death or the similarly inevitable, and often exceedingly expensive and emotionally wrenching, deaths of loved ones. Similarly, if one fears that the Constitution spells the death of state autonomy and the transfer of power to distant national elites with agendas of their own, the Elections Clause may similarly look like a ticking time bomb, ready to go off as soon as these elites, once ensconced in the House and Senate, feel politically able to consolidate their power and further weaken the states.

## FEDERALIST 60

### *Manipulating Elections*

SO WHAT ARE THE practical fears? What might Congress in fact do under the Elections Clause? A favorite charge of the Constitution's opponents was that Congress might require that the vote for members of the House be confined to one city. Just imagine—or engage in the dark fantasy—that the merchants and lawyers who Publius has earlier told us would be likely to dominate the House (along with landowners) have mandated that the only site of voting in all of Massachusetts will be Boston, and in Pennsylvania, Philadelphia. The honest yeomanry throughout these states will have to journey to these urban centers if they wish to vote. One can only imagine who would be elected under such circumstances.

Publius insists, quite plausibly, that such notions are "chimerical" and that no Congress would engage in "conduct so violent and extraordinary"—not least, he suggests, because such an attempt "could never be made without causing an immediate revolt of the great body of the people, headed and directed by the State governments." That Congress could take such an action "without occasioning a popular revolution, is altogether inconceivable and incredible."

These are strong words. Is it telling that Publius does not deny that the clause, especially as interpreted by lawyers committed to enhancing national power, could in fact authorize such "interpositions" in the conduct of elections by states? Legal arguments turn out to be less important than the spirit of the people to rise up in armed revolt as their means of protest. This is no small point, for it goes beyond the proposition that the people retain a right to revolt should the national government breach the new Constitution. That is an argument about fidelity to law. Here, however, Publius seems to acknowledge that the national government has been given powers that are potentially dangerous. It will ultimately be up to the people to keep the government within acceptable bounds, not merely (if at all) by making legalistic arguments, but by arguing that even if legally permissible, certain actions violate the basic (perhaps unwritten) terms of union.

After raising the specter of violent revolution as the ultimate safeguard against national overreaching, Publius returns to an extensive refutation of the argument that the "wealthy and the well-born" will establish permanent dominance through clever manipulation of the Elections Clause. One reason is simply that elites are distributed throughout states, not only in the great cities. The only truly effective way to entrench their power is by passage of a national law limiting state suffrage to those with sufficient property, but no one has suggested that the Elections Clause extends so far. "Times, Places and Manner" did not mean "eligibility to vote."

At the end, Publius returns to the role of sheer power in the enforcement of (or resistance to) unacceptable interpositions. If one can imagine that the national government has indeed amassed sufficient power to quell popular resistance—backed, one presumes, by state militias—then why, he asks, would national elites even bother to manipulate the conduct of elections? "Would they not rather boldly resolve to perpetuate themselves in office by one decisive act of usurpation, than to trust to precarious expedients, which in spite of all the precautions that might accompany them, might terminate in the dismission, disgrace, and ruin of their authors"? In any event, we are talking about potential "tyrants" who amply deserve "overthrow" in order "to avenge the violated majesty of the people."

One can only wonder whether Publius himself, having written these two overheated essays, considered it truly worthwhile to include the Elections Clause in the Constitution. It was almost guaranteed to be a red flag that would goad the raging bulls of anti-federalism. Did Publius's defense, however convincing, do anything more than reduce the clause to a de facto nullity? Is this much ado about what has turned out to be nothing, or could the Elections Clause have an important part to play in the twenty-first century?

## FEDERALIST 61

### *What Is a Propitious Time to Choose Representatives?*

PUBLIUS WINDS UP HIS defense of the Elections Clause not only by pointing out that some of the same problems are present in the New York constitution, which seemingly authorizes the legislature to require that everyone vote in their county seat, but also, and far more interestingly, by suggesting that one important outgrowth of the clause could be the establishment of a common national election date in order to prevent states from electing members of the House whenever they want. Just think of the spectacle of contemporary presidential campaigns, where New Hampshire and Iowa vie to make sure that no other state will conduct its primary or caucus (respectively) earlier than they do. Other states are willing to schedule late primaries in the hope that the earlier elections will not have produced a winner and that the close race will induce world-class pandering from candidates eager to procure key delegates. "It is more than possible," Publius writes, "that this uniformity [of election days] may be . . . of great importance to the public welfare."

It took almost a hundred years, until 1872, for Congress to pass legislation mandating the first Tuesday in November as the day on which all elections for the House of Representatives shall be held (save for "special elections" designed to fill unexpected vacancies), as well as for the electors formally charged with choosing presidents. To this day, of course, states hold elections for *state* officers whenever they want, though most, to save money and encourage turnout, make them coincide with national elections. An increasing number of states have adopted "early voting" options, which allow voters to cast their ballots beginning several weeks before election day. Though they are not counted until that day, early voting has the consequence of erasing the importance, for those who have voted, of any developments in the last week or two of the campaign. Harvard political theorist Dennis Thompson has criticized early voting precisely for diminishing the symbolic and practical importance of a shared national moment when we elect our leaders. Of course, one reason for early voting is the widely shared belief that the first Tuesday of November, whatever sense it might have made in 1872 as a national day of election, is grossly inappropriate in the twenty-first century. Almost no other country conducts its elections during the ordinary workweek, and many have weekend-long periods for casting ballots. As should be obvious, the Constitution says nothing about any given "election day." It is a matter for congressional determination, and one can well ask why Congress does not select a day better suited to contemporary American life.

An equally obvious question is this: What accounts for Congress's failure even to consider election-day reform, given that there is almost no rational argument for maintaining our adherence to the first Tuesday in November? The answer—and I think the words "of course" are all too appropriate—is that almost everything about elections has implications for political partisans. The late philosopher John Rawls famously created the conceit of a "veil of ignorance": We should design our basic constitutional structures and norms as if we did not know what our social position would be once the veil was lifted. This would assure that whatever we agreed to, behind the veil, would be regarded by everyone as fair. There are many reasons to praise this idea, but adherence to the actual circumstances of constitutional design is not one of them (nor did Rawls believe that he was actually positing a practical mode of designing constitutions). It is widely thought, for example, that holding elections on the first Tuesday in November diminishes the turnout of working-class Americans, for whom taking time off to vote is simply too expensive. And if one assumes that working-class voters—or those (disproportionately women) who are faced with child- or parental-care responsibilities—are more likely to vote Democratic than Republican, it is scarcely surprising, given Publius's emphasis on the importance of factional perspectives, that support for changing election day is higher among Democrats. Similar analyses could be offered with regard to registration rules—the United States probably has the most stringent such rules of any country in the "democratic" West—and even such particularities of election administration as design of ballots, hours of voting, number and reliability of machines, and the location of voting sites.[1] (The last, of course, was the subject of the original seemingly paranoid fantasies about the Elections Clause.) And American politics has been roiled for at least the past decade by frequently successful attempts by a number of American states—controlled, without exception, by conservative Republicans—to use their authority over suffrage criteria to impose voting identification requirements. As the noted Judge Richard Posner wrote in a scathing opinion, given the absence of any significant empirical evidence of "voter fraud," it is simply implausible that anything other than partisan motives explain the passage of such legislation.[2]

Since Publius wrote, in 1788, the Constitution has been amended to limit at least some state autonomy with regard to structuring the electorate, and Congress has used its authority under these amendments to pass a number of laws, none more important than the Voting Rights Act of 1965. Among the key aspects of that law was one requiring federal preapproval of every change to election law in so-called "covered" states to make sure that these changes, including moving the sites at which elections take place, did not discriminate against minority voters. As one can imagine, the continued application of federal "preclearance" a full half century after the passage of the Voting Rights Act angered a number of states, who no doubt viewed it as exactly the kind of congressional overreach the anti-federal critics of the Constitution feared would be enabled by the Elections Clause. A conservative Republican majority of the United States Supreme Court in a 2013 case arising out of Shelby County, Alabama, liberated states from the preclearance requirements by emphasizing that the coverage formula was based on data involving voting discrimination in 1964. Too much has changed in the subsequent fifty years, Chief Justice John Roberts wrote, to allow such incursions on state autonomy to be based on what he clearly believed was outdated information. That Congress (and George W. Bush, who signed the relevant legislation in 2007) relied on that information was beside the point.

It is worth considering in this context a July 8, 2014, story in *The New York Times* titled "Mistrust in North Carolina Over Plan to Reduce Precincts." The piece described efforts in Shelby, North Carolina, a town of about twenty thousand, to reduce the number of precincts from five to two. Although the evidence is mixed, opponents of the plan, mostly from the African American community, view it as a Republican effort to reduce the turnout of Democratic voters.[3] There are, of course, many other acrimonious controversies about changes in voting procedures, many of which almost certainly would not have survived the now-dormant pre-clearance process. Two things are especially interesting about the North Carolina story. First, it demonstrates the practical importance of the *Shelby County* decision. There is a huge debate among political scientists about the actual consequences of Supreme Court decisions, but in this case it seems impossible not to credit (or blame) *Shelby County* for actions taken in its aftermath. Second, because the North Carolina legislation concerns local and state officials, it easily fits into Publius's concern about the power of political factions in states, set out most memorably in *Federalist* 10.

The Voting Rights Act was based on the Fourteenth and Fifteenth Amendments, which authorize Congress to pass legislation designed to enforce its commands. But in a number of recent decisions, the Supreme Court has refused to allow Congress to offer more "liberal" interpretations of those amendments than the Court itself will tolerate. In a later case, the Court did strike down Arizona's refusal to accept compliance with federal law as dispositive with regard to the legitimacy of registering to vote. Arizona demanded more proof of U.S. citizenship than did the relevant federal legislation. In commenting on the decision, a number of election-law specialists suggested that Congress should make greater use of its powers under the Elections Clause in lieu of its presently diminished powers under the Fourteenth and Fifteenth Amendments. Readers could be forgiven if they viewed such discussions as "inside baseball" of interest primarily to constitutional lawyers, since the major point is that the currently polarized Congress is not likely to do anything about the conduct of elections. Still, the Elections Clause is there, waiting to be invigorated by a Congress that is persuaded that state autonomy may be just another term for factional overreach.

# PART 12

## *On the Senate*

## On the "Lesser Evil"

I N *FEDERALIST* 62, Publius turns his attention to the Senate, the subject of the next five essays (two fewer than he devoted to the House of Representatives). He begins with a short discussion of the "qualifications" to be a senator, which require both "a more advanced age" than House membership, thirty instead of twenty-five, and "a longer period of citizenship," nine years instead of seven. One can raise legitimate questions about whether either requirement should be laid out in the Constitution, as against leaving it up to the voters to decide whom they wish to represent them. The durational citizenship test assures that no newcomer to the United States could serve in the Senate until fourteen years after arrival—given five years to meet the naturalization requirement and then the additional nine years before she would be eligible for the Senate. It's important, as well, to realize that in 1788 there was no way of knowing how long the requirement for becoming a citizen would be. Federalists were briefly able to impose a fourteen-year requirement, though Jeffersonians, upon assuming power, were able to change it back to the original five.

I feel slightly embarrassed when reading Publius's defense of the requirement on the ground that "hasty admission" of naturalized citizens to the Senate "might create a channel for foreign influence on the national councils." Still, even though it is important to remember Justice Holmes's admonition that "we live by symbols" and therefore to object to the presence in the Constitution of what I term the "second-class citizenship clauses," it is difficult to believe that either requirement has practical significance. One might contrast these clauses, as they apply to would-be members of the House and Senate, with the absolute exclusion of naturalized citizens from the presidency; the latter could explain why the then governor, Arnold Schwarzenegger, did not run for that office in 2008, either as a Republican or as an independent hoping to overcome the polarization between the two parties.

With regard to what many might have seen as the Senate's most striking feature—that its members would be chosen by state legislatures instead of by direct vote of the public—Publius has remarkably little to say. "It is recommended," he assures the reader, "by the double advantage of favoring a select appointment, and of giving to the State governments such an agency in the formation of the federal government, as must secure the authority of the former, and may form a convenient link between the two systems." The paucity of comment beyond this sentence may show that in 1788 there was no real controversy about this mode of appointment. It did not, of course, last, and this is one of the Constitution's few basic institutional structures that has been changed by subsequent amendment. The Seventeenth Amendment stripped the appointment power from state legislatures and gave it to the general electorate. At the time the change was widely favored, to judge from the rapidity with which it was approved: it was proposed by Congress on May 13, 1912, and ratified by the requisite thirty-six states by April 8, 1913.

What is more interesting is that the Seventeenth Amendment has become controversial in the twenty-first century as a number of conservative Republicans have called for its repeal and a return to appointment of senators by state legislatures. Utah's Senator Mike Lee has described the amendment as "a mistake." Texas Governor Rick Perry ascribes its passage to "a fit of populist rage in the early twentieth century."[1] They could easily quote Justice Antonin Scalia in support; he told a University of Chicago audience in 2010 that he would recommend changing the Constitution "back to what they wrote, in some respects. The 17th Amendment has changed things enormously . . . [Y]ou can trace the decline of so-called states' rights throughout the rest of the 20th century."[2]

It is hard to deny that the Seventeenth Amendment fundamentally changed the constitutional order, for exactly the reason that Publius suggested while defending the initial method of selection: It *did* provide state officials with a direct way to influence the composition, and thus the legislative direction, of the Senate. They would have been even more influential had, for example, senators been vulnerable to recall by unhappy state legislators—which would have made senators the equivalent of ambassadors from the states to the national government, answerable to their masters back home. But even without this option, senators no doubt felt at least somewhat beholden to those who selected them and, perhaps more importantly, alert to the possibility of not being reappointed after six years if state legislators became unhappy with their performance. After the Seventeenth Amendment, senators certainly have an incentive to serve the wishes of their constituents, but they no longer have any particular concern about maintaining the prerogatives of state governments. It may be that their constituents have grown comfortable with the far more powerful national government that developed in the twentieth century and do not care if that has led to the diminution of state autonomy. It is understandable that some state officials might take a different view. We can be quite confident, however, that the Seventeenth Amendment will not be repealed, partly because it is difficult to imagine that modern national legislators, all of whom have gained their offices through popular election, would voluntarily place their futures in the hands of state legislators. It is also difficult to believe that enough Americans are so eager to lose their right to vote for senators, that they would delegate this power to their state legislatures. Thus, even if it could get through the Congress, a proposal to repeal could not draw the requisite support from thirty-eight of the fifty states. But this reality does not vitiate Justice Scalia's point about the importance of the Seventeenth Amendment for anyone wishing to understand how our institutions operate.

Publius spends the bulk of this essay on the total number of senators, which will always be far fewer the number than in the House of Representatives—if there were 65 original representatives from the thirteen states, there would be only 26 senators—and the advantages of the senators' longer terms. As to the former, he repeats his point that small assemblies are likely to function better than larger ones. It is not only that one feature of American bicameral government is that each house has an absolute veto over the other; Publius also appears to believe that the House is more likely to pass legislation in need of veto, as a function of both its greater size and its members' more frequent election. "Numerous assembles," Publius tells us (meaning assemblies with many members), are apt "to yield to the impulses of sudden and violent passions, and to be seduced by factious leaders, into intemperate and pernicious resolutions." Even if, as an empirical matter, the modern House of Representatives, with its 435 members, is more likely to respond to "sudden and violent passions" than the 100-member Senate—and how, one might ask, would one demonstrate this proposition to a skeptic?—one might still believe that the explanation for this tendency lay more in the frequency of elections than in the sheer effects of size.

But Publius, who defines "good government" not only by its "object" of achieving "the happiness of the people" but also by "a knowledge of the means by which that object can be attained," believes that the Senate, because of its longer terms as well as its nonpopular selection, will contain a far higher percentage of appropriately knowledgeable legislators. He is very critical of "mutable government," by which he means a high turnover of members. This produces too much "change of opinions" and thus an excess of destabilizing "change of measures." His final comment, though, concerns the importance of creating a psychological bond between the citizenry and the new constitutional order. "The most deplorable effect of all" from too much turnover and consequent change of policies (which may, after all, reflect public opinion), "is that diminution of attachment and reverence which steals into the hearts of the people, towards a political system which betrays so many marks of infirmity. . . . No government . . . will long be respected, without being truly respectable; nor be truly respectable, without possessing a certain portion of order and stability." Living in a time when all of the polls indicate ever diminishing respect for Congress—including, obviously, the Senate—we can only wonder how persuasive Publius's arguments would be today, especially his ill-concealed suspicion of any government that is too responsive to the vagaries of public opinion.

Publius's most interesting arguments, especially for a twenty-first-century reader, concern the third issue, the equal allocation of voting power in the Senate. Each state, whatever its size, has two and only two senators. There can be no doubt that Publius is appalled by this feature of the Constitution, but given his role, he must defend it rather than throw it to the wolves. So what does he say? First, and crucially, he describes it as "the result of compromise between the opposite pretensions of the large and the small States." We can be confident that he objects to the Senate's remarkable deviation from proportional representation, and to the tremendous advantage given to small states. He does admit that "it does not appear to be without some reason that in a compound republic, partaking both of the national and federal character, the government ought to be founded on a mixture of the principles of proportional and equal representation." But the next sentences capture how tepid this concession is: "But it is superfluous to try, by the standard of theory, a part of the Constitution which is allowed on all hands to be the result, not of theory, but 'of a

spirit of amity, and that mutual deference and concession which the peculiarity of our political situation rendered indispensable.'" If "standard[s]
of theory" are irrelevant, on what should we base our judgment? Publius
does not use the magic word "compromise," but his answer lies in the "exigencies" of the current "political situation" that absolutely require that the
people of the United States (however defined) create a "common government, with powers equal to its objects." It is crystal clear that the small
states would have withdrawn from the constitutional project rather than
accede to proportional representation in the Senate. Given the harsh realities facing the drafters in Philadelphia, "the advice of prudence must be to
*embrace the lesser evil*; and, instead of indulging a fruitless anticipation of
the possible mischiefs which may ensue, to contemplate rather the advantageous consequences which may qualify the sacrifice" (emphasis added).

Once more, Publius's advice to the reader across the centuries has far
less to do with the specifics under discussion—we did, after all, liberate
ourselves from legislative selection of senators, and one need not endorse
the allocation of senators simply because it is in the Constitution—than
with the need to recognize the constraints that actual "political situations" always generate. Those caught in the maelstrom of politics must
make what former Secretary of State Hillary Clinton has labeled the "hard
choices" that present themselves for resolution. One can always try to spin
the choices, as Publius does when he suggests that equality of representation may make it harder to pass legislation and thus prevent the "excess
of law-making" that seems to be one of "the diseases to which our governments are most liable." Still, his heart really is not in the defense.

Politics involves compromise, sometimes even "rotten compromises,"
including the Three-fifths Clause and other safeguards of slavery written
into the Constitution. Yet there may be lines in the sand that honorable
people should not cross, and from 1787 until today, some have believed
that the Constitution was not worth the price of appeasing slave owners.
Consider an exchange at the Virginia ratifying convention between George
Mason, who was with Patrick Henry the leading opponent of ratification,
and James Madison regarding the Constitution's guarantee of a twenty-year
ban on congressional regulation of the international slave trade. (Congress
passed on March 2, 1807, a law prohibiting the importation of slaves after
January 1, 1808.) Mason was willing to face the prospect of union without
"the Southern States," by which he meant Georgia and South Carolina,

which apparently would not accept a Constitution that did not protect the slave trade. Mason deplored "this disgraceful trade" and was, according to Pauline Meier in her magisterial history of the ratification debates, "ready to leave those states out of the Union" if they insisted on maintaining it. What was Madison's response? "'Great as the evil is, a dismemberment of the Union would be worse.'"[3]

Compromise may come at the stage of writing a constitution; it may come when deciding that "parchment barriers" are in effect made to be breached to achieve greater goods, such as the "self-preservation" that is given pride of place especially in *Federalist* 41. Compromise is not *all* that politics is about; we could not even identify why people would involve themselves in political battles unless driven by genuine ideals. But to imagine politics as only a struggle to the end over competing ideals is to concede that it will almost inevitably disintegrate into war. That is where compromise rears its head, ugly in the eyes of the "idealist," but perhaps quite beautiful from the perspective of someone terrified by the dogs of war.

## FEDERALIST 63

## *Let Sleeping Sovereigns Lie?*

PUBLIUS BEGINS *FEDERALIST* 63 by repeating his arguments from 62 regarding the advantages of a smaller group serving longer terms. What may particularly interest the modern reader, though, is his assertion that "national councils may be warped by some strong passion, or momentary interest," in which case "the presumed or known opinion of the impartial world, may be the best guide that can be followed." Here Publius echoes the Declaration of Independence and its appeal to a "decent respect to the opinions of mankind." Senators, he believes, are more likely to be cosmopolitan and therefore cognizant of world opinion, and as importantly, to have the disposition to be guided by it, at least in "doubtful cases" where the right answer is not clear. One wonders how many Americans in the twenty-first century would unequivocally accept this argument. How many of us today believe that American political leaders should openly prefer the views of "the impartial world" over their own convictions?

Consider the response, for example, of Justice Scalia, in a June 2012 case involving the duty of Arizona to submit to national law regarding unauthorized immigrants. The United States, defending the proposition that the national law "preempted" Arizona's legislation, gave as one of the supporting arguments that immigration involves delicate questions of foreign policy, and Arizona's measures inflamed the Mexican government and made our relationship with Mexico more difficult. The majority agreed that "foreign countries['] concern[s] about the status, safety, and security of their nationals in the United States" were relevant in deciding how much autonomy the "sovereign State" (as Scalia repeatedly called it) of Arizona could have in pursuing its own policy. For Scalia, on the other hand, "the fundamental sovereign powers of the States [cannot be] abridged to accommodate foreign countries' views. Even in its international relations, the Federal Government must live with the inconvenient fact that it is a Union of independent States, who have their own sovereign powers," even if the exercise of those powers turns out in effect to be "a nuisance and a bother in the conduct of foreign policy." Scalia reminds his readers (and his colleagues) that the Court in 2008 refused President George W. Bush's request that it "interfere" with the operation of Texas criminal courts in a case where those courts had sentenced a Mexican national to death without notifying the Mexican embassy of his arrest, as required by international treaty. Scalia interpreted that decision to mean that "Though it may upset foreign powers—and even when the Federal Government desperately wants to avoid upsetting foreign powers—the States" retain significant autonomy, including "the right to protect their borders against foreign nationals, just as they have the right to execute foreign nationals for murder" in circumstances where international law has been violated. It is, of course, possible to read this simply as a debate about the role of courts in monitoring these delicate questions, but it is hard not to read Justice Scalia's opinion as an implicit rejection of Publius's argument that at least the "impartial" views of the rest of the world should be of interest to American lawmakers. How many candidates for national office in the United States today emphasize their cosmopolitanism—for example, the ability to read or speak foreign languages or frequent travel abroad—and their willingness to take seriously the views of foreigners?

Given that Publius fears the consequences of "irregular passion" and a populace "misled by the artful misrepresentations of interested men," it is not surprising that the most important aspect of *Federalist* 63, then as now, is his resolute rejection of any genuine role for unmediated rule by "We the People." The Constitution might proclaim popular sovereignty as its basis, but it should be absolutely clear that the sovereign people, having spoken once through elected conventions and not, for example, through direct referenda, should in effect slip into a coma.

Publius proudly acknowledges that the leitmotif of the American experiment in republican government is to replace "direct democracy," where the people themselves are empowered to make decisions, with "representative democracy," where the role of "the people" is restricted to choosing, at suitable intervals, the officials who will be empowered to make decisions in the people's name. The British political scientist Anthony King titled a recent book *The Founding Fathers v. The People: Paradoxes of American Democracy,* in order to underline the anomalies presented by the Publian fear of direct rule. King points out not only that many countries make frequent use of referenda that place decision-making power in the hands of the populace itself, but also, and far more interesting, that almost all American states, whose constitutions with only two exceptions were written or revised after the 1787 national Constitution, include at least some opportunity for "direct democracy." This can range from the relatively modest grant of power to the general electorate to decide whether or not to ratify proposed amendments to state constitutions (forty-nine of fifty states do this; Delaware is the exception), to the well-known (and often maligned) "initiative and referendum" option in California and other western states, in which the electorate can force issues onto the public agenda by petition and then vote certain proposals (including state constitutional amendments) into law through subsequent referenda.

Publius wants none of this. For him the "true distinction" of the proposed constitutional order lies "IN THE TOTAL EXCLUSION OF THE PEOPLE IN THEIR COLLECTIVE CAPACITY from any share" in actual policy making, except insofar as representatives are attentive to public opinion. It is significant that the capitalized words appear as such in the original. Publius did not hesitate to embrace this fully as a feature, and not at all a bug, of the proposed system. We should not be surprised at this posture, given his frequent warnings about the propensity of the public to be dominated by factional concerns or irrational passions, compared to more public-spirited and knowledgeable characters who will "represent" the public. This stance generates important questions about what "represent" means.

Does it require faithful adherence to one's constituents' expressed desires? Or does it require that public officials construct an image of an idealized public, cleansed of the disfigurements generated by faction and passion and devoted to the public (as against private) good? One might think of "portraits" that show "warts and all" versus the idealization of ancient Greek statuary.

It is not surprising that Publius's denunciation of what might be termed "actualized popular sovereignty" should come in an essay devoted to the Senate, given its formal lack of popular accountability, at least prior to the Seventeenth Amendment. But even with that amendment in effect, vital questions remain about what we expect our "representatives" actually to represent. One function of the six-year term, obviously, is that it is takes far longer to fire a senator than a representative. King notes that many states (and localities) in the United States have recall procedures that in effect allow aroused electorates to fire public officials in midterm. The most famous twenty-first-century examples are surely California's recall of Democratic Governor Gray Davis and his replacement by the Republican Arnold Schwarzenegger, and the failed attempt in June 2012 to recall Republican Governor Scott Walker in Wisconsin.

It should be clear that Publius, when read in the twenty-first century, speaks only about the unique United States Constitution among the fifty-one separate constitutions within the overall American constitutional order. Forty-nine of the other fifty embody a more robust—some a far more robust—conception of "popular sovereignty" than does the United States Constitution. The question that any person faced with the task of drafting a constitution today must ask is, Which among the fifty-one constitutions (not to mention the many other national constitutions, especially those drafted after World War II) presents the best model of achieving the Goldilocks mixture of representative and direct democracy?

## FEDERALIST 64

### *The Senate's Superior Wisdom on Foreign Affairs*

ONE DEFENSE OF BICAMERALISM is simply that two heads are better than one. Most of the time, identical legislation is submitted to the House of Representatives and the Senate, and to become a law it must be passed in identical form by both chambers and then either signed by the president or passed over a presidential veto. Publius has already explained why the heads in the Senate might be both less passionate and better informed than those in the House. *Federalist* 64, however, concerns an important reversion to the "one head" principle, where the Senate has powers that the House totally lacks. The United States, as a sovereign nation within the international system, possesses the constitutional power to enter into treaties with foreign countries. But treaties become effective only if the Senate, by a two-thirds vote, ratifies them after submission by the president, who initially negotiated them with the relevant foreign powers. Why might we approve this exclusion of the House?

By now we should not be surprised that the answer lies in Publius's skepticism about the deficiencies of elections and, concomitantly, the dangers of too much sensitivity to the views of one's constituents. What he labels "party zeal" is all too likely to "tak[e] advantage of the supineness, the ignorance, and the hopes and fears of the unwary and interested," by which he means those who favor their own special interests ahead of the general welfare. Representatives who have been elected, often "by the [marginal] votes of a small proportion of the electors," are not likely to serve the national interest well. Instead, we want decisions about foreign policy to be made by those who "will not be liable to be deceived" by "transient meteors" that can "mislead as well as dazzle." When one combines the superiority of the Senate with the advantage of longer terms and the protection against "members constantly coming and going in quick succession," one ends up wondering why one would give the House much say in anything important, but that is another matter.

One might wonder what Publius would think of the modern practice of relying on "executive agreements" to do the work formerly done by formal treaties. The most famous modern such agreement is the North American Free Trade Agreement with Canada and Mexico. To be sure, it did require the concurrence, by majority vote, of both House and Senate, but that, of course, underscores the difference between an "agreement" and a treaty. If it had been unequivocally viewed as the latter, only two-thirds approval of the Senate (which would probably have not been forthcoming) would have been necessary. Yale Professor Bruce Ackerman and Harvard Professor Laurence Tribe conducted a notable debate some years ago about the de facto evisceration of the "Treaty Clause" in favor of the pervasive (but, to be sure, not exclusive) reliance on executive agreements. Ackerman, who agreed that the modern practice constitutes an "amendment," albeit outside Article V, of the Constitution, defended it as recognizing the dysfunctionality generated by overly fastidious reliance on the Treaty Clause. He also argued that it had gained the practical assent of "We the People" through the electoral process. Thus he answered an unequivocal yes to the question posed by a book he coauthored with NYU Professor David Golove, *Is NAFTA Constitutional?* Tribe disagreed, dismissing Ackerman's arguments as exemplifying "free-form" constitutional interpretation, willfully ignoring the dictate of the Constitution and the only legitimate way of amending it.

Do we care that executive agreements strip the Senate of not only its exclusivity, but also the particular power that comes with the requirement of a supermajority? Publius hardly mentions the fact that treaty ratification requires two-thirds of the Senate. In the twenty-first century one could easily compose a "blocking" minority of one-third-plus-one out of senators who represent less than 10 percent of the U.S. population. If there are no significant political differences between small (generally rural) states and their larger counterparts, one might be relatively complacent about this. But consider today's pressing issue of global warming and the concomitant need to reduce our use of coal and oil in favor of energy sources that do not emit $CO_2$. Some measures would require "only" the passage of national legislation, which is hard enough. But because climate change is a worldwide problem, addressing it will undoubtedly require the negotiation of an international treaty, and therefore the acquiescence of at least sixty-seven senators (assuming that all one hundred vote). Many American states do not mine substantial amounts of coal or produce other forms of energy, but enough *do* to make ratification of any such treaty precarious. Equally important is the fact that presidents charged with negotiating drafts to be laid before the Senate would have to count votes even as they bargained with other countries. Not only might they be reluctant to make concessions that disinterested analysts would readily agree to, but their felt need to get a treaty past a possibly obstructive minority might prevent them from taking a leadership role in the negotiations.

The preceding paragraph assumed that "executive agreements" would in fact be submitted to Congress, as was NAFTA. But American politics in 2015 are being roiled by the possibility of an "executive agreement" with Iran, regarding its potential ability to produce nuclear weapons, that would not be submitted to Congress at all (where it would almost certainly fail, given the adamant opposition of most Republicans and some Democrats). I confess to supporting President Obama in his willingness to reach agreement with Iran, but one can certainly understand the criticism that this places too much power in the hands of a single chief executive. Publius was writing about an entirely different vision of constitutional and political reality.

Perhaps Publius's valentine to the Senate was accurate in 1788. But it is significantly weakened by the passage of the Seventeenth Amendment and the switch to selection by popular vote. Is there any reason to believe that voters will be better at choosing senators than representatives, or that they will look for cosmopolitans when voting for the former? There remains, of course, the presumptive advantage of longer terms, but this too rests in part on the empirical assertion that the House features significantly greater turnover than the Senate. In the twenty-first century, there is little reason to believe this.

Both Houses of Congress are largely inhabited by professional politicians who are eager to secure reelection. There are distinctly different cultures in the 435-member House and the 100-member Senate, linked to the fact that the basic work of the House is done in committees. Specialization and expertise with regard to particular policy areas are more likely to be found in members of the House, whereas senators are called upon to profess expertise (or at least heartfelt views) about many different matters. It is highly unlikely, though, that contemporary candidates for the Senate would emphasize to the voters that they had lived abroad or, even more so, that they spoke French or Chinese. And some political scientists have argued that senators rarely seek out appointment to the Senate Foreign Relations Committee, which had once been extremely prestigious, in part because it is not a good base from which to raise badly needed campaign funds. Far better to be on the Senate Committee on Banking, Housing, and Urban Affairs, for example.

Finally, it is also worth mulling Publius's perspective on the sanctity of treaties. "[A] treaty," he writes, "is only another name for a bargain. . . . [I]t would be impossible to find a nation who would make any bargain with us, which should be binding on them ABSOLUTELY, but on us only so long and so far as we may think proper to be bound by it." He seems to be arguing that Congress's power to repeal existing legislation, which is basically absolute under the principle that no Congress can bind its successor, is limited when treaties are involved. "[T]reaties," Publius reminds us, "are made, not by only one of the contracting, but by both; and consequently, that as the consent of both was essential to their formation at first, so must it ever afterwards be to alter or cancel them." There might be a certain logic to this argument, but it is not followed in practice. Every nation believes it can get out of what it decides is a bad deal simply by renouncing it and paying whatever costs such behavior entails. The idea that any country would ever bind itself "absolutely" is fanciful. After all, a persistent theme of *The Federalist* has been the permeability of "parchment barriers" when vital national interests are thought to be at risk. If that applies even to clauses in the Constitution, it applies all the more to treaties made with foreign countries. The willingness of countries to enter into treaties with the United States (or any other country) is an extremely interesting mystery, especially given the lack of institutions with the power to enforce treaty obligations against breachers.

## FEDERALIST 65

### *The Senate's Confirmation and Impeachment Powers*

THE OTHER MOST IMPORTANT distinction between the Senate and House, with regard to their constitutionally granted powers, concerns the former's unique role in confirming presidential appointments. It is utterly irrelevant, as a formal matter, what the House thinks about any of the president's nominees; what is crucial is whether that person can get approved by the requisite majority of senators who are present and voting on a given day (as against an absolute majority of the entire one hundred senators). Anyone aware of contemporary American politics knows this is no easy task, whether one is thinking of nominees to the federal bench or even nominations for cabinet or subcabinet positions. Rather stunningly, Publius mentions this power only to scant any serious discussion of it. He does, to be sure, mention it again in *Federalist*s 76 and 77, when discussing the president's power to appoint officials, but one can only wonder at the absence of sustained discussion in the group of essays devoted to the

Senate. The answer surely cannot be that appointment and confirmation is without practical interest.

One might ask why the framers of the Twenty-fifth Amendment, added to the Constitution in 1965 to provide a way of filling vacancies in the vice presidency, dictated that *both* the House and Senate must approve the president's choice. Granted, the vice president, as a prospective president should anything happen to the incumbent, is more important than almost any other political official, but, given the infrequency of such succession and the uncertain powers of the vice president (whose only task under the Constitution is to preside over the Senate), is it really more important to gain the assent of both House and Senate for that office than, say, for the person chosen to be chief justice of the United States, secretary of state, chair of the Joint Chiefs of Staff of the armed forces, or head of the Federal Reserve Board? And it is worth noting as well that under the Succession in Office Act, members of the cabinet, beginning with the secretary of state (if a "natural born Citizen") would move into the Oval Office in certain extreme circumstances. The vice president may be only a heartbeat away from the presidency, but the secretary of state is only four beats away (with the speaker of the House and the president pro tempore of the Senate, unwisely I believe, being placed by the act between the vice president and the secretary). Were we redesigning our Constitution from scratch, would we again place the confirmation power entirely in the hands of the Senate?

Publius gives a good deal more attention to the Senate's unique role of determining whether to convict presidents (and other high officials) who have been impeached by the House. One can compare the House to the grand jury, which has only the power to indict. Conviction requires either a trial or a voluntary guilty plea. Some impeached officials have gone quietly into obscurity by resigning their offices, but most (especially federal judges) have insisted on their "day in court," that is, the Senate, and some have escaped conviction.

Publius is well aware that impeachments stir up popular passion and may reflect partisan or factional disputes. Readers should have little trouble thinking of contemporary examples. Although one might imagine that voters themselves be given the power to acquit or convict, as they do in recall elections, that is obviously not the path taken in Philadelphia, nor is it likely that Publius would have thought that a good idea. He writes, "The convention, it appears, thought the Senate the most fit depositary of this important public trust" to judge impeached officials fairly and impartially, as we would expect ordinary juries to do.

Publius compares the constitutional differentiation between House and Senate to that in Great Britain, where the House of Commons brings charges and the House of Lords assesses their merits. But are there no alternatives, even if one rejects a national "citizen jury" of electors? Publius addresses the possibility that the Supreme Court might be the final judge of an official's culpability. "It is much to be doubted," he writes, that the Court would have the "fortitude" necessary "in the execution of so difficult a task." Far more important, though, is his second concern, which is whether members of the Supreme Court "would possess the degree of credit and authority, which might, on certain occasions, be indispensable towards reconciling the people to a decision that should happen to clash with an accusation brought by their immediate representatives. A deficiency in [fortitude] would be fatal to the accused; in the last, dangerous to the public tranquillity." Again, the principal concern appears to be taming public passions, which requires that the decision makers have genuine public respect, and Publius apparently doubts whether Supreme Court members will be as highly respected as senators. This too raises empirical questions: One can wonder whether this is true in the contemporary United States. Perhaps, if we polled the public, we would discover that neither institution possesses "enough" respect to still the partisan clashes that at least some impeachments would provoke. Just as much to the point, perhaps, we might want senators to cast "prudential" votes, based on balancing the harm done even by a president's illegal conduct against his or her ability to serve the nation well by continuing in office (mixed, perhaps, with assessments of the abilities of the vice president, who would take over in case of a conviction). Justices, on the other hand, might be more legalistic in their approach and ask *only* whether the president in fact committed "high Crimes and Misdemeanors."

Publius points to another problem if we rely on the judiciary instead of the Senate, which is the limited size of the United States Supreme Court. While the Constitution does not specify the Court's size, Publius was likely not surprised that the first Congress gave it six members (as distinguished from the initial count of twenty-two senators, given that Rhode Island and North Carolina had not yet ratified the Constitution when the new government met for the first time). "The awful discretion which a court of impeachments must necessarily have, to doom to honor or to infamy the most confidential and the most distinguished characters of the community, forbids the commitment of the trust to a small number of persons." Once again Goldilocks renders her judgment: The Court provides "too few" members, even as the general electorate would undoubtedly have been far too many.

One "further consideration" reinforces the preference for the Senate over the Court. Impeachment is a special kind of trial in which conviction brings a unique form of punishment: the removal of the miscreant from office and, in certain circumstances, a ban on his holding any public office in the future. But this may not be the end of the matter. An impeached official can also be subjected to criminal trial and punishment, which is the function of the judiciary. "Would it be proper," Publius asks, "that the persons who had disposed of his fame, and his most valuable rights as a citizen in one trial, should, in another trial, for the same offense, be also the disposers of his life and his fortune?" There is surely something to be said for this concern, but then one wonders why the Constitution assigned the chief justice to preside over impeachment trials of the president. Some readers may recall that William Rehnquist wore special robes of his own design when crossing the street to take his seat as the presiding officer in the trial of President Clinton. Would he have recused himself in any subsequent case involving potential criminal liability of the impeached Clinton?

Publius goes on to consider the creation of what might be termed a "special court of impeachment," whose members' only duty is to try those charged by the House with impeachable offenses. He presents reasons both pro and con. What is ultimately most telling is the tepidness of the entire discussion and his reminder, once more, that we should not seek perfection in that human creation called a constitution. He readily concedes that "preferable" alternatives to the system set out in the Constitution might well have been "devised," but so what? "[I]t will not follow that the Constitution ought for this reason to be rejected. If mankind," Publius mordantly observes, "were to resolve to agree in no institution of government, until every part of it had been adjusted to the most exact standard of perfection, society would soon become a general scene of anarchy, and the world a desert." The search for a possibly utopian best—and, he asks,

"Where is the standard of perfection to be found?"—would truly become the enemy of an attainably adequate constitution. Thus, he states that "adversaries of the Constitution . . . ought to prove, not merely that particular provisions in it are not the best which might have been imagined," a proposition to which Publius readily assents, but instead "that the plan upon the whole is bad and pernicious."

It is one thing to predicate one's support or opposition to the Constitution on the compromises surrounding slavery or on the demands of small states for equal representation in the Senate. Perhaps they *should* have been deal breakers. But surely only a fanatic would be so concerned about the impeachment process as to reject the Constitution on that basis. We can read in this essay an "anti-fanaticism" principle, a maxim that we should draw lines in the sand only about truly fundamental issues. What might otherwise appear to be an esoteric discussion thus contains a strong and important lesson for twenty-first-century readers.

## FEDERALIST 66

### *The Past Is a Different Country*

IN *FEDERALIST* 66, PUBLIUS continues his discussion of the propriety of the Senate's sitting as the court of impeachment. The primary importance of this essay today is to underscore that the issues of greatest interest to those uncertain about the new Constitution in 1788 were often very different from anything we think about today. Just as reading *Reading Lolita in Tehran*,[1] especially after the Islamic Revolution of 1979, might be a different experience from reading it in contemporary New York or Los Angeles, so might we conclude that reading *The Federalist* in the twenty-first century will inevitably provoke different responses than if one had been part of its original audience in 1788.

We have already seen the near-paranoid concern that Congress would take advantage of the Elections Clause to favor urban interests by restricting voting sites to major cities. Sometimes people in 1788 spoke differently, even if the words were the same; the valence attached to the word "democracy," for example, has certainly shifted dramatically over time, from a term of near opprobrium among many of Publius's generation to an almost unanalyzed good today. But just as important is the shift with regard even to relatively unambiguous language from a high level of concern to one of indifference. It is difficult for most twenty-first-century readers to understand the depth of concern—what Publius describes as the "vehemence"—about the Senate's role in impeachment, even if one agrees, as Publius apparently does, that it is not one of the Constitution's more felicitous aspects. One criticism involved the violation of a "pure" theory of separation of powers, which would deny any legislative institution the ability to play a judicial role. Given Publius's earlier disdain for such purity, it is not surprising that he defends the "partial intermixture" of legislative and judicial roles. Moreover, he points out—not for the first time—that the constitutions of six states, including New York, Massachusetts, and Pennsylvania, assign decisive powers to one or another branch of the legislature when considering impeachment.

Perhaps the problem is the Senate itself. Some viewed the Senate's exclusive power over ratification of treaties, the confirmation of federal appointments, and now the resolution of impeachments as "an undue accumulation of powers" and an invitation to aristocracy. Publius not only does not share such fears; he also takes care to note some of the exclusive powers assigned to the House of Representatives. One of them, of course, is initiating impeachment in the first place; the Senate merely reacts to the House's actions. Another, which has turned out to have little practical importance, is that revenue bills must begin in the House. This could conceivably have been an important feature of our government insofar as it gives the House the ability to prevent any and all tax increases simply by refusing to initiate them. But, as a matter of fact, the Senate has long been accorded the right to amend existing legislative proposals by including provisions requiring tax increases. The House's third exclusive power has on two occasions, 1801 and 1825, proved extraordinarily important: the ability to choose a president when the Electoral College cannot name a clear winner. That power might have reemerged in 1948, 1968, and 2000, when a shift of relatively few votes in key states would have resulted in no candidate's gaining a majority of the electoral votes or, in 2000, a tie between George W. Bush and Al Gore.

Publius makes a sagacious observation with regard to the charge that the Senate will be reluctant to convict federal officials whose initial appointments it, after all, confirmed. He notes that the confirmation power is itself a reactive power. The Senate "may defeat one choice of the executive, and oblige him to make another; but they cannot themselves CHOOSE—they can only ratify or reject the choice, he may have made." Even in the twenty-first century, this remains a key point. Confirmation battles have now become a feature of our polarized political process, and Senate opponents of the president sometimes win. But presidents rarely lose the overall appointment wars inasmuch as they can continue sending nominees, all of whom will presumably be committed to the president's agenda.

That being said, it may be increasingly relevant that the ability of a partisan Senate to deny confirmation to *any* nominee can disrupt the ordinary operations of administrative agencies. Former Clinton speechwriter Jeff Shesol has caustically described the strategy of the congressional wing of the Republican Party as vindicating "the liberty of the American people to have a non-functioning government."[2] One would, of course, like to dismiss this as mere partisan hyperbole, but that could be a mistake. At least some Republican senators, angry over President Obama's declaration of a new policy regarding the treatment of unauthorized aliens who have lived for a substantial time within the United States (and who have children who are indeed "natural born Citizens" of the United States), proclaimed that they would simply refuse to confirm any of Obama's appointees at least when vital interests of national security are not at stake. The 2015–2017 Senate, firmly controlled by the Republican Party, will offer a natural test of the extent to which a president will be stymied in making practically any appointments that require Senate confirmation.

# PART 13

## On the Executive

# FEDERALIST 67

## *A Monarchical President?*

WITH ALMOST PALPABLE relief, Publius turns in *Federalist* 67 to the executive, a subject that will take up the next eleven essays. The concerns expressed by opponents of the Constitution—and Publius's counterarguments—continue to resonate today, as the powers of the chief executive appear ever greater. In our time, exertions of presidential authority are increasingly justified as a way of working around a polarized and gridlocked Congress that seems incapable of responding to the "exigencies" that face us. In any event, contemporary readers can find much in these essays to engage them.

"Monarch" was a key term of opprobrium used by opponents of the Constitution who feared the extent of the president's powers. As Harvard Professor Eric Nelson noted in a recent book, a key debate at the time concerned the difference between "monarchical" and "republican" forms of government. One view was that "monarch" referred only to the principle of selection, where bloodlines were all, and the role played by the public—or even "representatives" of the public—was nil. As a somewhat acerbic author of a letter to *The New York Times* put it on the occasion of Spanish King Juan Carlos's abdication in June 2014 in favor of his son, Felipe, "I found it amusing to read that Felipe, the current prince, 'has solid credentials' to replace his father. The only real 'credential' that matters is Felipe's bloodline."[1] One answer to the charge of "monarchy" directed at the American president is to point out that succession in office is not established by bloodline. Thus, the president by definition cannot be described as a "monarch."

A conflicting view, though scarcely ignoring the selection process, placed at least equal weight on the president's actual powers. Would he, for example, be seen as having "prerogative powers" that enabled him to act independently of legislative constraint, especially in times of "exigency"? Would the veto and appointment powers enable the president to capture control of the entire national government by "corrupting" those officials charged with oversight? This had been a key charge against King

George III. From this perspective, an "elective monarchy" was not at all a contradiction in terms. As Nelson emphasizes, proponents of a strong executive were often quite candid, at least in private, about their admiration for the British monarchy. Alexander Hamilton had given a remarkable speech at the Philadelphia Convention, which would certainly have become notorious had it been made public. (Because everyone honored the vow of secrecy, it was unknown to those engaging in the ratification debates about the Constitution in 1788.) In that speech, Hamilton admitted that "he had no scruple in declaring, supported as he was by the opinions of so many of the wise & good, that the British Govt. was the best in the world: and that he doubted much whether any thing short of it would do in America."[2] Obviously Hamilton, a key aide to George Washington during the Revolution, was an ardent "patriot" wholly untempted, so far as we know, to cast his lot with the Loyalists. But opposition to the mistakes made by the king and his ministers, which precipitated a revolution that was almost certainly avoidable, did not for Hamilton translate into opposition to placing in the hands of the president many of the political powers identified with "monarchy."

This division of opinion is alive and well in twenty-first-century American politics, especially with regard to the particular policies of particular presidents. It is one thing to say that George W. Bush or Barack Obama was wrong on the merits of some decision; it is quite another to describe either as behaving like a monarch or, more commonly in twenty-first-century rhetoric, like a "dictator." As someone who used such terminology against President Bush and has opposed its use by opponents of President Obama, I know personally the depth of feeling attached to exercises of presidential authority with which one does not agree. Indeed, President Obama certainly helped to encourage some of the outrage attached to his assertion of executive power regarding the treatment of unauthorized aliens; he had, after all, rebuffed earlier calls by political liberals to act by reminding them that he was not a "king" or an "emperor." What happened, apparently, is that the president's lawyers persuaded him that statutes passed by Congress in fact delegated to him sufficient power to make some of the changes set out in his postelection November 2014 proclamations. But, of course, many of Obama's opponents—and even some liberal observers as well—dismiss these lawyers as mere agents of the president willing to rubber-stamp whatever he wishes to do. Monarchs, after all, are able to appoint all sorts of courtiers who offer flattering assessments of their desires. A key question is whether the invocation of such loaded terms as "kingly" or "monarchical" aids our grasp about the nature of executive power within the American system of government (and the Constitution setting out that power).

After considerable harrumphing attacking the sincerity and good faith of those who question the power placed in the presidency, Publius turns to specifics. His first example, which takes up the rest of the essay, concerns a relatively esoteric but fascinating and sometimes important aspect of the Constitution, the "Recess Appointments Clause." Generally speaking, presidential appointments must be confirmed by the Senate. But there is an exception: "The President shall have Power to fill up all Vacancies that may happen during the Recess of the Senate, by granting Commissions which shall expire at the End of their next Session." George Washington used this clause to name John Rutledge as the second chief justice of the United States (succeeding John Jay, who resigned to run for governor of New York), though he had to leave the Supreme Court when the Senate, upon reconvening, voted down his nomination. Several nominations to the Supreme Court, including those of Chief Justice Earl Warren and Justice William J. Brennan by President Eisenhower, were made under the Recess Appointments Clause, though both were later confirmed. One still finds presidents using the clause as the basis of appointments to what the Constitution calls the "inferior" federal judiciary.

The easiest explanation for the clause, of course, is that the Senate was expected to be only relatively rarely in session, and it could prove embarrassing if, for example, the president could not replace a secretary of state or treasury on the death or resignation of an incumbent. It is hard not to agree with Publius that "it might be necessary for the public service to fill [a vacancy] without delay." He also takes care to rebut the charge that the clause would entitle the president to appoint a new senator should a vacancy occur. This charge, he writes, reflects "an intention to deceive the people, too palpable to be obscured by sophistry, too atrocious to be palliated by hypocrisy." One can understand his anger, inasmuch as the Constitution clearly places the power to fill Senate vacancies in the hands of the governor of the relevant state, and then only until the next session of the state legislature exercises its own constitutional prerogative to fill the seat.

Even if one readily agrees that the Recess Appointments Clause made sense in the context of the late eighteenth century, Publius's justifications scarcely seem persuasive today. The Senate meets throughout the year and can be quickly brought together, even if in temporary recess, by the Senate majority leader if a presidential appointee really requires rapid confirmation. Should a vacancy occur between the formal end of one session, sometime in December, and its reconvening in January, it is hard to imagine that the country could not rely on a subordinate, quite likely someone who was also subject to Senate confirmation, to serve ably and honorably until another nominee could be confirmed.

So why was the clause the subject of one of the most contentious cases before the Supreme Court in 2014? After all, if the opposition party controls the Senate and is irate at the president's nominees, the solution is obvious: Vote them down. As suggested in the previous essay, this might in fact turn out to be the approach taken by the majority Republican Senate elected in 2014. The highly acrimonious controversy that generated the 2014 *Noel Canning* case resulted from the fact that the Senate, though nominally controlled then by the president's own party, was prevented from voting on a nominee by a filibuster by the minority determined to prevent confirmation. This kind of partisanship, pervasive in American politics at least since the 1990s, helped to explain President Clinton's 139 recess appointments in his eight years in office, and George W. Bush's 171, the most notable of which was probably his choice of John Bolton to serve as the U.S. ambassador to the United Nations, an institution for which Bolton never concealed his disdain.

On March 7, 2010, President Obama made fifteen recess appointments, including that of a pro-labor lawyer to the National Labor Relations Board whose nomination had been blocked by presumptively pro-management Republicans. In that case, the acrimony was enhanced by the fact that Republican refusal to allow confirmation of any nominees to the NLRB had deprived it of the quorum of three members legally required for it to make decisions. If one can't abolish an agency or "defund" it, then, as Shesol suggested, one can render it impotent by preventing the appointments necessary for it to function. It is clear why Democratic and Republican presidents have both found the Recess Appointments Clause a handy port in certain political storms. In response to Republican obstructionism, the ability of Senate minorities to block votes—and thus give the president reason to use the Recess Appointments Clause—was significantly vitiated in November 2013, when the Democratic majority in the Senate voted to eliminate the filibuster for all presidential appointments save members of the Supreme Court.

The Supreme Court was moved to take the case by a remarkable decision by the United States Court of Appeals for the District of Columbia, which struck down the appointments by Obama mentioned above on the ground that the phrase "Vacancies that may happen during the Recess of the Senate" limits the power only to such vacancies as might arise while the Senate is in recess, and not to vacancies that arose at other times but continue because of the unwillingness or inability of the Senate to vote on the nominee. In addition, and just as remarkably, it limited "the Recess of the Senate" to the relatively few days between the end of one session, now almost certainly in December, and the beginning of the next one, which begins the first week in January. For decades, it had been customary to issue "recess appointments" any time the Senate had taken "a recess," for example to take a vacation. This had generated rancorous debate about whether there was any minimum time for a "recess" to count as authorizing the president to make a "recess appointment." Were three days sufficient? One day? And so on. As one might expect, given that the entire issue arises from partisan acrimony, there were even debates about what exactly counted as a genuine "recess." The Senate had taken to meeting in completely pro forma sessions with literally only two or three senators in attendance and agreement that it would conduct no official business. The Court of Appeals decision operated as a coup de main of grammatical exposition based on the difference between "*the* recess" and merely "*a* recess."

The Supreme Court handed down its decision in June 2014. For a six-justice majority, Justice Breyer determined that it was possible—and desirable—to read the text in a way that fundamentally accepted at least a century of practice by presidents who made "recess appointments" even if the vacancies had begun while Congress was meeting and the "recess" in question occurred "during" a given session of Congress rather than between them. But President Obama's victory was in fact minimal. The Court also announced—or, its critics might assert, declared by fiat—that a "recess" had to last at least ten days to legitimize a recess appointment. Along the way, the Court stated that it was up to the Senate, not the president, to declare exactly when the Senate was in recess.

There is much to be said for the sagacity of Justice Breyer's solution. But these arguments about the clause have almost nothing to do with the arguments set out by Publius, who was clearly assuming a world in which the Senate would rarely be in session and that there might therefore be a strong national interest in allowing the president to fill vacancies before the Senate could meet to approve them. Today the Senate is almost always in session, yet one cannot begin to understand its operations without giving full attention to what Publius was eager to deny—the reality of a highly polarized decision-making process in which the appointment of officials is simply one more occasion for partisan warfare. Reading *The Federalist* provides us not with a solution to the problem, but rather just one more reminder that we must apply our own "lessons of . . . experience."

## FEDERALIST 68

### *Selecting the President*

MODERN READERS COULD be excused for rubbing their eyes in disbelief at Publius's assertion, at the very beginning of *Federalist* 68, that "[t]he mode of appointment of the Chief Magistrate of the United States is almost the only part of the [new constitutional] system, of any consequence, which has escaped without severe censure" from the Constitution's opponents. That "mode of appointment," of course, is the Electoral College, by which voters in presidential elections cast their votes for "electors" from their own states, who in turn are pledged to the candidate. Actual election to the presidency requires getting a majority of the electoral votes, as distinguished from a majority or even a plurality of the popular vote. As most readers presumably know (and many, no doubt, vividly remember), George W. Bush, thanks in part to the Supreme Court's decision in *Bush v. Gore*, received a bare majority of the electoral vote in 2000 even though he lost the popular vote to then Vice President Al Gore by approximately half a million votes.

Contemporary opponents of the American way of selecting presidents are many and voluble. Every Gallup Poll taken since 1944 has shown that solid majorities of the American public would abolish the Electoral College if they could. That would, however, take a constitutional amendment, which the Constitution makes exceedingly difficult. Given that at least one-quarter plus one of the states would almost certainly consider it to their disadvantage if the United States shifted to popular election, it is difficult to be optimistic about such an amendment, even if it received the two-thirds majority in both the House and Senate necessary to send a proposal to the states for ratification. Yet there has been no shortage of proposed amendments. A report to Congress published in 2005 noted that "more proposed constitutional amendments have been introduced in Congress regarding electoral college reform than on any other subject. Between 1889 and 2004, approximately 595 such amendments were proposed."[1] The closest Congress came to actually proposing an amendment was after the 1968 election, when Alabama Governor and American Independent Party candidate George Wallace won forty-six electoral votes, all from the Deep South. Richard Nixon gained a majority of the electoral votes (and the presidency), but a change of relatively few votes in a few states would have left both Nixon and Hubert Humphrey without an electoral vote majority. The final choice would have been made by the House of Representatives.

The House, no doubt feeling it had dodged a bullet, in 1969 voted 338–70 for a proposed amendment that would have abolished the Electoral College and established a national popular election. Victory would go to the first-place finisher if he or she obtained more than 40 percent of the total vote; failing that, there would be a runoff between the top two finishers. The proposal died in the Senate in 1970 because of a filibuster that prevented the proposal from even coming to a vote. The objecting senators, according to *Congressional Quarterly Almanac*, were a coalition of southern senators who feared that a national election would lead to yet more national voting laws (beyond the Voting Rights Act of 1965) and small-state senators who feared that they would simply be forgotten as candidates campaigned only where the votes were highly concentrated.

At least one later proposal for popular election died, ironically, because senators from large states, aware of the clout their states possess because electoral votes are allocated by most states on a winner-take-all basis, believed that candidates were most motivated to go where the electoral votes are. As an empirical proposition, that is demonstrably false. Candidates rarely visit states that can be safely predicted to vote Democratic or Republican. Thus a Republican candidate in recent years might visit California to raise money—or the Democrat might do the same in Texas—but almost never to engage in serious campaigning. Why should they? As I write this paragraph on New Year's Day, 2015, I can safely predict that the Democratic candidate, whoever it is, will carry California in 2016, and the Republican candidate will sweep Texas. Where do candidates spend their time (and their advertising dollars)? By now we are all familiar with the phenomenon of "battleground states," like Ohio, Florida, Wisconsin, or Colorado, who profit handsomely both from pandering candidates and from the money spent on campaigning.

An organization called FairVote is trying to mobilize a joint decision by a sufficient number of states, regardless of size, to account for 270 or more electoral votes among them, to agree to appoint slates of electors pledged to the winner of the national popular vote.[2] This would obviously require ignoring the possibility that the state's own particular vote might have supported the loser in the national popular vote. As of the beginning of 2015, it has received the endorsements of ten states plus the District of Columbia, who together cast 165 of the 270 votes necessary to constitute a majority of the electoral votes. The most significant of the states agreeing to the plan is surely California, which itself possesses 55 electoral votes, but Illinois and New York, with 49 electoral votes between them, have also agreed to the proposal. Besides ordinary political calculations, including the loss of presumptive advantages attached to being a "battleground state," other states may remain dubious about making such a commitment if the "winner," as has been common in post–World War II elections, though coming in first, in fact received less than a majority of the overall vote because of the votes cast for third or fourth parties. The two most dramatic examples are Richard Nixon in 1968 and Bill Clinton in 1992, each of whom received approximately 43 percent of the popular vote. If one is a little-"d" democrat, the Nixon and Clinton elections might be more troublesome even than the 2000 election. Many statisticians would pronounce the Bush-Gore election basically as a tie, not to mention the fact that one cannot in any way be confident that the popular vote would have been the same if we in fact elected presidents by popular vote instead of electoral vote. Surely many Democrats in states like Texas or Republicans in New York decided to stay home rather than cast ballots that were sure to be swamped, at least in those states, by those of their adversaries; in a truly national election, candidates might have visited such states in order to mobilize their voters to turn out, since their votes would no longer be irrelevant. Neither Bush nor Gore could claim the support of a majority, given the votes that went to Pat Buchanan and Ralph Nader (among others), as was the case, far more significantly, with Nixon or Clinton. Countries around the world, and several states within the United States, provide for runoffs in case no candidate in the initial election receives a majority of the vote. Why would a twenty-first-century system ostensibly committed to "majority rule" support selecting a chief executive who cannot demonstrate majority support? The FairVote proposal speaks only to the Bush-Gore contretemps and not at all to the system that placed in office presidents who fell far short of amassing a majority of the vote.

Still, one might find certain advantage in the FairVote proposal, whatever its limitations. It would abolish the distinction between "battleground" and "spectator" states, where 80 percent of the voters might live but nonetheless are ignored because of the predictability of the outcome in their states. There would presumably be less pandering to the lucky residents of the "battlegrounds." It has also been suggested that the role of huge campaign contributions would be diminished, even if not minimized, by the fact that the amounts available to campaigns and unrelated organizations would now have to be spread out among the fifty states instead of being concentrated on the dozen or so "battlegrounds." And one should not forget the elimination of the possibility that a president would be chosen by the House of Representatives in a process that gives Wyoming and Vermont equal weight with California and Texas. Finally, for better or worse, most elections within the United States are "first-past-the-post," where winners need only get more votes than any of their opponents, whether or not they in fact add up to a majority of the votes cast. There is the additional technical question of whether any such agreement among the states would be enforceable without what the Constitution calls for as an interstate compact approved by Congress. At least one commentator has suggested that Congress is without the power to approve such a compact inasmuch as it would in effect amend the Constitution by replacing the Electoral College system with a popular election of the president.[3]

We might well wonder why Publius (in contrast to his lukewarm endorsement of the Senate as the venue for trying impeachments, or his even cooler enthusiasm for equal voting power in the Senate) seems genuinely supportive of "committing the right" to choose the president "to men chosen by the people" for that purpose. We have consistently observed his general skepticism about the actual capacities of "the people" to engage in self-government. He much prefers to filter the views of ordinary folk through "representatives" who will be superior in several respects. So he is altogether consistent in declaring that "the immediate election should be made by men most capable of analyzing the qualities" we desire in a president, who will presumably be "acting under circumstances favorable to deliberation and to a judicious combination of all the reasons and inducements which were proper to govern their choice." Here, especially, it is important to recognize that Publius was writing under the professed assumption that even if the new political system could not prevent the emergence of "factions," it could limit or even eliminate political parties. Only this assumption makes it sensible that the person finishing second in the electoral vote, assuming the winner received a majority, would automatically become vice president. This is what led to the "odd couple" of John Adams as president and his ever more vigorous adversary (and successor) Thomas Jefferson as vice president.

The elector is envisioned as a disinterested patriot, devoted to the general welfare and the public happiness, eager to meet with his fellow decision makers away from the madding crowd. This is why the Constitution requires that they meet in "their respective States" and not, for example, all together in the nation's capital, where they might be exposed to the "heats and ferments" of popular demonstrations. We can trust the electors to deliberate carefully about who is most fit to serve the public weal. Moreover, the odds of finding such public-spirited citizens are presumably increased by the Constitution's bar of any currently serving United States official, including representatives or senators, from serving as electors, lest they be tempted to engage in self-dealing. The electors are to be the finest people in the community, at least among those not serving in national offices, who will ask only who is best for the country. Sitting presidents who might be thinking of running for reelection will temper their decisions with the knowledge that they will have to run the gauntlet of a brand-new group of civic worthies, given that electors are chosen for that election only. A noble vision indeed!

Should a majority of electors, distributed among the states, fail to agree on who is best fit to become president, the decision will be made by the House of Representatives, on a one-state/one-vote basis (the same allocation of voting power as in the Senate). The original Constitution confined the House to choosing among the five candidates receiving the highest number of votes; the Twelfth Amendment, proposed and ratified in the aftermath of the near-fiasco of the 1800 election, made two important changes. First, the final list from which the House could choose was reduced from five to three; second and more importantly in its consequences for the political system, electors now cast their votes separately for the offices of president and vice president. This is the closest the Constitution comes to recognizing that the Edenic absence of political parties, and thus of partisanship, could not last. Beginning in 1804, electors, whether chosen by voters or by state legislators, would be presumptively loyal to a given party ticket consisting of two candidates, rather than for a putative "best man" on the assumption that the second best would make an apt successor should anything happen to the incumbent.

Publius thus expresses confidence that "[this] process of election affords a moral certainty, that the office of President will seldom fall to the lot of any man who is not in an eminent degree endowed with the requisite qualifications." If this is not enough, he asserts as well "a constant probability of seeing the station filled by characters pre-eminent for ability and virtue." Readers will have to decide for themselves if Publius's endorsement has withstood the corrosive test of experience whose virtues he often praises. One might ponder Professor Mark Graber's suggestion that this essay especially justifies classifying *The Federalist* as "fiction."

## FEDERALIST 69

### *Comparing the President with the/a King*

IN SOME WAYS, FEDERALIST 69 is at once the least relevant and yet perhaps the most illuminating of Publius's essays. On the surface, it is a thoroughly time-bound comparison of the president's powers under the new Constitution with those of the British monarch and the governor of New York in 1788. Whatever historical interest this comparison may hold, few twenty-first-century readers are likely to find it relevant that King George III possessed more power than would the American president. Yet precisely because the issue of presidential power and the degree to which it is subject to congressional control remains a subject of passionate argument, one can mine this essay for sentences and offhand observations that illuminate our present political situation.

One aspect of Publius's comparison of presidential and monarchical power deserves mention at the outset: What he tells us about the British monarchy is not always accurate. It very much serves his interests to portray the king as an all-powerful leader, in contrast to the more-limited powers possessed by the president (not to mention, of course the basic difference that the president would be elected, while the monarch relied on hereditary succession). Yet as the British historian J. R. Pole notes, Publius is best read as what literary theorists label an "unreliable narrator." An interesting question is whether the misinformation is deliberate. Publius was not engaging in detached academic analysis but intervening in real-time politics to encourage ratification of the Constitution and discredit any and all arguments brought against it. Isn't it naive to expect him to be more fastidious with his factual assertions than political operatives in the twenty-first century, who routinely offer decidedly self-interested versions of reality? There is a reason, after all, that Stephen Colbert (who never, in Russell Baker's wonderful formulation, confused seriousness with "seriosity") contributed the term "truthiness" to our vocabulary. *Merriam-Webster Dictionary* named "truthiness" its 2006 "Word of the Year" and offered, as one of its definitions, "the quality of preferring concepts or facts one wishes to be true, rather than concepts of facts known to be true."[1] One picture of the world is chosen over another simply because it is agreeable to do so and not, for example, because it is actually true under standard definitions of that elusive concept. Publius was not above engaging in his own versions of "truthiness," which may itself be an important lesson for twenty-first century devotees of *The Federalist* to acknowledge, even if not to praise.

Thus, when Publius refers to "the crown as a patrimony descendible to his heirs forever," he ignores not only that English revolutionaries in the seventeenth century had abolished the monarchy and executed King Charles I, but also, perhaps more tellingly, that the "Glorious Revolution" of 1688 featured a far more peaceful displacement of King James II and the proclamation by Parliament that William of Orange and his wife, Mary, who was King James's daughter but certainly not next in line for the throne, would become the new king and queen of Great Britain. And descent would be permanently barred to a Catholic, which was the basis of James's displacement.

A far more serious problem is Publius's assertion that King George III possessed an "absolute negative" (that is, veto power) over laws passed by Parliament, whereas the president would possess only a "qualified negative" that could be overridden by Congress, albeit only if two-thirds of the members of both the House and Senate vote to do so. At the time Publius was writing, in 1788, the last royal veto had been cast by Queen Anne in 1708. In the eighty years since, it had become part of the unwritten "British constitution" that the Act of Settlement that defined the Glorious Revolution included the de facto subordination of the monarch to Parliament and elimination of the veto power. Queen Anne's veto, of a minor piece of legislation, was the first since 1688 and the last in recorded history. As Pole writes, its "disuse" following her reign "amounted to a convention of the constitution; its reuse would have provoked a constitutional crisis."[2] Today, no serious person believes that Queen Elizabeth II could in fact veto an act of Parliament, whatever her ostensible status as the "sovereign" head of the British state. But even in 1788, Publius should have known that the royal veto had disappeared, and that the president's "qualified veto" was a considerably greater power than his British counterpart possessed.

What makes Publius's discussion of the veto relevant, both here and in a later essay, is that a surprising number of leaders of the American Revolution were in fact highly critical of King George for *not* exercising what they insisted was his continuing power to veto laws passed by Parliament that ran counter to the interests of the American colonies and, therefore, they claimed, to the general welfare of the British Empire. Harvard's Eric Nelson has audaciously argued that some of these "patriots" were the last proponents of the Stuart theory of the British monarchy, which otherwise literally died with the execution of King Charles I and was explicitly repudiated in the Act of Settlement. Many of these patriots, Nelson argues, became leaders of the new American nation and played important roles at the Convention. Recall Hamilton's confession of his admiration for the British monarchy (though not for George III); one of the most important implications of that admiration indeed involved the president's authority to resist what he viewed as legislative fiat by vetoing it.

In any event, one can compare the American president to the British king (or governor of New York) as of 1788, or one can compare twenty-first-century presidents with those counterparts today. Publius asserts, for example, that the monarch's power was far greater than the president's inasmuch as the former could declare war and raise armies to engage in the hostilities, whereas the American president had no power to declare war, "which by the Constitution under consideration, would appertain to the legislature." But here in the twenty-first century, one may be more inclined to describe the president's war powers as at least quasi-monarchical, especially if we compare them with actual monarchs like Queen Elizabeth or the sitting kings and queens of Denmark, Sweden, Spain, or Belgium. The United States has not "declared" war since December 8, 1941. Harry Truman notably went to war in Korea in June 1950 without seeking any congressional authorization at all, basing his claim of unilateral authority on his duties as president to enforce the new constitutional order ostensibly created by the United Nations Charter, ratified by the United States by an 89–2 vote on July 28, 1945, even before the formal end of World War II.[3] Subsequent "big" wars—Vietnam, the two wars in Iraq, and the war in Afghanistan—were authorized by congressional resolutions that served, in effect, to hand the president a blank check to decide whether and when to initiate hostilities and how to carry them out. Moreover, in several smaller wars, in Granada, Panama, and Serbia, Presidents Reagan, George H. W. Bush, and Clinton acted unilaterally without even the pretense of explicit congressional authorization. And President George H. W. Bush argued that he had no duty to get Congress's authority to invade Iraq in 1991 after its seizure of Kuwait; it was, he insisted, a courtesy that served to bolster the war's political legitimacy. President Obama notably intervened in Libya in 2011 without authorization; he also threatened unilateral intervention in Syria in 2013, though he backed down. However, the 2014–2015 American bombing campaign against the "Islamic State" seeking to establish a new caliphate in the territory now belonging to Syria and Iraq began without explicit authorization, as emphasized particularly by Kentucky Senator Rand Paul.

President Obama generated a major political controversy in 2014 when he traded five Taliban prisoners confined at the Guantanamo Bay prison camp for an American soldier held as a prisoner of war in Afghanistan. The problem was that a statute passed by Congress and signed by the president required him to notify Congress thirty days in advance of any movement of a prisoner detained at Guantanamo, and Obama clearly and unequivocally violated the statutory command. Law professors and others subsequently debated the statute, suggesting that it placed constitutionally illegitimate fetters on the commander in chief's authority to make tactical decisions as to when exchanges of prisoners, quite common during times of war, were merited. The point is not to determine whether these arguments were correct but to note the conflict between two visions of presidential authority, one of which can fairly be described as more "monarchical" in its origin and implications than the other. To be sure, there were certainly ways that the English king, as of 1788, possessed more power than the president would, even if some of Publius's arguments were misleading. But when we look at the British or any of the other constitutional monarchs in the West, we must acknowledge that they are all hollow shells of what the monarchy once represented, even as the president of the United States has become ever more powerful.

## FEDERALIST 70

### Unity in the Executive

IF *FEDERALIST* 69 SEEMS at least on the surface to be a candidate for the dustbin of history, its successor certainly is not. *Federalist* 70 remains a canonical defense of a conception of the presidency that is alive and well in the twenty-first century. "Energy in the Executive," Publius writes, "is a leading character in the definition of good government." One might read the Constitution as creating a reasonably passive president whose primary contribution would be to "take care" that the laws passed by Congress will be "faithfully executed." From this perspective, energy is more something we look for in those "policy entrepreneurs" (a decidedly un-Publian term) that we call legislators. This is definitely not Publius's view.

What is quite stunning is his overt reference to the Roman dictatorship, by which that noble "republic was obliged to take refuge in the absolute power of a single man" to protect liberty, either by resisting a foreign invasion or by cracking down "against the intrigues of ambitious individuals, who aspired to the tyranny, and the seditions of whole classes of the community, whose conduct threatened the existence of all government." The United States must be prepared for any eventuality, and part of that preparation is the willingness to place great powers in the hands of a properly chosen, virtuous, and energetic leader. "The ingredients which constitute energy in the Executive," Publius tells us, "are, first, unity; secondly, duration; and thirdly, adequate provision for its support; fourthly, competent powers." What provides us with suitable "safety in the republican sense," in turn "are, first, a due dependence on the people, secondly, a due responsibility." The rest of *Federalist* 70 is devoted to defending this proposition. We have a direct interest today in engaging in suitable "reflection and choice" as to whether the Publian vision of the presidency created in Philadelphia calms us or frightens us.

Most observers would consider it naive to talk about "the president" rather than "the presidency." The latter connotes a complex institution, presided over by someone we call "the president" but not single-handedly operated by that person. Presidents often complain about their *lack* of power. Richard Neustadt's famous book *Presidential Power* reduced the operative power of the president mainly to the ability to persuade people, whether in Congress or even those serving in his own administration, to adopt his policies in contrast to purporting to "command" them.[1]

One might say that Publius offers a far more romantic "Great Man" evocation of the president, a noble colossus stepping in to serve (and sometimes save) the republic. And before one agrees too much with Neustadt's picture of the president as a glorified "clerk," we must remember as well, for good or ill, a host of presidents who happily accepted the term made famous by George W. Bush: "I'm the decider, and I decide what's best."[2] He was referring to his ability to decide who stays and goes in his cabinet, but it is not difficult to think of a host of other decisions, ranging from the invasion of Iraq in 2003 to his veto, in 2006, of a bill that would have allowed research on stem cells and cell lines taken from aborted embryos. And of course it was President Obama who decided to violate Pakistan's sovereignty—formally an act of war—in order to kill Osama bin Laden, or to order drone strikes in a number of countries, at least one of which was for the purpose of killing Anwar al-Awlaki, an American citizen, not to mention even more recent decisions with regard to the treatment of unauthorized aliens or restoration of diplomatic relations with Cuba.

Publius unabashedly declares that "[d]ecision, activity, secrecy, and despatch will generally characterize the proceedings of one man." As the number of decision-making officials increases, "these qualities will be diminished." We might remember, after all, the defense of relatively few initial members of the House of Representatives, and then even more so the defense of the always-smaller-in-number Senate, on the grounds that excessive numbers are fatal to sound government. Too many cooks spoil the broth. But is one master chef the answer?

Some readers may remember the notorious advertisement that Hillary Clinton ran against Barack Obama during the primary campaign of 2008, which featured a phone ringing at 3:00 A.M., awakening the president with presumably dire news. The gist of the ad was that we wanted a president capable of making quick decisions, without excessive reliance on staff or advisers, and Senator Obama was portrayed, perhaps accurately, as insufficiently experienced to be trusted with such decisions. The advertisement provoked at least two reactions from those not persuaded by its emotional appeal: First, of course, did Senator Clinton herself have the requisite experience? Second, and perhaps far more important, do we really want such decisions in the hands of a single individual, even if they convey Publian "energy" and "unity"? This latter question takes on special import during what Publius calls "the most critical emergencies of the state." To be sure, the United States will often need to respond to such emergencies with dispatch, but we should still ask ourselves if there is not some danger in overemphasizing the need to do it at 3:00 A.M. Should we really favor candidates who consider themselves ready, willing, and able to act quickly, without taking the time to check all relevant intelligence sources or consult a wide range of people, who are likely to be far more expert in specific areas than the president? Interestingly, Publius also commends the "differences of opinion" common to legislatures; "though they may sometimes obstruct salutary plans," they "often promote deliberation and circumspection, and serve to check excesses in the majority." But, he insists, "no favorable circumstances palliate or atone for the disadvantages of dissension in the executive department." It is surely anachronistic to accuse Publius of advocating what Irving Janis, analyzing the Vietnam debacle, labeled "groupthink," but a twenty-first-century reader may well believe that the "lessons of . . . experience" that Publius has earlier insisted should be our guide might make us skeptical of his enthusiasm for a conception of the unitary executive that seems antagonistic to adequate debate.

One reason for Publius's zeal for single executives is that they can be held responsible by electorates for all decisions issued within their administration. Even if this made some sense in 1788, one can wonder if it still makes sense today, when even the most exceptionally capable president presides over an executive branch that has unimaginably more responsibilities (and employees) than Publius could have dreamed of. It may be fair to hold President Obama accountable for the decision to release detainees from Guantanamo in return for an American prisoner of war, but it seems zany to believe he is truly responsible, in any genuine sense, for the difficulties veterans have in obtaining timely care from the Department of Veterans Affairs. It is not even clear why Secretary of Veterans Affairs Eric Shinseki had to be sacrificed, except to appease an aroused public. As we live our lives within increasingly complex institutional structures, it becomes ever harder to generate plausible chains of responsibility for actions taken in the name of "We the People." The fantasy of a single executive making decisions may be psychologically soothing, but one wonders if any account of the modern presidency shouldn't begin by liberating itself from Publian simplicity.

FEDERALIST 71

## *How Long Should a President Be Able to Serve?*

ONE REASON *The Federalist* has endured as an icon of American political thought is that many consider it a fount of wisdom about the proper organization of government. *Federalists* 71 and 72 present one of the sharpest tests of this claim, inasmuch as they unequivocally argue that a particularly popular president could remain in office for life, whereas by far the most significant constitutional amendment in the last seventy-five years explicitly rejected this possibility in favor of a two-term limit. Publius perhaps reflects his respect, however closeted, for the British monarchy when he suggests a direct linkage between long duration in office and "the probability of obtaining" the important advantages attached to "the stability of the system of administration which may have been adopted under [the] auspices" of a specific president.

Part of his argument depends on his view of the likely character of those seeking the nation's highest office. The best presidents, he tells us, will possess a broad and sweeping vision of what the public good requires and will, in contemporary jargon, want to leave the kind of compelling legacy that leads to the building of public monuments memorializing their service. "[A] man acting in the capacity of chief magistrate," who lives under the realization "that in a very short time he MUST lay down his office, will be apt to feel himself too little interested in it" to take the risks attached to truly significant public leadership. Thus "feebleness and irresolution must be the characteristics of the station" if the presidential term is too brief. To be sure, "[t]here are some who would be inclined to regard the servile pliancy of the Executive to a prevailing current, either in the community, or in the legislature, as its best recommendation." One need not be a particularly skilled decoder of the rhetorical arts to realize that, in Publius's view, a true republican would want something other than "servile pliancy" in a president. Yes, "the deliberate sense of the community" is needed, but this is not at all equivalent to "an unqualified complaisance to every sudden breeze of passion, or to every transient impulse which the people may receive from the arts of men, who flatter their prejudices to betray their interests."

Not for the first time, Publius describes democratic politics, sensitive to the vagaries of public opinion, as submission to "the wiles of parasites and sycophants" who can play on popular sentiment to gain support for measures that ill serve "the PUBLIC GOOD," even if it is true, as he concedes, that "the people commonly INTEND" (his capitals) that worthy goal. But as we are all taught from an early age, the road to hell is paved with good intentions. "When occasions present themselves, in which the interests of the people are at variance with their inclinations," Publius writes, it is "the duty of the persons whom they have appointed to be the guardians of those interests, to withstand the temporary delusion, in order to give them time and opportunity for more cool and sedate reflection." Objective needs or interests should always take priority over mere wants, however passionately expressed. The president is like the wise father (or doctor) who has a proper sense of priorities.

Publius would surely be contemptuous of presidents who pore over polls, either for guidance on particular issues or out of concern for their "approval rating," just as he would be contemptuous of pundits who put real stock in such ratings. If some poll showed that a president was approved of by less than a quarter of all Americans (as Harry Truman, Richard Nixon, and George W. Bush were at different points in their presidencies), this would not be terribly relevant. The only question anyone should ask is whether their policies truly served the public good. Why, Publius seems to ask, do we believe that ordinary people are capable of providing reliable answers to such questions? In any event, "it is certainly desirable that the Executive should be in a situation to dare to act his own opinion with vigor and decision." The word "certainly" speaks volumes.

Who truly "represents" the people in a representative democracy? One might argue that the collectivity of legislators, if they are chosen in reasonably fair elections, are likely in the aggregate not only to mirror public opinion but to display the "wisdom of crowds" that give overall better answers than even the most capable individuals. Publius appears to dismiss any such argument. "The representatives of the people, in a popular assembly, seem sometimes to fancy that they are the people themselves, and betray strong symptoms of impatience and disgust at the least sign of opposition from any other quarter," such as the president. This attitude threatens the separation of powers that Publius has been keen to defend in *Federalist* 47 and elsewhere. But Publius seems to want more than an executive check on possible legislative overreaching. He clearly has more faith in the capacities of the disinterested president, chosen, as he argued earlier, by a process that guarantees that the presidency "will be filled by characters pre-eminent for ability and virtue." To be sure, we should not place *all* power in that person's hands, but we want to retain his services for as long as possible.

Perhaps Publius would have preferred a longer term of office, but his task is to defend the handiwork of Philadelphia, not to give any aid to its enemies by conceding to any significant imperfections (save those, like equal voting power in the Senate, that represent compromises made in order to save the Union). Four years is far better than any shorter term precisely because it permits the president to serve, at least until the year before the next election, without giving undue attention to a public opinion or a legislature that he might believe to be unwise.

FEDERALIST 72

*You Can't Get Too Much of a Good President*

AFTER OFFERING a somewhat romantic vision of the chief executive as the Lone Ranger, Publius begins *Federalist* 72 with a recognition that the success of a president's administration will depend also on the quality of his appointments. These assistants will operate on some of the same incentive structure Publius has already ascribed to the president: They will also want the possibility of long terms in office in order to achieve their own legacies. So, he argues, everyone wants and benefits from longer, as against shorter, terms of office.

While the Constitution limits presidents to terms of four years, the crucial question is their eligibility for continued service. That, Publius argues, "is necessary to give to the officer himself the inclination and the resolution to act his part well, and to the community time and leisure to observe the tendency of his measures, and thence to form an experimental estimate of their merits." It also enables "the people," or whoever actually chooses presidents, "when they see reason to approve of his conduct, to continue him in his station, in order to prolong the utility of his talents and virtues, and to secure to the government the advantage of permanency in a wise system of administration." Although Publius purports to concede that "respectable advocates" might endorse only limited eligibility to serve as president, he almost ruthlessly dismisses all such arguments as "for the most part rather pernicious than salutary," not least because new incoming presidents would be prone to replacing even the most capable cabinet officials with persons of their own choosing (and loyalties). This would inevitably generate instability, especially unfortunate if the incumbents had been truly fine public servants.

Still, one cannot underline too strongly the extent to which Publius's argument is rooted in an analysis of the psychology of those likely to assume the mantle of leadership. We will procure the very best presidents by evoking their *"love of fame, the ruling passion of the noblest minds,* which would prompt a man to plan and undertake extensive and arduous enterprises for the public benefit" (emphasis added). Such enterprises will likely require "considerable time to mature and perfect them, if he could flatter himself with the prospect of being allowed to finish what he had begun." It would be in every way unfortunate if a president were deterred "from the undertaking, when he foresaw that he must quit the scene before he could accomplish the work, and must commit that, together with his own reputation, to hands which might be unequal or unfriendly to the task. The most to be expected from the generality of men, in such a situation, is the negative merit of not doing harm, instead of the positive merit of doing good."

Publius attributes to presidents—and *all* would-be political leaders?—a decidedly mixed psychology. Their motivation is not merely detached public service, but also individual glory and undying fame. Presidents are, lest there be any doubt, *ambitious* men who, Publius warns us, might be tempted to resist leaving office at the assigned time and, like Caesar, "usurp" continued power. It is also possible that public opinion might support such usurpation, lest the adherence to legalistic form deprive it of its hero's services. Indefinite eligibility for reelection solves this problem.

Publius has already spoken to the cost of forgoing the experience and wisdom built up over a given period of service. But he also plays what might be called the "exigency card." Exclusion from re-eligibility is the equivalent of "banishing men from stations, in which in certain emergencies of the state their presence might be of the greatest moment to the public interest or safety." Think only of the United States in 1944. Whatever one thinks of Franklin Roosevelt's decision to violate the two-term tradition established by George Washington, would it really have made sense to *require* in 1944 the election of a replacement who almost certainly did not know the other players in the war as Roosevelt did? Perhaps we should have considered emulating the British and simply *suspending* the 1944 election until the completion of the war, but that would have raised obvious problems with regard to the notion of constitutional fidelity, in addition to the fact that Henry Wallace would have presumably continued as vice president and thus succeeded Roosevelt, with unknowable consequences, in 1945. (This latter point either calls the office of the vice presidency into question or, more moderately, at least suggests that whatever virtue is attached to a fixed-term presidency may not extend to the president's designated successor. Why shouldn't a president be able to fire a vice president, just as he can dismiss any member of his cabinet in whom he loses confidence?)

"There is an excess of refinement," Publius concludes, "in the idea of disabling the people to continue in office men who had entitled themselves, in their opinion, to approbation and confidence; the advantages of which are at best speculative and equivocal, and are overbalanced by disadvantages far more certain and decisive." So the issue is clearly joined. In ratifying the Twenty-second Amendment, initially proposed by both houses of Congress in 1947, three-quarters of the state legislatures by 1951 apparently concluded that there was something amiss in Roosevelt's refusal to step down after two terms, even as World War II had broken out with the German invasion of Poland in 1939 and the fall of France in 1940. Were they correct in making such a repetition impossible without the repeal of the Twenty-second Amendment?[1] To say yes requires that one reject Publius's arguments. One should have no hesitation in doing so if one is not persuaded by him. That is, after all, what "reflection and choice" requires: that one listen to arguments without necessarily accepting them, especially if the strongest reason for acceptance is merely the "name" making the argument. But if Publius is wrong on something as important as presidential term limits, why stop there? Where else might he have been mistaken, though with the best of intentions? If, on the other hand, one agrees with him and therefore rejects the wisdom of the Twenty-second Amendment, what does *that* suggest, even about a proposal that can run the gauntlet required to ratify a constitutional amendment, let alone ordinary legislation that can pass through Congress perhaps in response to the heated passions of an aroused but ignorant public that is all too eager to reject Publius's cautionary wisdom?

## FEDERALIST 73

### *Why the Presidential Veto?*

MANY OF PUBLIUS'S essays emphasize the importance of a chief executive with adequate "energy" and "vigor" to serve the nation's interest. *Federalist* 73 is especially interesting in its application of this criterion to one of the president's most notable powers—the ability to veto, and as a practical matter often to kill, legislation that otherwise has the support of sometimes substantial majorities of both the House and Senate. As should already be clear, the veto violates the strongest version of "separation of powers" that distinguishes between the lawmaking function assigned to the legislature and the enforcement function given to the executive. Instead, the veto power—tellingly found in Article I of the Constitution, dealing with the legislative branches—gives the president a voice in deciding which proposals will become law in the first place.

There have been, since the inauguration of George Washington, more than 2,500 presidential vetoes, but the first several presidents rarely exercised this power. The first truly major vetoes were issued by Andrew Jackson, who, not at all coincidentally, viewed himself as the tribune of the general American public. Still, his major vetoes relied on constitutional arguments that challenged the legitimacy of congressional legislation (as did James Madison in his literal last act as president, a veto in March 1817 of a "public roads" bill that he agreed might be good for the country but was, alas, unconstitutional in his view). Most presidential veto messages included such constitutional argument, until the administration of Ulysses Grant, who, like most presidents since then, relied more on policy disagreement than constitutional fastidiousness about limitations on congressional power.

Grant vetoed 45 bills, of which only 4 were overridden, a quite typical success rate (at least from the president's point of view). Of 2,506 vetoes as of 2012, only 110 have been overridden, a rate of less than 5 percent. Even if one breaks them into two groups—"pocket vetoes," in which a president simply refuses to sign legislation after Congress has adjourned, providing no opportunity to attempt an override, and regular vetoes, which occur while Congress is in session and therefore at least theoretically is able to override—one discovers that only 7 percent of the latter have been overridden. This should occasion no surprise, given the difficulty of amassing the two-thirds majority in each house of Congress necessary to override a presidential veto. Only three presidents (Franklin Pierce, Andrew Johnson, and George W. Bush) have had more than 20 percent of their vetoes overridden. Far more had fewer than 2 percent rejected. John F. Kennedy and Lyndon Johnson are the most recent presidents to have been completely successful, though Barack Obama, who has vetoed only two bills, the fewest since James Garfield, also seems poised to achieve 100 percent success, even if (or perhaps especially if) a Republican-controlled Congress is able to pass and send to the White House a plethora of controversial legislation.

Why should the executive be able to intrude into the process of legislation, especially if the very threat of a veto is often all it takes to shape legislation, even against what could well have been a congressional majority? We have in effect a tricameral legislative system whose "third house" consists of a single individual who can, with the stroke of a pen, render irrelevant decisions made, perhaps after extensive debate and compromise, by the other two houses.

Publius offers a defense of the veto: It is, he suggests, "[t]he propensity of the legislative department to intrude upon the rights, and to absorb the powers, of the other departments." Once again we read of "the insufficiency of a mere parchment delineation of the boundaries" of congressional power. Instead, it is a merit of the Constitution that it furnishes the executive "with constitutional arms for its own defense." Without the veto, a president "would be absolutely unable to defend himself against the depredations" of a rampaging Congress tempted to strip him "of his authorities." It is logical and just that the executive should "possess a constitutional and effectual power of self-defense."

This is, in fact, a remarkably limited defense of the veto power. Even if one agrees that a president should be able to protect the executive branch against "depredations" of a legislature designed to illegitimately limit executive powers, this has almost nothing to do with how modern executives actually exercise their veto power. Few contemporary bills are vetoed because the legislature has threatened executive authority by violating some separation of powers principle; most often, the reason is simply that the chief executive disagrees with the policy Congress wants to enact.

Why is it not sufficient for a proposed law to pass the hurdles presented by bicameralism? Perhaps a gubernatorial veto is justified in Nebraska, our one unicameral state, if we think "two heads" are necessarily better than one. But why aren't two heads—the House of Representatives and the Senate—good enough at the national level?

Publius has an answer, but it relies on a totally different argument than a president's right to "self-defense." Instead, he shifts to defending the presidential veto as "an additional security against the enaction of improper laws." Returning to one of his central points, he suggests that the veto "guards the community against the effects of faction, precipitancy, or of any impulse unfriendly to the public good, which may happen to influence a majority" of Congress. Elections may not suffice to throw factional rascals out of office, because they may mirror the preferences of a factional *majority* of the population. There is no relationship between majority rule and genuine attainment of the public good. It is a happy accident when they coincide, but we should not rely on it.

One may still wonder why presidents and governors are not themselves likely to be leaders of factions. Publius's faith in the president seems connected with the classic defense of the monarch as above petty politics and devoted only to the good of the commonwealth. Even if the Framers looked to George Washington as a uniquely Roman-like leader concerned only with the public good, by 1800 it had become clear that Washington's successors were not Olympian gods standing above politics, but the dedicated, often highly partisan leaders of political parties.

In any event, Publius insouciantly declares that the "the injury which may possibly be done by defeating a few good laws will be amply compensated by the advantage of preventing a number of bad ones." He gives us no good reason to have more faith in a president than in what we today might refer to as the "wisdom of the legislative crowd," but asks his readers to accept this assertion on faith. Perhaps one wishes to justify Publius's claim by suggesting, as some contemporary libertarians do, that preventing legislation is a good thing in itself. "That government is best which governs least," wrote Henry David Thoreau in *Civil Disobedience*. If one believes that passing laws generally enhances "government" rather than serves the public, then impediments to legislation become goods in themselves.

But what about those of us who are not libertarians, who believe that government is necessary to provide a host of social goods? Recall the vision set out in *Federalist* 45, which presents the national government as the means of achieving the general welfare and public happiness. All constitutions inevitably reflect the fears and aspirations of their authors and of the polity that accepts being governed by them. The U.S. Constitution's Preamble sets out magnificent aspirations. But at least equally as strong were the fears, perhaps touching on paranoia, that the government charged with establishing justice and providing for the general welfare would be so much in danger of being captured by factions that, like Gulliver, it must be tied down lest the sleeping giant awaken and take our liberties from us.

The presidential veto, especially when its domain is expanded far beyond plausible guardianship of the president's institutional prerogatives, represents the triumph of fear over hope. Too many cooks not only spoil the broth; their propensity to squabble may assure that there will ultimately be no broth at all, that we must be satisfied with the status quo of leftovers rather than take the risk that a new broth will include poisons placed in it by malicious and self-interested chefs.

### FEDERALIST 74

## *The Presidential Prerogative to Pardon*

IN ONE OF HIS LAST acts as governor of California, Arnold Schwarzenegger reduced the sentence of the son of a political associate who had pleaded guilty to participating in the murder of twenty-two-year-old Luis Santos. By doing so, Schwarzenegger violated a California law that seemingly required that Santos's parents be informed before any such reduction was granted. Although he admitted to *Newsweek* that he had made a mistake in not notifying the parents, the now-former governor was unrepentant about the decision itself: "I mean, of course you help a friend."[1] A California court later upheld the pardon, saying that it was Schwarzenegger's prerogative under the California constitution, though the judge described his action as "repugnant to the bulk of the citizenry of this state."

A similar controversy broke out in Mississippi when then Governor Haley Barbour, in his last act before leaving office, pardoned 214 persons, including more than two dozen who had been convicted of murder or manslaughter. Barbour defended his actions in an op-ed piece in *The Washington Post*: "In Mississippi the constitutional power of pardon is based on our Christian belief in repentance, forgiveness and redemption—a second chance for those who are rehabilitated and who redeem themselves." And he recognized that other traditions as well include similar tenets.[2]

Many people have not forgiven Bill Clinton for his last-minute pardon, as he was leaving the White House in 2001, of Marc Rich, then living abroad after being charged with multiple counts of stock fraud; he was also the ex-husband of (and still presumably friendly with) Denise Rich, who had been a fund-raiser for Clinton and the Clinton Library. And, of course, a lead item in many of the obituaries of former President Gerald Ford was probably the most famous pardon in American history, in which Ford exempted Richard Nixon from liability for any crimes that he might have committed as president. Nixon, Ford suggested, had "suffered enough," though it was also suggested—and by the time of Ford's death most people seemed to agree—that the country would be best served by shutting the door on the further national trauma that would have inevitably followed had a former president actually been charged with crimes, taken to trial, and perhaps jailed.

One of the more interesting powers of presidents and of many, though certainly not all, state governors is the power to pardon. If the presidential veto violates a pristine model of separation of powers by injecting the executive into the legislative process, pardons allow the executive to take at least a quasi-judicial role, though with none of the formalized process that we normally identify with the "rule of law." The pardoning power is perhaps the most truly monarchical aspect of the presidency.

In *Federalist* 74, Publius attempts to justify the president's power to pardon. "Humanity and good policy conspire to dictate," he writes, "that the benign prerogative of pardoning should be as little as possible fettered or embarrassed." It should be clear that Publius once more, as with his defense of the president's veto power, is engaging in what lawyers call "pleading in the alternative." Just as the veto can be justified, he believes, by reference either to a president's defense of executive powers or to the ability of a president to block the passage of bad laws, here he offers two quite different rationales for giving executives the pardoning power. The first involves mercy. Without what he calls "easy access to exceptions in favor of unfortunate guilt, justice would wear a countenance too sanguinary and cruel." Even devotees of the "rule of law" must recognize that overly rigorous application of the law has little or nothing to do with achieving justice. One way of accommodating this tension is by giving juries the de facto power of "nullification": They may, for reasons of justice, acquit persons who are "clearly guilty" of violating the letter of the law. Or, as happened most notably in Staten Island, New York, in December 2014, grand juries can refuse to indict persons. In that particular case, it was difficult to believe that the actions of the police officer who most certainly caused the death of Eric Garner were not sufficient also to justify a finding by the jury of "probable cause" of violation of Garner's rights. Those opposed to jury nullification fear not only that it discredits the notion of the "rule of law" but, just as importantly, that there is no good reason to believe that juries will always behave justly in making such decisions. The demonstrations objecting to the grand jury's actions certainly exhibited no such faith in their wisdom.

Similarly, too many older Americans can easily recall "nullifications" by all-white juries in the South, when persons charged with deathly violence against African Americans or white civil rights workers were acquitted almost casually. Younger Americans, perhaps, can recall the acquittal of O. J. Simpson, following a plea by his lawyer, the late Johnnie Cochran, to "send a message" to the Los Angeles Police Department condemning its history of racism by acquitting Simpson, who was almost certainly guilty. Perhaps it is better that the only legitimate nullification is by a president or governor. Or so Publius seems to suggest: "The reflection that the fate of a fellow-creature depended on his sole fiat, would naturally inspire scrupulousness and caution. . . . [O]ne man appears to be a more eligible dispenser of the mercy of government, than a body of men."

It is difficult to argue that there should not be some mechanism in a legal system for dispensing mercy as well as rigorous (perhaps rigid) justice, though one might still doubt the judgment of particular executives. Ironically, one might well argue that contemporary presidents are too stingy in demonstrating a capacity for mercy rather than too soft. But Publius does not restrict himself to such "soft" arguments as the kind Portia made to the Venetian court, in Shakespeare's *The Merchant of Venice*, about the "quality of mercy."

The other argument concerns "policy." Once again, Mae West seems an appropriate guide: "Goodness has nothing to do with it"—nor does mercy when, for example, a president pardons someone accused of or sentenced to death for treason. As Publius quite sagaciously argues, "in seasons of insurrection or rebellion, there are often critical moments, when a well-timed offer of pardon to the insurgents or rebels may restore the tranquility of the commonwealth; and which, if suffered to pass unimproved, it may never be possible afterwards to recall." The Constitution's Preamble, after all, declares that a principal purpose of the new constitutional order is to "insure domestic Tranquility," and this might counsel a wise chief executive to exercise what appears to be mercy, not because the miscreant does not deserve punishment but because it will be best for the society if one shuts the door on what happened and declares that it is time to move on. This was arguably the case with the Nixon pardon. Sometimes time is of the essence: "The dilatory process of convening the legislature, or one of its branches, for the purpose of obtaining its sanction to the measure, would frequently be the occasion of letting slip the golden opportunity. The loss of a week, a day, an hour, may sometimes be fatal." This is another illustration of Publius's preference for "energy" and "vigor" in a chief executive who, presumably, can be trusted to know what will best serve the public interest.

It is perhaps easier to be skeptical of Publius's arguments about "mercy." Unless the person to be pardoned is scheduled to be executed, time is rarely of the essence. In addition, one might wish for more heads than one to decide what mercy requires. This is why many states have established "pardoning boards" or "commissions" that restrain unilateral gubernatorial power. The Department of Justice has established elaborate procedures for presidents to follow before exercising the pardoning power. These days, one is more likely to hear complaints that the procedures have become too elaborate and that contemporary presidents, perhaps fearful of making even a single mistake, have become much too restrictive in their use of the pardoning power. The political fallout from Clinton's pardon of Rich seems to have made it more difficult for his successors to escape a mixture of excessive political caution and an "iron cage" of legalistic procedures designed to limit presidential prerogative.

Harry S. Truman pardoned his first prisoner only eight days after taking office. The two twenty-first-century presidents after Clinton have been remarkably cautious, perhaps even cowardly. President Obama waited 682 days into his presidency before using his power, and then he did so sparingly, almost trivially. Even following his reelection, well into his fifth year as president, he had pardoned only thirty-nine people, twenty-five of whom had been sentenced only to probation. For what it is worth, his 2012 opponent, Mitt Romney, had declined to pardon anyone during his four-year tenure as Massachusetts governor. Perhaps it would be better, both for chief executives and for people seeking mercy-based pardons, to place such decisions in the hands of an entirely independent board that could make decisions (relatively) free of political considerations.

But Publius's policy arguments retain genuine strength. One of President Jimmy Carter's first major acts was to declare an "amnesty" for those who had fled the United States rather than submit to the draft during the Vietnam War. As with Ford's pardon of Nixon, one can believe that, however controversial, it contributed to healing the national trauma over that war. But we should not seduce ourselves into believing that all such examples will be so happy. Andrew Johnson, known for his copious use of the veto power to try to torpedo Reconstruction following the Civil War, also was free in his use of the pardon for those who could well be regarded as traitors for their support of secession. And President Obama most recently chose, immediately on taking office, to make it clear that he had no interest at all in pursuing those persons who might have been responsible for the use of torture and other illegal modes of interrogation during the wars in Iraq or Afghanistan or at the American prison at Guantanamo Bay Naval Base. Though not technically the exercise of his pardoning power, it was the kind of policy judgment to which Publius alluded. To have tried high officials of the Bush administration for their role in establishing systematic torture would surely have split the country. From Obama's perspective, it was better to "move on."

Was he wrong? Any answer to this question requires one to wrestle with what one means by "rule of law," including the possibility not only that certain rules are made to be broken but also that those who break them, even if not truly excusable, should be freed from legal liability out of some conception of the wider public good. One might believe, however, that this kind of "domestic Tranquility" is purchased at the price of failure to confront important aspects of our past. It allows us to hide from the actualities of what was done in our collective name and damages our moral compass. It appears that even torturers and murderers—as well as bankers and other architects of the near-collapse of the American economy—can indeed "get away with it" so long as they have sympathetic friends in sufficiently high places. Is this the lesson that the American Bar Association wishes to teach foreigners when it distributes Publius's essays around the world?

### FEDERALIST 75

## *The Complicated Process of Making or Refusing to Make Treaties*

FEDERALIST 75, ONE OF Publius's shorter essays, is devoted almost exclusively to the president's power to make treaties with the consent of two-thirds of the Senate. Given that treaties, once ratified, become the law of the land, this power is one of the most dramatic illustrations of the rejection of pure separation of powers, inasmuch as the president is obviously a necessary, although not sufficient, actor in the process by which the United States enters into treaties. As one could readily predict from his earlier discussions, Publius has little difficulty defending the propriety of presidential participation. What is interesting is that he supports participation by the Senate—not because two institutional heads are better than one, but because there is always some finite risk that a president would be corrupt and open to the blandishments of a foreign power. "The history of human conduct does not warrant that exalted opinion of human virtue which would make it wise in a nation to commit interests of so delicate and momentous a kind, as those which concern its intercourse with the rest of the world, to the sole disposal of a magistrate created and circumstanced as would be a President of the United States." As if recognizing the unsettling implications of this description, a paragraph later he shifts tone and insists that "whoever has maturely weighed the circumstances which must concur in the appointment of a President, will be satisfied that the office will *always* bid fair to be filled by men of such characters as to render their concurrence in the formation of treaties peculiarly desirable, as well on the score of wisdom, as on that of integrity" (emphasis added).

It is difficult to prove that the treaty power in the twenty-first century is more important than it was in the eighteenth, nineteenth, or twentieth. We know, however, that the United States, acting through the president and Senate, is constantly engaged in discussions of treaties about matters ranging from climate control to nuclear proliferation to participation in the International Criminal Court. Some executive-backed treaties are "dead on arrival" in the Senate because they will never gain the required support; indeed, the president may simply refrain from sending them to the Senate rather than risk overt rejection. The Clinton administration, for instance, signed the Kyoto Protocol on climate change on November 12, 1998 (very shortly after the November congressional elections of that year), but never submitted it to the Senate for ratification, knowing that it would be voted down. George W. Bush, in one of his very first acts as president, formally withdrew the support given it by his predecessor.

One of the most significant aspects of the Constitution is precisely the requirement that the Senate give its assent to treaties by two-thirds support of those "present." Publius supports the decision not to require two-thirds of the entire membership of the Senate on a very interesting ground. Recall that he had earlier expressed skepticism about any supermajoritarian requirement, inasmuch as this empowers minorities to block important legislation. Here he repeats his concern that "all provisions which require more than the majority of any body to its resolutions have a direct tendency to embarrass the operations of the government and an indirect one to subject the sense of the majority to that of the minority." In the contemporary Senate, approval by two-thirds of the entire membership would require at least 67 votes. If, on the other hand, only two-thirds of those "present" must assent, the actual number goes down as more senators are absent. One can imagine circumstances where, say, the Senate is exquisitely divided 67–33, and a member of the supermajority suffers a debilitating illness or accident that makes it impossible to appear and cast a vote. *That* would change the ayes from a winning 67 to 66; under one procedure, the treaty would be doomed, but under the actual one, it would still have the support of two-thirds of those actually present.

Whether or not this is often important as a practical matter, it underscores both the importance of what Harvard Law Professor Adrian Vermeule has labeled the "micro-rules" of the Constitution and, as importantly, Publius's concern about the costs to the political order of minority vetoes of majority views. Today one might wonder why majority support of the Senate should not suffice to ratify a treaty, as it does for, say, a lifetime appointment to the federal bench. After all, no treaty will even reach the Senate without the president's strong support. One can readily imagine that a given president would support an international environmental treaty or a deal with Iran concerning its nuclear program, either of which might gain majority support if the Senate is controlled by the president's party. But that might not suffice if the Senate is split. Consider that the Panama Canal treaties were ratified by the Senate in 1977 by the constitutionally narrow vote of 68–32, with 52 Democrats and 16 Republicans voting in favor, and 10 Democrats and 22 Republicans against. One might look back to this as an example of the halcyon days of bipartisanship. It is almost impossible to imagine a similar vote in our own time. Thirty-eight Republicans, should they be in collective opposition, could torpedo a treaty thought vital to American national interests by a Democratic president and by 60 percent of the Senate. It is hard to believe that Publius would be encouraged by this state of American politics.

But what Publius does not discuss is that the power to make treaties is also necessarily the power to refuse to make them, even if two-thirds of the Senate were quite willing to ratify a treaty should it be submitted to them. Although, as a political matter, most contemporary legislation might be said to begin with bills prepared by the executive branch and introduced in the Congress by friendly legislators, it still sometimes happens that legislators themselves can take the lead and even override the president's opposition. That is impossible with treaties. Perhaps this is as it should be: Publius and many other analysts note the problems that would be posed if the Senate, with no authoritative leader, were to negotiate directly with foreign powers, even putting to one side the question of whether they could be trusted to keep the negotiations secret and not use them to score domestic political points. But the power given to a president in effect to veto, on whatever grounds, agreements painstakingly negotiated by professional diplomats, only underscores the importance of having confidence in those who occupy the Oval Office.

Publius's ambivalence on this point is telling. For obvious reasons, he wants to reassure us that only the most capable and most virtuous will attain that office, but he justifies a procedure that seems to depend for its justification on retaining some doubts on that score. Today it is truly paranoid to believe that a president will come under the sway of a foreign power. But is it so paranoid to believe we might find ourselves with a president in whom we have little confidence and who, nonetheless, can unilaterally reject what might be "necessary and proper" agreements with foreign countries? Some readers might regard this as a wild speculation, but even those who do not should wonder what the costs are of placing such power in a single man or woman over matters that may be of consummate importance.

## FEDERALIST 76

### *The Appointment Power*

*F*EDERALIST 76, another relatively short essay, concerns the president's power to appoint officials, not only within the executive branch but also the judiciary. Once again, Publius emphasizes the desirability of placing initial authority in one person, relying as before on the "great probability" that the chief executive will always be "by a man of abilities, at least respectable." The key question for readers today (setting aside the gendered language) may be our estimate of the "abilities" possessed by whomever we choose for that office. But Publius "lay[s] it down as a rule, that one man of discernment is better fitted to analyze and estimate the peculiar qualities adapted to particular offices, than a body of men of equal or perhaps even of superior discernment."

Publius rather dramatically rejects the so-called Condorcet jury theorem, much discussed today by decision theorists, which suggests that under certain conditions, decisions reached collectively are likely to be better than decisions made by a single individual, *even if the latter is more able, on some metric, than every one of the former*. That is, even if we stipulate that a given individual is likely to be right 75 percent of the time about some issue, and all individuals in the group are likely to be right only 51 percent of the time, the decision of the former is likely to be wrong 25 percent of the time. The ability of the larger group, on the other hand, to agree on what they deem a "correct answer" will, under the right conditions, guarantee the near certainty of actual correctness, even if reliance on a single member of the group would produce a 49 percent likelihood of error. The larger the group, the closer they will come to perfection. This is clearly the case with regard to "facts," and at least some theorists have argued that one should rely on such collective judgment even with regard to "values." Some version of this theorem underlies the strongest defense of democracy (or what is sometimes called the "wisdom of crowds").[1]

But Publius does not rely simply on the president's unusual skills of "discernment." He also makes a more plausible argument: A president has an unusual incentive to seek out only the best, precisely because any maladroitness in their own execution of the offices to which they are appointed will create political pain for the president. One need only think, in recent times, of attempts to blame the president for problems arising at relatively low levels of the Internal Revenue Service and the Department of Veterans Affairs.

While Publius seems to anticipate the rise of political parties within American politics, he also asserts that the president will be above partisan considerations when making appointments. After all, he proclaims, "it will rarely happen that the advancement of the public service will be the primary object either of party victories or of party negotiations." Thus we should have faith in presidential appointment not because of the executive's better cognitive abilities but, rather, because he or she will be nonpartisan. Few serious observers would defend the presidential appointment power on that ground today. What does survive into the twenty-first century is a credible belief that presidents have an incentive to choose people who will not embarrass their administrations and cause them political difficulties, and perhaps that is enough to justify the power entrusted to our contemporary, highly partisan (and often not intellectually distinguished) presidents.

Of course, as we know, presidents do not have unilateral authority to place nominees in office. They need a majority of the Senate to confirm their choices. Over our nearly 230-year history, that has proved a relatively weak, though not completely inconsequential barrier. Twelve nominees for the Supreme Court have been rejected, beginning with the Senate's rejection of George Washington's nomination of John Rutledge to be chief justice and extending through the refusal of the Senate, on a 58–42 vote, to confirm Ronald Reagan's nomination of Robert Bork. It took until 1834 for any cabinet nominee to be rejected: Andrew Jackson could not get a Whig Senate to approve Roger Taney as secretary of the treasury. Needless to say, that was not fatal to Taney's career, as Jackson successfully named him to succeed Chief Justice John Marshall on the Supreme Court, a nomination confirmed by a Senate then narrowly Democratic.

John Tyler, the first vice president to succeed to the presidency (and called by his opponents "His Accidency"), saw no fewer than four of his nominations defeated by the Senate.[2] The next rejection occurred in the administration of another accidental (and even worse) president, Andrew Johnson, the unworthy successor to Abraham Lincoln. The next rejection was not until 1925, when Calvin Coolidge's nomination of Charles Warren as attorney general lost by a vote of 39–41. Dwight Eisenhower saw the defeat of Lewis Strauss's nomination as secretary of commerce in a 46–49 vote by a Democratic Senate in 1959, and John Tower was defeated, also by a Democratic Senate, when nominated by George H. W. Bush to serve as secretary of defense in 1989. Several nominations have been withdrawn prior to vote in the face of senatorial opposition, and no doubt many others were never made out of fear of the senatorial gauntlet.

Still, as Publius emphasizes, the president's political opponents may gain only limited pleasure from these defeats. Even if a nominee is "overruled" by the Senate, this will only "make place for another nomination" by the same president. "The person ultimately appointed must be the object of his preference, though perhaps not in the first degree." This may help to explain why the Senate in fact rarely rejects nominees: "because they could not assure themselves, that the person they might wish would be brought forward by a second or by any subsequent nomination." Consider that the replacement for the defeated John Tower was Richard Cheney! The president has an important "first mover" advantage, even if frustrated on the first name he submits.

So why, one might ask Publius, should we bother with Senate confirmations? The answer involves yet another twist in his description of the president. We might hope that presidents will be persons of exemplary knowledge and virtue who have an incentive to staff their administrations only with the best and the brightest, but we must guard against the possibility that an "elective magistrate" will betray "a spirit of favoritism, or an unbecoming pursuit of popularity." Senate confirmation (by only a majority of those "present," it is vital to emphasize) provides an important check against such temptations.

Any evaluation of such a system, whether in the eighteenth or twenty-first century, must depend on one's estimation of the likelihood of "partisanship" and other tendencies that Publius would have found suspicious, first in the president and then in the Senate. One might consider this estimation not only difficult to carry out but, at least since 1801, perhaps impossibly foolish, inasmuch as presidents are also the leaders of political parties and not austerely "above politics" in the way Publius suggests. If we assume that presidents and senators are equally political creatures, the value of Senate confirmation is unclear, unless it is to give a Senate controlled by the opposing party the ability to stymie the president's ability to choose those best equipped to carry out the administration's programs. But it is also true that Senate confirmation forces that institution to take some "ownership" of the appointments and to bless successful nominees with whatever additional legitimacy comes from receiving legislative as well as executive support.

There is one important caveat, which Publius does not take up. Should there be a "one size fits all" practice regarding presidential appointments?

Why, for example, should only a majority be enough to confirm individuals for lifetime appointments to the federal judiciary? Perhaps a requirement of supermajority support would be preferable, not in spite of the fact that this would hand the opposition a de facto veto, but, rather, *because* it would assure that federal judges command bipartisan support. At least, it would suggest that not all presidential appointments are created equal, and some may deserve greater scrutiny, and opportunity for defeat, than others.

## FEDERALIST 77

## *The Constitutional Bona Fides of a Unilateral Authority to Remove Executive Branch Officials*

*F*EDERALIST 77 COMPLETES Publius's review of presidential authority. Most of it is taken up with a comparison of the appointment process given in the United States Constitution with that in the New York constitution. This is unlikely to interest many twenty-first-century readers. What does remain relevant, though, is the first paragraph, which is worth quoting:

> It has been mentioned as one of the advantages to be expected from the co-operation of the Senate, in the business of appointments, that it would contribute to the stability of the administration. *The consent of that body would be necessary to displace as well as to appoint.* A change of the Chief Magistrate, therefore, would not occasion so violent or so general a revolution in the officers of the government as might be expected, if he were the sole disposer of offices. Where a man in any station had given satisfactory evidence of his fitness for it, a new President would be restrained from attempting a change in favor of a person more agreeable to him, by the apprehension that a discountenance of the Senate might frustrate the attempt, and bring some degree of discredit upon himself. Those who can best estimate the value of a steady administration, will be most disposed to prize a provision which connects the official existence of public men with the approbation or disapprobation of that body which, from the greater permanency of its own composition, will in all probability be less subject to inconstancy than any other member of the government. (emphasis added)

There are at least two major points of compelling interest in this paragraph. The first is that Publius was completely, unequivocally, wrong in thinking either that the Senate would retain any say at all in the dismissal of executive branch officials, or that the United States would develop a political tradition of expecting able cabinet officials to be retained even as new presidents take office. Neither supposition remotely describes our present political order.

As to the Senate's continuing role regarding the fate of cabinet officials in whom the president had lost confidence, in one of its first great debates after the organization of the American government in 1789, Congress—with the strong support, incidentally, of James Madison—decided that the president need not get the Senate's permission to sack an executive branch official. The vote in the Senate was tied, and decided in the president's favor by the president of the Senate, Vice President John Adams. Thus the removal power is altogether different from the appointment power. It lies within the president's sole discretion and is limited only by calculations of the potential political costs of retaining or firing a popular official. President Obama's firing of Defense Secretary Chuck Hagel in late 2014, for example, might not have received Senate approval, to judge from some of the reactions of individual senators. But their comments were a matter of politics, not law. George Washington himself removed seventeen officials whose appointments had been confirmed by the Senate. If, as suggested above, Senate confirmation gives that body a certain "ownership" of the appointment, one should realize that it is a decidedly limited kind of property interest. Publius obviously expected, and defended, more.

It is not that Publius was demonstrably wrong in his normative argument. But as we have seen throughout our tour through *The Federalist,* some of his arguments serve mainly to show us how different the eighteenth-century United States was from the country we now live in. Publius assumes that the executive branch will be largely free of the partisan juices that rile up the rest of the political order. If the apolitical "best" persons have been appointed to the cabinet, it follows that "We the People" would wish to retain them even when control of the executive branch passes to a different political party. This, after all, is the theory behind the Civil Service Reform Act of 1883 that began the drastic limitation of presidents' (and their political parties') ability to hand out federal jobs to their supporters, which requires the ability to fire incumbents in order to make way for the preferred hires. For this view to make sense, one has to view civil servants as capable professionals without genuine political commitments of their own, capable and willing to take direction from whomever their superiors might be. As we saw with President Obama's retention of Robert Gates, originally appointed by George W. Bush to succeed Donald Rumsfeld as secretary of defense, remnants of this view even with regard to members of a president's cabinet persist into our own time. Still, what might be most telling about Gates's retention is how very few similar instances come to mind.

The situation is different when a president is succeeded by a member of the same party, especially when the succession is unplanned. One might believe that George H. W. Bush might have felt constrained to keep much of the Reagan cabinet had John Hinckley's assassination attempt against Ronald Reagan not failed, just as Lyndon Johnson kept even his hated rival Robert F. Kennedy as attorney general following John Kennedy's assassination in 1963. There, as with Truman's succession of FDR in 1945, the Publian theme of stability took precedence over practically any other value, and even a relatively limited housecleaning of cabinet members—especially of the "big four," the Departments of State, Treasury, Defense, and Justice—would have been deeply unsettling to a traumatized public. Robert Caro, in *The Path to Power: The Years of Lyndon Johnson* (2011), his magisterial treatment of Johnson's ascension to the Oval Office, emphasizes Johnson's entreaties to understandably devastated officials like Robert McNamara and Robert Kennedy, as well as to important Kennedy assistants like Theodore Sorensen and Larry O'Brien, to stay on at least until the 1964 election provided Johnson with independent legitimacy. But those are surely exceptional cases. Most presidential campaigns, particularly if they involve incumbents, involve promises by the challenger to sweep clean with a new broom and bring fresh faces to replace the presumptively failed leaders of the previous administration. Even if party control does not shift, as with George H. W. Bush's succession of Reagan in 1989, one still expects a new president to appoint his (or in the future, her) own cabinet.

The second reason that Publius's argument is of interest to a twenty-first-century reader, beyond the fact that it was so wrong in actually predicting the future, has to do with how we read *The Federalist* itself. At the very least, it is impossible to sustain the proposition that it was ever viewed as an unbroken fount of wisdom as to the best way to organize our polity. Similar problems are raised for those who believe that judges have an obligation to adhere to the "original understanding" of the Constitution—and that *The Federalist* is an infallible guide to that understanding. How is it that the very first Congress, made up entirely of members of the founding generation, felt authorized to reject Publius's arguments? Must one engage in an entirely fruitless debate over whether *The Federalist* or members of the First Congress better instantiate a single true "original understanding"? This is not the only such embarrassment for originalists, but it is surely one of the most blatant.

"Originalists" must concede either that *The Federalist* must be recognized as a distinctly flawed source—and Publius as an "unreliable narrator"—or the members of the First Congress must be acknowledged to have developed a theory of "living constitutionalism" in which decisions were based on something other than original understanding. But, of course, Publius's emphasis on "reflection and choice" might itself suggest the fatuity of submitting even to an unequivocal "original understanding" that thoughtful deliberators believe disserves the public interest. It is basically a fallacy to believe that 1787–1788 represented a completed "transition" from the constitutional order represented by the Articles of Confederation to a new one whose meaning was clear. As almost any competent historian—though perhaps too few modern judges—would readily concede, the "transition" is never truly complete, particularly if we pay attention, as Publius has emphasized throughout, to the role of "exigencies" in shaping our thought and decisions. To be sure, it is especially striking that the confident assertions of *Federalist* 77 were so completely rejected within two years, but that only underscores the point. We must recognize that the members of the First Congress were "Framers" in their own important ways, as were many of their successors, for good and for ill. In pleading for fidelity to the ostensible intentions of the Framers, or even, as has become fashionable, the original meanings purportedly assigned to constitutional language by the readers at the time in 1788, one must always ask "which Framers" or which members of the audience and why they should uniquely be selected out as privileged authorities.

# PART 14

## *The Roles of the National Judiciary*

## Is the Judiciary "Above Politics"?

IF READERS OF THIS BOOK have previously read any of *The Federalist* essays, the odds are very high that they include *Federalist* 78, in which Publius defends the practice of judicial review, that is, the assessment by federal courts of the constitutionality of legislation. Before turning to Publius's specific arguments, however, it is worth noting how seldom he has mentioned the judiciary before this. The only previous discussions occur in *Federalist*s 16 and 39. The latter mention is confined to the fact that boundary disputes, which were expected to be relatively frequent and potentially acrimonious, will be decided by "the tribunal which . . . is to be established under the general government," which will ostensibly assure that any "decision is to be impartially made, according to the rules of the Constitution." More important, but still quite brief is the earlier reflection on the implications of the fact that the new national government will be able to pass laws that apply directly to individuals, without requiring any cooperation from potentially hostile state governments. States might then try to torpedo this legislation by passing their own laws designed to block the national measures. What then? "The success" of such an effort, Publius writes in *Federalist* 16, "would require not merely a factious majority in the [state] legislature, but the concurrence of the courts. . . . If the judges were not embarked in a conspiracy with the legislature they would pronounce the resolutions of such a majority to be contrary to the supreme law of the land, *unconstitutional, and void*" (emphasis added). It is taken as a matter of course that courts would be authorized to invalidate constitutionally offensive state legislation. This is suggested by the fact that Article VI requires all public officials, national and state, to take an oath of allegiance to the national Constitution, and also establishes the supremacy of all national laws passed "in Pursuance" of the Constitution.

But the brunt of the ensuing essays is to explain why liberty and the other goals set out in the Preamble are best protected by the full range of the institutional structures established by the Constitution. There is nothing special about the judiciary in this regard, since a properly composed legislature and well-chosen chief executive will have every incentive to remain within constitutional limits. Now, however, Publius does turn to the judiciary.

As we have also seen in earlier essays, Publius generally shies away from extreme "separationist" arguments. He explains at length the advantages of giving the president certain powers that might be defined as legislative and that go beyond the faithful execution of laws passed by another branch. With regard to the judiciary, though, he adopts far more categorical language: "The complete independence of the courts of justice is peculiarly essential in a limited Constitution," meaning one that "contains certain specified exceptions to the legislative authority" that might prove frustrating to a legislature. The primary way Publius defines this "independence" is by reference to tenure of office, which the Constitution sets out as coterminous with "good Behaviour." This has been interpreted by most (though not all) lawyers to mean life tenure. This differs substantially from the practice of almost every state within the United States and most countries abroad, which have either specific term limits (often around ten to fourteen years) or age limits (usually between seventy and seventy-five).[1]

One can agree with Publius about the risks posed by "judges who hold their office by a temporary commission," though we seem to have accepted that presidents may apply their power of recess appointment to the judiciary as well as the cabinet. This entails the presence of federal judges who are in effect auditioning for confirmation. It takes little imagination to believe that such a judge will be less than resolute in antagonizing members of the Senate on a delicate constitutional issue. If, on the other hand, one views the previous sentence as a slander on the capable men and women who have filled judicial posts via initial recess appointments (including, among many others, Chief Justice Earl Warren and Justice William J. Brennan), then perhaps one might wonder why *life* tenure is necessary to procure a suitably independent judiciary. One might still cavil at "temporary commissions" of, say, two or four years but believe that twelve to eighteen years, with reappointment (and the need for renewed Senate confirmation) prohibited, would be more than sufficient, especially if linked to a lifetime pension sufficient to remove any temptation to think of potential future employers, particularly as a judge reaches the end of her term.

In any event, Publius clearly believes (or at least argues) that life tenure is not only necessary but sufficient to provide the necessary independence, which must be protected against the possibility of "being overpowered, awed, or influenced" by the "co-ordinate branches." Publius's emphasis on the importance of institutional "ambition," most clearly spelled out in *Federalist* 51, might lead him to predict that ambitious legislators or presidents would try to pack the judiciary with individuals more likely to uphold their overreaching than to enforce the limits established by the Constitution. The analysis is hardly affected if one replaces the "institutional ambition" articulated in *Federalist* 51 with the "party ambition" described by Richard Pildes and Daryl Levinson in their essay "Separation of Parties, Not Powers." Instead of Congress attempting to assure the selection of judges prone to favor that branch, we will see Democrats and Republicans seeking out judges who are sympathetic to their respective parties' quite different constitutional programs. Life tenure seems far more an inducement to partisanship at the selection stage than a guard against it, even before we consider the encouragement judges might have, knowing they cannot be fired save through impeachment, to give free rein to their particular and perhaps quite partisan readings of the Constitution.

Consider in this context perhaps the most famous debate in American history, between Abraham Lincoln and Stephen A. Douglas in their bid to win over the "court of public opinion" with regard to their candidacies for the United States Senate (even though the Illinois legislature would make the actual selection). A key issue was the Supreme Court's 1857 decision in the *Dred Scott* case, which held, among other things, that the key plank of the Republican Party's 1856 presidential platform was unconstitutional. Republicans had pledged to prohibit the further spread of slavery into the territories added to the United States as a result of the Louisiana Purchase and of James K. Polk's 1847 war against Mexico. Chief Justice Taney, writing for the Court, proclaimed that Congress had no power to block such expansion. Slave owners and non–slave owners alike must have equal access to the territories, though new states could decide upon their admission to the Union (but not before) whether to be slave or free states. One can readily understand why Lincoln denounced *Dred Scott* and suggested that it should be overruled.

But how was such overruling to be done? Lincoln didn't talk about a constitutional amendment, perhaps because he realized the hopelessness of getting the necessary approval of three-fourths of the states, even if one could surmount the hurdle posed by the requirement that assent first be gained from two-thirds of both the House and Senate. Instead, he suggested, basically, that as nature took its course and new vacancies emerged on the Court, he would, as a senator, use his confirmation power to limit appointment to compatible judges. Of course, senators can do only so much. The real need was to elect in 1860 a president committed to nominate such judges; Senator Lincoln would then be ready to use his power to confirm the nominee. This elicited the following response from Douglas:

> [Lincoln] is going to appeal to the people to elect a President who will appoint judges who will reverse the Dred Scott decision. Well, let us see how that is going to be done. . . . [W]hy, the Republican President is to call upon the candidates and catechise them, and ask them, "How will you decide this case if I appoint you judge?" [Shouts of laughter.] . . . Suppose you get a Supreme Court composed of such judges, who have been appointed by a partisan President upon their giving pledges how they would decide a case before it arose, what confidence would you have in such a court? ["None, none."] . . . It is a proposition to make that court the corrupt, unscrupulous tool of a political party. But Mr. Lincoln cannot conscientiously submit, he thinks, to the decision of a court composed of a majority of Democrats. If he cannot, how can he expect us to have confidence in a court composed of a majority of Republicans, selected for the purpose of deciding against the Democracy, and in favor of the Republicans?[2]

The issues Douglas raised, whatever we may think of the cause for which he raised them, are no laughing matter. A steady theme throughout *The Federalist* is the importance of confidence in the decision makers. For all of Publius's attempts to construct a complicated set of institutions that can control "faction" and other inevitable human failings, he returns, over and over, to assuring his readers that we are likely, far more often than not, to get virtuous leaders committed to the "common good" or the "public happiness." The same must be true of judges. The question, though, is why we should believe life tenure suffices to ensure this virtue. Why shouldn't we pay far more attention to the process by which judges are chosen in the first place, and ask whether that process inspires our confidence or fear with regard to judges' "independence" from ordinary politics?

One's answer to these questions may depend on one's overall theory of what it means to be an interpreter of the Constitution. *Federalist* 78 is beloved by lawyers (and even more by judges) because it justifies the exercise of judicial review by describing the judiciary as the faithful agent of "We the People," standing between them and overreaching political officials who do not recognize the limits placed on their power. "[C]ourts of justice," Publius writes, "are to be considered as the bulwarks of a limited Constitution against legislative encroachments." We cannot trust legislatures to guard against their own temptations to overreach. That will be the province of judges.

The problem is that Publius's own theory of "ambition" predicts that judges will not be free of the desire to use their power for their own particular ends, whatever the Constitution might be said to mean. "The courts must declare the sense of the law," says Publius, but he recognizes that they might be "disposed to exercise WILL instead of JUDGMENT, the consequence" of which "would equally be the substitution of their pleasure to that of the legislative body." Anyone reading this essay today should wonder why one would think that life tenure will tame a judge's will instead of encourage its exercise.

Perhaps this is why Publius concludes with a paragraph on the talents and dispositions that appointing presidents and confirming senators will presumably seek out: "To avoid an arbitrary discretion in the courts, it is indispensable that they should be bound down by strict rules and precedents," which will "demand long and laborious study to acquire a competent knowledge of them." This entails that there are "but few men in the society who will have sufficient skill in the laws to qualify them for the stations of judges. And making the proper deductions for the ordinary depravity of human nature, the number must be still smaller of those who unite the requisite integrity with the requisite knowledge." One could obviously write an entire book—many of which in fact exist—on the plausibility of viewing judges, especially those who are selected for the truly peculiar institution of the Supreme Court, as the impersonal enforcers of "strict rules and precedents" with no "will" or political views of their own. And this before we even get to the question of how many candidates for the judiciary have displayed the "long and laborious study" necessary to encompass the "requisite knowledge." Some judges surely fulfill the latter condition, but few analysts believe that judges, especially those we usually deem "great," are without will or what Jack Balkin and I have called a "high politics," which involves decided (and controversial) views about how best to fulfill the great purposes set out in the Preamble.[3]

Richard Posner, one of the most brilliant and influential of contemporary judges, once proclaimed in a notable essay in *The New Republic* that he was not a "potted plant" devoid of views of his own. It may literally be a "legal fiction," therefore, to expect that Supreme Court justices would have the characteristics suggested by Publius. As with so many other *Federalist* essays, one can wonder how plausible *Federalist* 78 can be to a twenty-first-century reader, even if one agrees with its critique of simply placing trust in legislative and executive officials to stay within their constitutional limitations. The ultimate question may be whether judicial review is itself a "parchment barrier," at least if we expect it to provide a bulwark against the intrusion of politics into law. Most political scientists, and many lawyers as well, would be skeptical. Judicial appointments have been thoroughly politicized from the time of John Adams and his "midnight" appointments, days before leaving the White House, of Federalist judges—most importantly including Chief Justice John Marshall, who would presumably stand firm against the Jeffersonian menace.

## FEDERALIST 79

### *Fixed Salaries—but What about Inflation?*

I F THE CANONICAL *Federalist* 78 is one of the longest of *The Federalist* essays, *Federalist* 79 is one of the shortest. Publius begins with the assertion that "[n]ext to permanency in office, nothing can contribute more to the independence of the judges" than a fixed salary, as is provided by the Constitution. "In the general course of human nature, *a power over a man's subsistence amounts to a power over his will*" (emphasis added). The Constitution prohibits judges' salaries from being "diminished" during their presumptive lifetime on the bench, but enhancement is entirely up to the legislature and president. There is surely much to be said for this, though Publius recognizes a potentially fatal flaw in his argument. There are "fluctuations in the value of money." A salary that is quite generous at one time can be turned by inflation into something really quite inadequate.

In the last century, the most generously compensated justices of the Supreme Court, in inflation-adjusted dollars, were those on the bench in 1969, when the chief justice received $62,500, and associate justices, $60,000.[1] In March 2015 inflation-adjusted dollars, these amounts came to $399,731 and $383,742, respectively.[2] As of 2014, the chief justice received $255,500 per year, $11,100 more than each of the associate justices. These salaries are, of course, well above the median income of Americans; they place the justices comfortably in the top 5 percent of salaried individuals but outside the top 1 percent, for which the cutoff, at least in the District of Columbia (the highest in the nation) was, in 2012, $688,000.[3] Moreover, Justices on the Supreme Court, like all federal judges, can continue to receive these salaries until the end of their lives, assuming a certain period of service on the bench. Perhaps uniquely in our society, they need not concern themselves with saving money for their retirement years. It is at least worth noting that few members of the Supreme Court—David Souter is a splendid exception—take advantage of this very attractive retirement plan established by Congress at least in part to encourage retirements and thus make way for new blood on the Court. As of 2015, Justices Ginsburg, Breyer, Scalia, Kennedy, and even Justice Thomas, because he was appointed at age forty-two in 1991, have accrued more than enough years of service to be able to retire and receive full pay for the rest of their lives. They are, from an economist's perspective, working "for free." Perhaps they are simply public-spirited; or perhaps they enjoy exercising the power that comes with membership on the Court. In any event, they remain on the Court well into their third decades (and in Scalia's case, fourth decade) of service, seemingly indifferent to the fact that they could be otherwise engaged while receiving the same income.

Although judges of what the Constitution terms "inferior courts" make considerably less—in 2014, $199,100 for federal district judges, and $211,200 for judges serving on the circuit courts of appeals—they may in fact be considerably closer to the top 1 percent in at least certain localities. Thus, one need earn "only" $274,000 to be in the top 1 percent in Idaho or $300,000 to reach that exalted status in South Carolina, even if most states require more than that. An independently interesting question is why these judicial salaries should vary in the way they do. By almost any measure, for example, district and appellate judges work far harder—as measured, for example, by the sheer number of cases they must hear and decide per year—than do Supreme Court justices.

Chief Justice Roberts has complained about judicial salaries throughout his tenure. Each year he writes a "state of the judiciary report," and the "sole" topic of his 2007 report, according to *The New York Times*, was what he termed the "constitutional crisis" provoked by inadequate salaries for the federal judiciary.[4] Roberts, who is said to have earned over a million dollars in the year before his appointment to the Court in 2005, argued that it was growing substantially harder to recruit federal judges from the higher echelons of the private bar. (Even if this is true for those asked to join "inferior" courts, there is no evidence whatsoever that denizens of the bar have turned down the opportunity to become justices of the Supreme Court.) And he noted that judicial salaries overall, adjusting for inflation, had declined by 23.9 percent since 1969, even as the national average for all wages rose by 17.8 percent. There have been raises, but it remains true that any partner at a "leading" law firm and (to be candid) many professors at leading law schools are better paid than the chief justice—and law professors have life tenure as well.

One of the causes of the epic struggle between President Franklin D. Roosevelt and the "Nine Old Men" on the Supreme Court during the New Deal was simply that judges were not assured a decent pension upon retirement. One of the ways the struggle was resolved, after the failure of FDR's notorious "court-packing" proposal, which would simply have increased the membership of the Court, was by congressional passage of a pension plan that assured that former judges would not have to live in penury. Such mundane details underscore the importance, when thinking about the design or operation of any political system, of addressing the issue of salary as an inducement to service. One may hope, of course, that salary will never be the sole incentive for public service, but in an age when living expenses are perpetually rising—think only of the cost of educating one's children—it is naive to dismiss as irrelevant the salaries that judges (and other public servants) receive. Still, one should wonder why judges, especially with life tenure and handsome benefits, should be viewed as more worthy than other public servants. Commenting on an earlier version of this essay, Professor Mark Graber described *Federalist* 79 as "a very crucial paper" inasmuch as it is about the importance of maintaining "government by an elite committed" to what ordinary Americans (even if not, perhaps, the top .5 percent) might define as "very lavish lifestyles." As someone who lives a very privileged life, I can well appreciate the goods that money can buy. I would even support being taxed more highly so that many more Americans could enjoy them. That is different, obviously, from suggesting that federal judges (or any other public officials) should be paid salaries that distinguish them quite sharply from those they purportedly serve.

For Publius, public service was perhaps the most honorable of all vocations. One wonders how many Americans today agree. One aspect of the "Reagan Revolution" was the unsubtle suggestion that public service is for losers (save those who see a brief period of such service as a stepping-stone to lucrative private-sector employment), and such losers should not expect to be paid very much. One wonders whether such attitudes, which I suspect are far more widespread in the twenty-first century than the eighteenth, threaten the project of maintaining a "Republican Form of Government."

## FEDERALIST 80

## *The Importance of Federal Courts*

IN *FEDERALIST* 80, PUBLIUS continues his analysis of the judiciary by emphasizing the crucial role that federal—that is, national—courts will play in the new political system. This emphasis only underscores a barely concealed motif of many of these essays: Publius's mistrust of state governments and his sense that the new national government is needed to set things right. A key role of the federal judiciary is to guard against "[w]hatever practices" of individual states "may have a tendency to disturb the harmony between the States." One of the fundamental struggles at the Philadelphia Convention concerned the wisdom of giving Congress the power to veto any and all state laws deemed contrary to the great purposes of the Union. James Madison was bitterly disappointed that he could not persuade his colleagues to give Congress this power. Instead, as historians such as Jack Rakove and Alison LaCroix have argued, the federal courts assumed the power to monitor state laws that unduly subordinated national interests to selfish local concerns. Though, of course, so long as federal courts are limited to invalidating only *unconstitutional* assertions of state authority, that may still leave a wide berth for state laws that are merely unwise or otherwise disserve the public interest.

Why could state judges not be trusted to enforce the norms of the new constitutional order? All of them were required to take an oath of fidelity. It appears clear, though, that Publius regarded this aspect of Article VI as just another "parchment barrier," unlikely to have genuine operational importance. Instead, he returned to political sociology and emphasized the overriding importance of state judges' "local attachments," in contrast, presumably, to the far different attachments of federal judges.

What is mysterious about Publius's argument is that only state judges seem to have questionable "attachments." He expects federal judges to be relentlessly "impartial" and "never . . . likely to feel any bias inauspicious to the principles" on which the Union was founded. But commitment to the national government is scarcely impartiality, at least in the eyes of those suspicious of what the Constitution's opponents called its "consolidation-ist" tendencies. They could even quote Publius against himself, inasmuch as he stresses, when giving his reasons for suspicion of state judges, that "it would be natural that the judges, as men, should feel a strong predilec-tion to the claims of their own government." This, of course, simply reiter-ates the argument about the linkages between individual ambition and institutional settings made in *Federalist* 51. But if state judges will unduly protect state prerogatives, why would we expect federal judges to be less solicitous of the prerogatives of the national government?

Probably the most brilliant critic of the new Constitution—and its consolidationist tendencies—was "Brutus," whose identity has never been definitively established. Brutus noted that the new federal courts would be "totally independent of the states, deriving their authority from the United States, and receiving from them fixed salaries; and in the course of human events it is to be expected, that they will swallow up all the powers of the courts in the respective states."[1] For Brutus, "independence" was a decid-edly mixed attribute that made judges basically unaccountable. "There is no power above them," he wrote, "to controul any of their decisions. There is no authority that can remove them, and they cannot be controuled by the laws of the legislature. In short, they are independent of the people, of the legislature, and of every power under heaven. Men placed in this situa-tion will generally soon feel themselves independent of heaven itself."[2]

Brutus could be read as summoning up two different fears. First, as national officials, federal judges will be indifferent to state autonomy, including that of state courts. Second, judges with lifetime tenure and fixed salaries will use their independence to impose their favorite political views on the country. It should be obvious that the degree to which one is concerned about the first possibility is a function of one's prior support for state autonomy from federal control. The primary way that federalism cases come before the Court is when they are asked to decide the validity of federal legislation that allegedly trenches on state autonomy, or of state legislation that pays insufficient respect, as Publius feared, to the commitments entailed in being part of the Union. In the former instance, the Court, for better or worse, functions primarily to legitimize actions taken by Congress; in the second, federal courts may play a somewhat more creative role, but it surely is relevant that the Supreme Court does not have the last word in such cases. Instead, it is subordinate to the ultimate power of Congress. If the Court decides, in the language of lawyers, that state laws are "pre-empted" by federal laws, or by the clause of the Constitution that assigns Congress the power to regulate interstate commerce, then Congress can simply pass new legislation licensing the state activities in question. This contrasts sharply with most constitutional cases, where Supreme Court decisions can be overridden only by constitutional amendment or by a decision of the Court itself to overrule its own precedent.

Enforcement of individual rights, however, may require the Court to override congressional as well as state legislation. One might think only of the Court's decision in 2013 to invalidate the Defense of Marriage Act, passed by Congress and signed by President Clinton in 1996. That decision has led a number of state and federal courts to strike down state laws prohibiting same-sex marriage. One might applaud that, as I do, but such decisions obviously raise questions about the role of courts in a democratic society. A 2014 Gallup Poll made headlines when it determined that public confidence in Congress was at an historic low of 7 percent.[3] But surely it was at least as significant that only 30 percent of the American public had "a great deal" or "quite a lot" of confidence in the Supreme Court. One may speculate on the causes for this remarkable ebb in confidence in the nation's top court; perhaps Republicans are upset about its upholding the health insurance mandate that is a central part of the Affordable Care Act, or its seeming reluctance to stop the onrushing legalization of same-sex marriage. Democrats may be upset that the Court gutted a key aspect of the Voting Rights Act of 1965 or permitted moneyed interests to spend as much as they want on political contests so long as certain meaningless technicalities are adhered to, not to mention lingering hostility to the Court's remarkable intervention in the 2000 election, *Bush v. Gore*. In any event, only a minority seem to hold the Supreme Court in high regard.

Publius consistently reminds us that American institutions are not self-validating. If adherence to constitutional forms alone provided what political scientists call "legitimation," then the task of fitting constitutions to particular societies would not be all that difficult. One would have only to establish the "rules of the game," so to speak, and everyone would happily play. But even games are not completely self-legitimating, and their governing bodies often make rule changes in response to what Publius would recognize as "lessons of . . . experience." Think only of the rule changes in football as a result of greater knowledge about the effects of concussions. All institutions, including the judiciary, must constantly persuade the public that they are operating in a manner conducive to "public happiness." Failure to do so may provoke important movements for change, or even, as in 1776, revolution. Or, perhaps, the consequence is ever-increasing sullenness and public unhappiness, including a perception that nothing can be done to change the situation for the better. It remains an open question whether the federal judiciary is "part of the problem" or "part of the solution" to what Publius, in the concluding sentence of *Federalist* 80, calls "general mischiefs," which most analysts clearly believe are troubling the American political system in the twenty-first century as well.

FEDERALIST 81

## *Disciplining Judges by Threatening Impeachment?*

IN *FEDERALIST* 81, PUBLIUS continues his defense of *federal* courts (as opposed to the judiciary in general). Returning to a consistent theme, he tells us that "the prevalency of a local spirit may be found to disqualify the local tribunals for the jurisdiction of national causes." Yet he does not acknowledge that one might speak of an equal "prevalency" of a *national* spirit that might lead to insufficient attention to the merits of local governance. And he reiterates his reliance on life tenure as an important ad-vantage of the federal judiciary. "State judges, holding their offices during pleasure, or from year to year, will be far too little independent to be relied upon for the inflexible execution of the national laws." One can easily as-sume that Publius would be appalled at the practice in most American states of electing judges and making them campaign for reelection or, in some states, "retention" elections, in which the voters assess their fitness to continue in office.

Is there no danger that one person's "inflexible execution of the na-tional laws" will be another's overreach? Recall Brutus's fear of federal judicial power. Some opponents of the 1787 Constitution expressed con-cern that federal judges might summon up the "spirit" of the Constitution simply by citing the Preamble and suggesting that their task was to make sure that "Justice" or the "general Welfare" was "established" throughout the nation, inevitably according to the judge's own criteria. Publius replies that "there is not a syllable in [the Constitution] which DIRECTLY empow-ers the national courts to construe the laws according to the spirit of the Constitution." One might agree with Publius as a descriptive matter but still call on the "lessons of . . . experience" to argue that judges have scarcely remained within the tight boundaries Publius suggests. Part of the reason, perhaps, is the addition, following ratification of the Constitution, of sev-eral amendments of unusually capacious language, whose interpretation inevitably generates controversy and sometimes acrimony. Think only of trying to discern the meaning of "equal protection of the laws." Things do not get much clearer when we must figure out "freedom of speech," "free exercise" of religion, or the right of "the people" to "keep and bear Arms."

As if recognizing the weakness of his argument, Publius continues with what, to a twenty-first-century reader, will appear to be a truly remarkable suggestion. Congress's impeachment power is available to discipline what in other writing I have called "judges on a rampage," who improperly im-pose their ideological predispositions on the rest of us. Publius dismisses as "a phantom" any concerns about judicial "encroachments on the legisla-tive authority." To be sure, there will be occasional "misconstructions and contraventions of the will of the legislature," but, we are reassured, "they can never be so extensive as to amount to an inconvenience, or in any sen-sible degree to affect the order of the political system." This "certainty" is derived "from the general nature of the judicial power, from the objects to which it relates, from the manner in which it is exercised, from its comparative weakness, and from its total incapacity to support its usurpations by force." In addition, there remains "the important constitutional check which the power of instituting impeachments in one part of the legislative body, and of determining upon them in the other, would give to that body upon the members of the judicial department. This is alone a complete security. There never can be danger that the judges, by a series of *deliberate usurpations* on the authority of the legislature, would hazard the united resentment of the body intrusted with it, while this body was possessed of the means of punishing their presumption, by degrading them from their stations" (emphasis added).

Modern readers can be forgiven for rubbing their eyes in disbelief, not, of course, that Publius wrote this (or even possibly believed it), but because we know that the "Impeachment Clause" has proved of no value whatsoever in limiting judicial "encroachments" or "presumption." Some judges have been removed, but only for conduct that is both clearly criminal and totally unlinked to the merits of any of their decisions. Early on, the Jeffersonians tried to impeach judges affiliated with the Federalist Party, especially Justice Samuel Chase, for what they perceived as the egregious overreach of their power in the service of Federalist politics—but Chase was acquitted by a majority-Jeffersonian Senate unable to muster the two-thirds vote necessary for conviction. More than two centuries since Chase's acquittal, Congress has never again tried to impeach a federal judge for ideological reasons. It has become a maxim of American politics—perhaps part of what Yale Professor Akhil Reed Amar calls America's "unwritten Constitution"—that federal judges need not answer for the quality of their decisions. Occasional calls, in recent years by right-wing Republicans, for the impeachment of federal judges have been consistently dismissed as political demagoguery.

In 1971, when he was Republican minority leader of the House of Representatives, Gerald Ford attempted to impeach Justice William O. Douglas, famously proclaiming that "an impeachable offense is whatever a majority of the House of Representatives considers it to be at a given moment in history; conviction results from whatever offense or offenses two-thirds of the other body [the Senate] considers to be sufficiently serious to require removal of the accused from office."[1] The context can be seen as softening the carte blanche that Ford apparently gives a partisan

Congress, but more importantly, his effort generated widespread condemnation at the time and has stood ever since as exemplifying what Publius in *Federalist* 81 called "the pestilential breath of faction" rather than a serious constitutional interpretation.

One obvious explanation is that we do not agree on what counts as "encroachment," accidental or otherwise. Just as it remains true, even after September 11, that one person's terrorist may be another's freedom fighter, it is equally true that one American's "judge on a rampage," engaging in "usurpation" and even betraying his or her oath to uphold the Constitution, may be another's model of a judge's behaving with the highest standards of judicial fidelity to stand up to political officials, even if supported by zealous majorities, who infringe on our constitutional rights. The need to tolerate judges, serving with lifetime tenure, whom we legitimately view as "usurpers" may be a price we pay for the American constitutional order. We may console ourselves that others are just as repelled by judges whom we admire as beacons of justice in difficult times. But such mutual toleration of those we view as fools or knaves is quite different than expressing Publian confidence in the federal judiciary per se and, more particularly, in the wisdom of lifetime tenure.

## FEDERALIST 82

### *A Judiciary for the Whole*

THE CENTRAL TOPIC OF *Federalist* 82 might appear arcane to nonlawyers, but it goes to the heart of the conception of the new constitutional Union. We have already seen how important Publius considers the federal courts; he sees them as faithful (and, he believes, "impartial") agents of the national government against states that may be all too tempted to renege on their commitments to the new Union. Here he addresses the question of "concurrent" jurisdiction of state and federal courts. That is, to what extent should state courts have any role in enforcing federal law, as against leaving its enforcement exclusively to federal courts? The latter, one might expect, will not only be sympathetic to the national project but will also have the relevant expertise, especially as more federal statutes and judicial cases accumulate.

Given that the Constitution mandates only one federal court—the Supreme Court—and leaves to Congress the establishment of any additional "inferior" federal courts, it is impossible to argue that the Convention expected jurisdiction to be placed exclusively in federal courts. No one could have believed that the Supreme Court could handle all federal cases, and Congress might have decided (though, predictably, it did not, when passing the framework Judiciary Act of 1789) to avoid chartering any other federal courts at all, in favor of relying on state courts. Publius readily concedes that "state courts will RETAIN the jurisdiction they now have, unless it appears to be taken away in one of the enumerated modes. . . . [A]s parts of ONE WHOLE, the inference seems to be conclusive, that the State courts would have a concurrent jurisdiction in all cases arising under the laws of the Union," at least in the absence of an "express" prohibition. Obviously, the capitalization is Publius's own, emphasizing his hope for a true Union in which the states would accept their status as de facto junior partners in the national project.

This means, however, not only that state courts will be entitled to hear cases based on federal laws but also that, as significantly, losing litigants in such cases will have the right to appeal the state verdicts to federal courts. This ability to appeal is, for Publius, a necessary condition of concurrent jurisdiction. Without it, "local courts must be excluded from a concurrent jurisdiction in matters of national concern, else the judicial authority of the Union may be eluded at the pleasure of every plaintiff or prosecutor." Once more—as if we needed additional confirmation—Publius expresses his basic mistrust of state officialdom and the need for an institutional check, the federal judiciary, against their temptation to prefer their local interests over national ones. He repeats his earlier statement (and capitalization) that "the national and State systems are to be regarded as ONE WHOLE," with the state courts "of course [as] natural auxiliaries" of their national counterparts, "and an appeal from them will as naturally lie to that tribunal which is destined to unite and assimilate the principles of national justice and the rules of national decisions."

But to what federal court will appeals go? If there are no federal courts other than the Supreme Court, the answer is self-evident. But what if there are additional federal courts? Could Congress allow losers before a state supreme court to appeal the result to the local federal district judge? Or is it required, perhaps as a rule of constitutionally mandated etiquette, that only the national Supreme Court can displace the decision of a state's highest court? Publius devotes only a paragraph to this question, and he clearly seems to believe that the Constitution gives Congress the ability to lodge the jurisdiction to hear appeals from state courts in any federal court it chooses. That would have two distinct advantages. First, it would be far easier for litigants to appeal their cases; they would no longer have to travel to the site of the Supreme Court but could perhaps find a federal district court in the same city as the state court. Second, it would be far easier for federal court decisions and federal law to enter the consciousness of officials and lawyers whose primary practice was state law.

As a matter of fact, most appeals from the final decisions of state courts are heard only by the Supreme Court. Originally, the Court was required to hear all cases in which the state courts upheld a challenged state law as constitutional under the national constitution, presumably reflecting the fear that state judges would be predisposed to validate state laws against such challenges whatever the legal merits. That requirement persisted well into the second part of the twentieth century, when the Supreme Court was given almost complete discretion in deciding what cases to take. Given that the modern Supreme Court takes only about seventy-five cases a year—as against a likely total of nearly fifty thousand cases decided by the highest courts of the fifty states and District of Columbia[1]—it is highly unlikely that even those minority of adjudications by state courts on the constitutionality of state laws will be heard by the Supreme Court. On the other hand, since 1871—not coincidentally, in the aftermath of the Civil War—federal district courts have had expanded jurisdiction *not* to hear appeals from state courts but rather to serve as the initial site of litigation over the constitutionality of state laws. What remains clear, even in the twenty-first century, is that the actual allocation of power to state and federal courts with regard to enforcement of federal legal norms remains a subject of both theoretical interest and, more to the point, political contention. Committed "nationalists," who look primarily to the federal government for resolution of basic political issues, are inclined to be suspicious of the degree to which state officials conceive of themselves as members of ONE WHOLE, just as one might imagine that partisans of local government are often suspicious of federal overreach. The ongoing dispute about "federal jurisdiction" turns out, after all, not to be so arcane.

## FEDERALIST 83

### *Trial by Jury*

PUBLIUS WINDS UP HIS extended considerations of the judiciary by addressing one of the most contentious issues raised in the ratification debates, the role of juries. The Constitution explicitly provided for jury trials in criminal cases: "The Trial of all Crimes, except in Cases of Impeachment [which will be tried by the Senate], shall be by Jury." But this specification played into the hands of well-trained lawyers who argued that the failure to include civil cases licensed the abolition of jury trials in such cases. The strongest version of this argument held that civil jury trials had been silently abolished; the more moderate version held that it was up to Congress to decide whether to retain what had come to be regarded as a precious right of the people to participate in law enforcement through service on juries. Most twenty-first-century readers can hardly appreciate the degree to which jury service was seen as an essential aspect of citizenship. Not only did it allow citizens good and true (assuming until well into the twentieth century that they were white and male) to serve as de facto public officials; it also meant that "We the People" would have yet another check on potentially unscrupulous or overreaching prosecutors. Alexis de Tocqueville, writing fifty years after the Constitution was adopted, emphasized the jury as one of the most important institutions of "democracy in America."

In addition, at the time Publius was writing, there was a serious debate about whether juries had the power not only of deciding what the facts were—Did X contract with Y to sell a cow at a certain price?—but also to decide what the law was. I have written elsewhere of a "protestant" conception of the Constitution that culminated in as radical a rejection of the authority of elite judges as that of dissenting Protestants vis-à-vis priests or even the clerics of less radical Protestant sects.[1] There is an analogy between the notion of "the priesthood of all believers" and the "lawyerhood of all citizens." Virtue and the presumed commitment to the public good took precedence over book knowledge and professional training. So it should not surprise that these basic fault lines about the comparative roles of elites and ordinary citizens were reflected in contentious debates over who had ultimate authority to determine the meaning of a statute or even of the Constitution itself. It was, therefore, no small point whether the Constitution reinforced or limited the role of juries in enforcing federal laws.

Publius readily agrees that the Constitution should not be read to abolish the right to a jury trial in civil cases. But he clearly believes it is up to Congress to decide to what degree jury trials will be allowed. The reason is twofold. First, he expresses some doubt that the right to a jury trial is as important in civil cases as it is in criminal cases. Civil juries may often be regarded as "valuable safeguard[s] to liberty," but criminal juries are "the very palladium of free government." The states had created a variety of courts, some of which recognized the right to a jury trial in civil cases, others of which did not, and Publius suggests that the United States will have at least as complicated a set of federal courts. One therefore should not adopt a one-size-fits-all approach. Congress should be trusted to know when juries are advisable and when decision making by judges themselves is adequate. "In short," he summarizes near the end of this essay, in which he canvasses the approaches of a number of states, "the more it is considered, the more arduous will appear the task of fashioning a provision in such a form, as not to express too little to answer the purpose, or too much to be advisable." Publius here states once more the "Goldilocks principle" of constitutional design. One should not spell out a rigid institutional requirement in a constitution unless one is confident that what is spelled out is "just right" and not, when applied to the complexities of government or the inevitable changes in circumstances, likely to emerge as too hot or too cold. Trust Congress, he tells us, to know what will be needed.

For better or worse, it is clear that Publius's advice was not followed. The Seventh Amendment, adopted in 1791 as part of what we have learned to call the Bill of Rights, requires that "In Suits at common law, where the value in controversy shall exceed twenty dollars, the right of trial by jury shall be preserved. . . ." Of course, few suits heard in federal courts actually involve the "common law" instead of statutory rights created by Congress. The primary example of common-law cases in federal courts is so-called "diversity" litigation, where a citizen of one state sues a citizen of another state in federal courts. This was allowed by the Constitution as a way of overcoming the bias that a state court might feel toward protecting its own citizen against the claims of an "outsider." Congress, however, has placed significant limits on the cases that can be brought via diversity jurisdiction, by providing that the "matter in controversy" must exceed "the sum or value of $75,000."[2]

But it is also important that, for better or worse, twenty-first-century attitudes toward the jury are very different from those of our eighteenth-century predecessors. Not only do most people consider jury service an onerous burden rather than a basic task of citizenship, but there also seems to be greater doubt about the basic capacities of ordinary people who are called upon for jury service. There is, of course, a connection between the two clauses. A cynical question establishes the linkage: Who would want to be tried by a jury composed of people not smart enough to get out of jury duty? For Publius, a "Republican Form of Government" depended on a large enough group of virtuous citizens willing to recognize *duties* as well as *liberties* (including, perhaps, the duty to participate in sometimes onerous institutions, such as juries or militias, in order to preserve liberty).

Great Britain, the ostensible source of the American commitment to trial by jury, has basically abolished jury trials in civil cases, and there are certainly many who would support doing the same with federal trials, especially in "complex cases." Publius himself doubted whether civil jurors would be "competent" to adjudicate disputes "that require a thorough knowledge of the law of nations," and one can easily imagine his expressing similar skepticism today about long, drawn-out trials involving antitrust issues or patent infringement. Certain cases, he writes, are "so nice and intricate, that they are incompatible with the genius of trials by jury" inasmuch as "[t]hey require often such long, deliberate, and critical investigation as would be impracticable to men called from their occupations, and obliged to decide before they were permitted to return to them." Trial by jury is suited to deciding "some single and obvious point"—Did the defendant pull the trigger or not?—as against cases involving "a long train of minute and independent particulars."

These cavils by Publius may have greater purchase for twenty-first-century readers than for his eighteenth-century audience, who insisted on the Seventh Amendment to safeguard what they thought of as an important safeguard of liberty. It is conceivable that a civil jury could serve to protect a defendant against overreaching by plaintiffs, whether the federal government or private litigants, but it is just as likely that jurors would be in over their heads in trying to evaluate the complex testimony of expert witnesses about, say, the nature of the derivatives markets or the operation of computer software. Indeed, it is hard to know who *is* competent to adjudicate these kinds of disputes, since federal judges are unlikely to have professional training in the disciplines relevant to many modern cases.

Ultimately, of course, this raises fundamental questions about *any* structures of governance regarding many issues that confront us today. What is true about climate change? If one believes (as I do) that it is a clear and present danger, if not to my life than certainly to the lives of my four grandchildren, what kinds of policies will effectively prevent environmental catastrophe? A final, decidedly nonrhetorical, question is whether we are more likely to get enlightened policies through explicit congressional mandates or, instead, through rules set by the Environmental Protection Agency on the basis of its delegated authority to make decisions that Congress clearly does not have the capacity to make. And, importantly, should courts "defer" to the decisions of the EPA rather than engage in any truly significant independent review of their basis?

My final point is perhaps the most troublesome of all: If we (properly) reject jury trials in more and more cases because we doubt the capacity of ordinary Americans to understand the issues presented—or because we doubt their virtuous commitment to the "public good" that would lead them readily to be willing to enforce laws that challenged their own factional interests—why do we continue to value elections and other mechanisms of decision making by "We the People"? One answer is that we now view elections as nothing more than occasions for measuring popular preferences, and that majority preferences are equivalent to the "public interest." But why limit this view, often described as "interest-group politics," to elections and then legislators who will simply do as their constituents desire? Why not extend it to judges and juries as well?

As we have seen, Publius is an adamant opponent of direct democracy. He is no great friend even of much representative democracy, insofar as it reflects popular "passions" instead of reasoned deliberation. We fool ourselves if we believe that trial by jury is an inconsequential part of our political system, easily cabined off from the rest of our political order. That is certainly not what most eighteenth-century Americans believed, nor is it really true in the twenty-first century. Nothing less than the meaning of "self-government" is at issue.

# PART 15

## *Reprise*

*The Importance of Institutions and the*
*Necessity of a Strong National Government*

# FEDERALIST 84

## The Limited Importance—If Not Outright Dangers—of Bills of Rights

On ITS INITIAL PUBLICATION on May 28, 1788, *Federalist* 84, the penultimate essay in the series, was titled "Concerning Several Miscellaneous Objections." Surely the most important and sustained of these objections was the failure to include a "bill of rights" like those found in several state constitutions, most prominently including Virginia's. We also know, of course, as Publius did not, that the Constitution would gain ten amendments in 1791 that we today call the "Bill of Rights." So one might wonder if it matters today that Publius was content with the Constitution as it emerged from Philadelphia. The question is especially important for modern drafters of constitutions, especially those abroad who have received copies of *The Federalist* from the American Bar Association or others enamored of the ostensible wisdom within its pages. Since Publius obviously did not convince most of his contemporary readers on this point, why should anyone today find anything of value in his musings? Perhaps the lesson, especially for admirers of Publius, is that even Homer occasionally nodded.

Some of Publius's arguments are specific to the text of the Constitution. He insisted, for example, that the prohibition of titles of nobility or the seeming guarantee of a preexisting right of habeas corpus (even though it could be suspended by Congress under carefully delineated conditions) worked as powerful guarantees against oppression, the equivalent of a bill of rights even if not so denominated. But his most audacious argument was that "bills of rights . . . are not only unnecessary in the proposed Constitution, but would even be dangerous." Similar sentiments were voiced by James Wilson of Pennsylvania, probably second in importance only to Madison at the Philadelphia Convention, by James Iredell in North Carolina, and Roger Sherman in Connecticut.

Why should we take such views seriously? One answer lies in the different conceptions of state constitutions, like those of New York and Virginia, and the new national Constitution. The former were written with the presumption that state governments had basically unlimited ("plenary") powers, unless the given state constitution specified limitations. The national government, on the other hand, would have only the "limited powers" assigned in the constitutional text itself. The absence of assignment was sufficient to justify an argument that the national government lacked a particular power. "[W]hy declare that things shall not be done which there is no power to do?" The example proffered by Publius involves regulation of the press. It is a canard to fear that the new national government could restrain "the liberty of the press," given that "no power is given by which restrictions may be imposed."

But his argument is actually more subtle (or, perhaps, simply intellectually conflicted). He adverts as well to the difficulty, perhaps even impossibility, of so carefully delineating "liberty of the press" that "any definition . . . would not leave the utmost latitude for evasion" by a government determined to crack down on the press. Thus, as one might expect from someone who has consistently warned against relying on mere "parchment barriers," Publius declares that the security of the press, and presumably of the other rights we might wish to protect in a bill of rights, "must altogether depend on public opinion, and on the general spirit of the people and of the government." Here alone, he seems to suggest, is where we must "seek for the only solid basis of our rights."

For some well-trained lawyers, specifying certain rights may imply that those not specified are not protected at all, just as for them the notion of "a limited government of enumerated powers" suggests that if a given power is not enumerated, the government does not possess it. Many people think this is why the federal Bill of Rights includes the Ninth Amendment, which declares that "[t]he enumeration in the Constitution, of certain rights, shall not be construed to deny or disparage others retained by the people." To this day the meaning and implications of the Ninth Amendment remain a subject of controversy among lawyers and judges. One might believe the most obvious meaning is that judges should feel free to implement unenumerated rights—think of the right to privacy or the right to reproductive choice—in addition to any rights, such as "the freedom of speech" that are set forth in the amended text of the Constitution.

There is, of course, a certain tension between Publius's first argument, that the Constitution, read carefully, is "in every rational sense, and to every useful purpose, A BILL OF RIGHTS" (capitalization obviously Publius's), and his seeming dismissal of the utility of writing down specific protections in the foundational document. But as we have seen many times, the presence of contradictions is not enough to dismiss the force of an argument, else no one could survive close scrutiny. The real question is whether we are wise today to identify constitutions almost exclusively with their protection of rights, and thus often to ignore the implications of institutional structures in facilitating various responses to political challenges. There is a reason that Publius confines his discussion of bills of rights to part of one essay and devotes the overwhelming bulk of his essays to the structures of governance. Even, or perhaps especially, if we disagree with his analyses of some of these structures—Has the Electoral College really guaranteed us uniformly capable presidents?—we are led, nonetheless, to realize that institutions count.

Anyone deeply familiar with the actual implementation of the Bill of Rights may realize that for at least a century after 1791, these ten amendments did very little to truly limit the power of the national government— and they were deemed not to apply at all to the states until the end of the nineteenth and into the twentieth century. The First Amendment, with its declaration that "Congress shall make no law . . . abridging the freedom of speech, or of the press" was thought by the Federalist Party majority in Congress (and by President John Adams) to have no application to the Sedition Act of 1798, under which the Federalists' critics were prosecuted and sometimes jailed. Almost all modern constitutions include clauses protecting rights, but they also typically include "limitations clauses," which recognize that few, if any, rights can be deemed "absolute" and impervious to all restriction.

The Canadian Charter of Rights and Freedoms, for example, passed in 1982 and since then of tremendous significance throughout the world— more so than the United States Constitution for those drafting new constitutions—explicitly provides in its very first article that "the rights and freedoms" it sets out are "subject only to such reasonable limits prescribed by law as can be demonstrably justified in a free and democratic society." The "freedom of expression" article of the European Convention on Human Rights, which has been vigorously enforced by the transnational European Court of Human Rights in Strasbourg against many of the now forty-six signatories to the convention, states resolutely in Article 10, Section 1 that "Everyone has the right to freedom of expression. This right shall include freedom to hold opinions and to receive and impart information and ideas without interference by public authority and regardless of frontiers." But Section 2 of this same article goes on, just as resolutely, to proclaim,

> The exercise of these freedoms, since it carries with it duties and responsibilities, may be subject to such formalities, conditions, restrictions or penalties as are prescribed by law and are necessary in a democratic society, in the interests of national security, territorial integrity or public safety, for the prevention of disorder or crime, for the protection of health or morals, for the protection of the reputation or rights of others, for preventing the disclosure of information received in confidence, or for maintaining the authority and impartiality of the judiciary.

Most law students—and, no doubt, many lawyers and judges as well—are appalled by the latitude conveyed by Section 2. Yet most law professors familiar with judicial decisions interpreting our own First Amendment's ostensibly categorical language will recognize in it many of the rationales that American courts have given for restricting freedom of speech or of the press. Still, obnoxious speech is far more protected in the United States than in Europe. The question is whether this difference in the operational meaning of "freedom of expression" comes from the particular linguistic formulations of our First Amendment against their Article 10, or instead reflects underlying differences in American and European culture. Canada provides an interesting test case as well: The Supreme Court of Canada has in some ways been more "European" than "American" in interpreting freedom of expression. Is it because of Article I of the Canadian Charter of Rights and Freedoms? Or does it reflect the continuing influence of the Loyalists and other subjects of the British Crown who settled in Canada and formed its basic cultural traditions regarding expression and its limitations? These questions are probably impossible to answer, given that the judges interpreting the written laws are themselves steeped in the cultural presuppositions.

It may be that contemporary constitution drafters, whether in the United States or around the world, should spend more time trying to figure out the implications of institutional structure in their societies, or studying how to create a more inclusive and tolerant political culture, than on crafting splendidly wrought sentences designed to protect particular rights. This applies especially to what University of California Law School Dean Sujit Choudhry has defined as "severely divided societies."[1] These are composed of groups, whether divided by race, ethnicity, religion, or access to economic resources, who fundamentally do not trust one another. Yet they also agree with Publius about the wisdom of uniting in order to protect themselves against the inevitable predators who are part of the international political order. If they wish to establish a viable political order, as political scientist and Duke University Law Professor Donald Horowitz has long emphasized, above all they need electoral institutions that offer people some reason to believe that they will not simply be swamped by oppressive majorities. These are far more important than "parchment barriers" announcing what rights will ostensibly be protected.

## FEDERALIST 85

### *"A Nation [with] a National Government"*

A ND SO WE COME TO the end. In *Federalist* 85, Publius offers a valediction on his entire enterprise, which ended with the publication, on May 28, 1788, of what he simply titled "Concluding Remarks." Perhaps he is entitled to his self-satisfied declaration of "entire confidence in the arguments" he has presented, "which recommend the proposed system to your adoption," coupled with his professed inability to "discern any real force in those by which it has been opposed." As he has said, he does not believe the Constitution is perfect, only that it is the best that could realistically be hoped for. "The compacts which are to embrace thirteen distinct States in a common bond of amity and union, must as necessarily be a compromise of as many dissimilar interests and inclinations. How," he asks, "can perfection spring from such materials?" The overwhelming necessity that counsels ratification by the New York delegates is "the dangers of a longer continuance in our present situation. . . . a nation, without a national government, is, in my view, an awful spectacle." If they reject the Constitution, they will not achieve, after a second convention, an even better document. Instead, they will subject the struggling nation to the likelihood of failure and the dissolution of the Union, with all of the consequences against which Publius warned at the outset.

Two other observations are worth making. First, when Publius, near the beginning of the essay, summarizes the advantages of the new Constitution—its "additional securities to republican government, to liberty and to property"—he mentions only the constraints on factions within states. The "preservation of the Union" will require reining in the power of "local factions" and

> the ambition of powerful individuals in single States, who may acquire credit and influence enough, from leaders and favorites, to become the despots of the people; in the diminution of the opportunities to foreign intrigue, which the dissolution of the Confederacy would invite and facilitate; in the prevention of extensive military establishments, which could not fail to grow out of wars between the States in a disunited situation; in the express guaranty of a republican form of government to each; in the absolute and universal exclusion of titles of nobility; and in the precautions against the repetition of those practices on the part of the State governments which have undermined the foundations of property and credit, have planted mutual distrust in the breasts of all classes of citizens, and have occasioned an almost universal prostration of morals.

University of Texas Law Professor Calvin Johnson titled his examination of the origins of the Constitution *Righteous Anger at the Wicked States.* One can doubt that righteous anger is really what the Framers in their entirety felt; if they had, the Philadelphia Convention might have adopted, for example, James Madison's heartfelt plea for congressional authority to veto any state legislation viewed as inimical to the national interest. Still, it is hard to deny that Publius almost nowhere expressed any real confidence in states, their peoples, or their governments. *The Federalist* is, with rare exceptions, a hymn to a truly *United* States of America, with a strong national government undergirding that unity.

But, again, he did not think the Constitution was perfect, and much of the conclusion addresses the mode of amendment. What is most interesting to a contemporary reader may involve a part of Article V that generally gets extremely little attention, which is the ability of *states* in effect to call a new national convention by petition of two-thirds of them. "By the fifth article of the plan," writes Publius, "the Congress will be obliged 'on the application of the legislatures of two thirds of the States' . . . to call a convention for proposing amendments. . . .'" Just in case we don't get the point, Publius repeats that "[t]he words of this article are peremptory.

The Congress 'shall call a convention.' Nothing in this particular is left to the discretion of that body." Should such a convention be called, he suggests, we "may safely rely on the disposition of the State legislatures to erect barriers against the encroachments of the national authority."

Perhaps we will soon have occasion to test Publius's confidence in Congress's obligation to call a new convention. There is a campaign in a number of state legislatures to petition just such a convention in order to propose a national balanced-budget amendment. The Michigan legislature, for example, in March 2014 passed such a petition, and the number of states that have done so is apparently somewhere in the twenties.[1] A mandate for Congress to act on the petition requires the agreement of thirty-four states, with at least sixty-seven legislative houses (assuming that Nebraska, with its unicameral legislature, is one of the petitioning states), and then, even if a convention is called and proposes a balanced-budget amendment (or any other amendment) it must presumably get the support of at least seventy-seven legislative houses in thirty-eight states (again assuming Nebraska is one of these states).

Publius began by challenging Americans to exercise their capacities for "reflection and choice" about the mechanisms of government. He concludes by suggesting that the possibilities for such reflection and choice will continue into the indefinite future, if only Americans take advantage of the opportunity presented by Article V to consider amendments to the Constitution. As we have seen, Article V has, like many other aspects of the Constitution, not quite lived up to the promises made in 1788. It is up to us, acting in the best Publian spirit, to draw our own "lessons of . . . experience" from this history.

# *Acknowledgments*

The truly happiest pages to write are those acknowledging the persons and institutions whose support were vital to this book's actually being written (and, importantly, revised). Pride of place among helpful readers include my friends Jack Balkin, Steve Gutsein, and Scot Powe, as well as my wife, Cynthia Levinson, with her never-ending concern for the ability of the general reader to overcome my various writing tics (including, if not reined in, too many parentheticals and overly long sentences). Hendrik Hertzberg provided essential help on the essay dealing with the Electoral College and the ideas of FairVote with regard to eliminating at least some of its pernicious effects. Special mention, though, should be made of Mark Graber's careful readings and many suggestions; to have taken sufficient heed of all of them and to respond as well to his own important reflections on the original *Federalist* essays would have led to a much, much longer book.

I am especially pleased to dedicate this book to Michael Walzer. It was almost fifty years ago that I was privileged to serve as his teaching assistant in a Harvard course on political obligation. That began a lifelong friendship in which he has also served as an important role model. Although the author of many important books, he is also a master of the essay, often devoted to reflections on pressing, even anguishing issues of contemporary relevance. I usually find myself in agreement with him, but, even when I do not, his arguments are illuminating and must be answered in the same fair and reflective spirit in which he has always presented his own conclusions. I can no more live up to his model than to that provided by Publius, but I hope, nonetheless, that he recognizes a kindred spirit and the importance set by his instantiation of the morally and politically engaged intellectual life.

Perhaps the main emphasis of *The Federalist* is the importance of institutions, and I certainly have reason to be grateful to a number of institutions. The University of Texas Law School has provided me a fully supportive home for over a third of a century. This book was conceived and then written during the deanships of Larry Sager and Ward Farnsworth, both of whom earned my continued gratitude. In my acknowledgments to my previous book, *Framed,* I expressed my appreciation as well to the Harvard Law School, which has allowed me now for more than a dozen years to present short "reading courses" about whatever has interested me. This would not have happened without the support of two deans (and friends), Elena Kagan and Martha Minow, for which I am deeply grateful. My ability to present such a course, "Riffing on *The Federalist*" during the fall semester of 2012, was essential in getting this project under way, as well as in eliciting almost unanimous advice to find another title for the overall project.

It was especially helpful to have the opportunity to try out some of these ideas in public forums. Thus I am also grateful to another longtime supporter and friend, Kim Lane Scheppele, who, basically at my request, invited me to give a talk at Princeton University in which I set out my vision of what might be learned by looking at each of the eighty-five essays of *The Federalist* separately and from a decidedly presentist perspective. Her encouragement was much appreciated, as was true also of that extended by Ran Hirschl, who invited me to make a similar presentation at the University of Toronto. Dean Susan Poser's invitation to deliver the Roscoe Pound Lecture at the University of Nebraska Law School in March 2013 allowed me to elaborate some of my views, particularly of *Federalist* 1. It was published as "'Reflection and Choice': A One-Time Experience?" in *Nebraska Law Review* 92 (2013): 239–258. I also took full advantage of the invitation to deliver the Kenneth Burke Lecture at Pennsylvania State University in April 2013, and I am grateful to Rosa Eberly for engineering that invitation. Finally, the opportunity to deliver the Knowlton Lecture at the University of South Carolina Law School on March 19, 2015, almost literally as the final copy was being prepared, provided one last occasion for extremely helpful feedback that resulted in some last-minute additions to the text. I therefore especially appreciate Thomas Crocker's arranging that lecture.

For the first time in nearly forty years, I worked with an agent, and I am truly grateful to Andrew Stuart for his encouragement and effort. It was he who prodded me to submit the proposal to Yale University Press, and I am delighted that I followed his advice. William Frucht has been an exceptional editor, reading the initial manuscript with remarkable care and suggesting always-useful ways of tightening the arguments. He also deserves full credit for suggesting what I think is an excellent title. Similarly, Kate Davis has been an exemplary copy editor.

It has become customary over several years (and books) to acknowledge the "splendid" members of my family whether or not they contributed to the manuscript (as my wife certainly did) in more than spirit. But it is certainly true that I depend on and cherish the general love and support I receive from my two daughters, Meira and Rachel, and their wonderful husbands, Marc Lipsitch and Ariel Levinson-Waldman. As it happens, both Meira, as a faculty member at the Harvard Graduate School of Education, and Rachel, as a lawyer with the Brennan Center for Justice, are themselves professionally concerned with some of the central issues that are raised by Publius. What kinds of civic education are necessary in order to generate a commitment to the vision of a genuinely "Republican Form of Government" and the active citizenship that the best versions of that vision require? And what dangers might be presented by a national government ever more fixated on what Admiral John Poindexter once labeled "total information awareness" as a means of achieving the "common Defence"? Meira and Rachel have each written essential works on these respective subjects.

Rebecca, Ella, Sarah, and Eli are all too young to be likely readers in the near future—Eli arrived only in April 2014—but, as with my earlier books, much of my energy is generated by my concern about the kind of future they are likely to inherit and the relevance of our present political institutions to providing an answer to that question. Of course they are splendid, but so, undoubtedly, are millions of other children whom I do not know and who equally deserve to live in a better world. Indeed, perhaps the most fundamental challenge set out—though scarcely resolved—by Publius is whether we as human beings are capable of subordinating our "factional" interests, including those generated by our families, to a more inclusive "general Welfare." As Rabbi Hillel unforgettably put it, "If I am not for myself, who will be for me? But if I am only for myself, what am I?"

# Notes

## Publius, Our Contemporary: An Introduction

1. As Ray Raphael notes, the now-common name *The Federalist Papers* is in fact a twentieth-century invention. The original collection was published under the simple name *The Federalist,* attributed to Publius. See Ray Raphael, *Constitutional Myths: What We Get Wrong and How to Get It Right* (New York: New Press, 2013), 106–107.

2. Ibid., 125.

3. My own view is that the best such book is Jack M. Balkin, *Living Originalism* (Cambridge, MA: Harvard University Press, 2012).

4. Sanford Levinson, *Our Undemocratic Constitution: Where Our Constitution Goes Wrong (and How We the People Can Correct It)* (New York: Oxford University Press, 2006, expanded pbk. ed. 2008).

5. Sanford Levinson, *Framed: America's 51 Constitutions and the Crisis of Governance* (New York, Oxford University Press, 2012).

6. As one might imagine, there are sometimes differences among these various versions, almost always involving punctuation or capitalization, though on occasion differences in wording. My favorite print edition is the one edited by the late English historian of American political thought J. R. Pole, published by Hackett Publishing Company in 2005. It has the advantages of not only being quite easy to read, unlike a number of editions where many words are crammed onto too few pages, but also includes Pole's helpful historical notes. As I was writing the book, I made use of several online editions. When differences emerged, I chose to use the version available at the Avalon Project of the Yale Law School, http://avalon.law.yale.edu/subject_menus/fed.asp.

## FEDERALIST 2. How Much *Pluribus* within a Single *Unum*?

1. Huntington's best-known book is surely *The Clash of Civilizations and the Remaking of World Order* (New York: Simon and Shuster, 1996), a key text for those who see contemporary world history as an epic conflict between Islamic and non-Islamic (primarily Christian) states. All the quotations in this chapter are taken from Samuel P. Huntington, *Who Are We? The Challenges to America's National Identity* (New York: Simon and Shuster, 2004).

2. Huntington, *Who Are We?*, 11.

3. Ibid.

4. Ibid., 19.

5. I treat this subject at some length in chapter 4 of *Constitutional Faith,* 2nd ed. (Princeton, NJ: Princeton University Press, 2011).

FEDERALIST 6. Humankind as "Ambitious, Vindictive, and Rapacious"

1. See http://pgpf.org/Chart-Archive/0053_defense-comparison. A helpful earlier discussion, including charts, can be found in Peter W. Singer, "Comparing Defense Budgets, Apples to Apples," *Time*, September 25, 2012, available at http://nation.time.com/2012/09/25/comparing-defense-budgets-apples-to-apples/.

2. See http://hansard.millbanksystems.com/commons/1848/mar/01/treaty-of-adrianople-charges-against, p. 122.

3. Ibid., 83.

4. When quoting from the Constitution, as here, "defence" will be used; otherwise, the reader should expect to find the more contemporary spelling "defense," which, indeed, was sometimes used in the eighteenth century as well.

5. Sebastian Rosato, "The Flawed Logic of Democratic Peace Theory," *American Political Science Review* 586 (November 2003): 97.


FEDERALIST 7. Endless Sources of Conflict (and War),
Even within the United States

1. Michael S. Greve, *The Upside-Down Constitution* (Cambridge, MA: Harvard University Press, 2012).


FEDERALIST 8. On the Rise of a Militarized State

1. Dunlap's essay was originally published in *Parameters*, Winter 1992–1993, and is available at http://strategicstudiesinstitute.army.mil/pubs/parameters/Articles/1992/1992%20dunlap.pdf.

2. Robert L. Goldrich, "American Military Culture from Colony to Empire," *Dædalus* 140 (2011): 58.

3. See http://www.gallup.com/poll/171710/public-faith-congress-falls-again-hits-historic-low.aspx.


FEDERALIST 9. The New (and Improved) Science of Politics

1. Cromwell's comment is worth quoting at length: "I am persuaded that divers of you, who lead the People, have laboured to build yourselves in these things; wherein you have censured others, and established yourselves 'upon the Word of God.' Is it therefore infallibly agreeable to the Word of God, all that *you* say? I beseech you, in the bowels of Christ, think it possible you may be mistaken." Oliver Cromwell, To the General Assembly of the Kirk of Scotland, letter no. 136, in Thomas Carlyle, *Oliver Cromwell's Letters and Speeches: With Elucidations*, vol. 3 of 5 vols. (New York: Scribner, Welford, 1871), available at http://www.gasl.org/refbib/Carlyle__Cromwell.pdf.


FEDERALIST 10. Can Moral or Religious Education
Overcome Natural Tendencies toward Faction?

1. "The Path of the Law," in *The Collected Works Of Justice Holmes: Complete Public Writings And Selected Judicial Opinions Of Oliver Wendell Holmes*, ed. Sheldon Novick, vol. 3, 391–406 (Chicago: University of Chicago Press, 1995); "cynical acid" is at p. 394. Also available at http://www.constitution.org/lrev/owh/path_law.htm.

2. George Washington, "Farewell Address," in *Washington: Writings* (New York: Library of America, 1997), 971.

3. See Mark Osiel, "The Mental State of Torturers: Argentina's Dirty War," in Sanford Levinson, ed., *Torture: A Collection*, expanded pbk. ed., 129–141 (New York: Oxford University Press, 2006); Osiel, *Mass Atrocity, Ordinary Evil, and Hannah Arendt: Criminal Consciousness in Argentina's Dirty War* (New Haven, CT: Yale University Press, 2002).

### FEDERALIST 12. Commerce and State Finance

1. See particularly Ira Katznelson's *Fear Itself: The New Deal and the Origins of Our Time* (New York: Liveright, 2013), which emphasizes the limitations of a number of New Deal measures at the behest of racist Southern Democrats unwilling to support the grant of any governmental largesse to African Americans.

### FEDERALIST 13. Economies of Scale

1. See http://www.guardian.co.uk/news/datablog/2010/apr/01/information-is-beautiful-military-spending.

### FEDERALIST 16. Why Confederation Is "Odious" and a National Government Is Necessary

1. Jessica Bulman-Pozen and Heather K. Gerken, "Uncooperative Federalism," *Yale Law Journal* 118 (May 2009): 1256.

### FEDERALIST 17. The Political Sociology of Federalism (Part 1)

1. See http://www.census.gov/popclock/.

### FEDERALIST 20. The Dutch Provide the Final Cautionary Example

1. Niccolò Machiavelli, *Discourses on Livy*, trans. Julia Conaway Bondanella and Peter Bondanella (1531; Oxford: Oxford University Press, 1997), 95.

2. *Medellín v. Texas*, 552 U.S. 491 (2008); Justice Breyer's dissent is available at https://supreme.justia.com/cases/federal/us/552/491/dissent.html.

### FEDERALIST 21. On the Importance of Sanctions

1. See Oliver Wendell Holmes, Jr., "The Path of the Law," *Harvard Law Review* 10 (1897): 457, available at http://www.constitution.org/lrev/owh/path_law.htm. All subsequent quotations from Holmes are taken from this seminal essay.

2. See http://www.governing.com/gov-data/state-marijuana-laws-map-medical-recreational.html.

### FEDERALIST 22. Publius as Majoritarian

1. See http://en.wikipedia.org/wiki/List_of_U.S._states_and_territories_by_population.

FEDERALIST 23. "Common Defence" and (Un)limited Government

1. Justice Roberts's concurrence in *Korematsu v. United States,* 323 U.S. 214 (1944), 226, is available at https://supreme.justia.com/cases/federal/us/323/214/case .html: "On the contrary, it is the case of convicting a citizen as a punishment for not submitting to imprisonment in a concentration camp, based on his ancestry, and solely because of his ancestry, without evidence or inquiry concerning his loyalty and good disposition towards the United States."

FEDERALIST 24. The Inconvenience of Militia Service

1. Thom Shankar and Helene Cooper, "Pentagon Plans to Shrink Army to Prewar Level," *New York Times,* February 24, 2014, A1; article titled "Pentagon Plans to Shrink Army to Pre–World War II Level" appears online on February 23, available at http://www.nytimes.com/2014/02/24/us/politics/pentagon-plans-to-shrink-army-to-pre -world-war-ii-level.html?_r=0.

2. See http://www.pbs.org/pov/wheresoldierscomefrom/photo_gallery_back ground.php?photo=2#.U3zy57dOXIV.

3. See http://www.defense.gov/news/newsarticle.aspx?id=121390.

4. See http://www.cnn.com/interactive/2012/04/us/table.military.troops/. Also see https://www.vetfriends.com/US-deployments-overseas/.

FEDERALIST 26. In Whom Do We Place Our "Confidence"?

1. Nagl is quoted in an important article by James Fallows, "The Tragedy of the American Military," *Atlantic,* January/February 2015, 89.

2. See http://avalon.law.yale.edu/20th_century/eisenhower001.asp.

FEDERALIST 27. Further Reflections on Confidence
in the National Government

1. Julia Vitullo-Martin and J. Robert Moskin, *The Executive's Book of Quotations* (New York: Oxford University Press, 1994), 130.

FEDERALIST 28. The Necessity of Force

1. Woody Allen, "The Scrolls," *New Republic,* August 31, 1974, available at http://www.newrepublic.com/article/113899/scrolls-woody-allen, reprinted in *Without Feathers* (New York: Random House, 1975).

FEDERALIST 30. First Death, Now Taxes

1. *Callins v. Collins,* 510 U.S. 1141 (1994), as quoted in Fred R. Shapiro, ed., *Yale Book of Quotations* (New Haven, CT: Yale University Press, 2006), 87.

2. *Los Angeles Times,* March 31, 1963, as quoted in ibid., 785.

3. See http://www.treasury.gov/ticdata/Publish/deb2a2013q4.html.

FEDERALIST 31. On the Inutility of Specified Limits

1. See http://www.usgovernmentrevenue.com/total_2013USrt_15rs1n.

FEDERALIST 34. Drafting a Constitution with the Long View in Mind

1. Hugh Rockoff, "Veterans," in *Historical Statistics of the United States: Governance and International Relations,* vol. 5 (New York: Cambridge University Press, 2006), 341.
2. See http://www.nytimes.com/2014/05/27/us/veterans-groups-lash-out-at
-republican-senator.html?contentCollection=us&action=click&module=NextInCollec
tion&region=Footer&pgtype=article.

FEDERALIST 39. Federalism, "Compact," and the Specter of Secession

1. Speech at Indianapolis, Indiana, February 11, 1861, in *Lincoln 1859–1865: Speeches, Letters, Miscellaneous Writings, Presidential Messages and Proclamations* (New York: Library of America, 1989), 202.
2. For Jefferson's draft, see http://www.ushistory.org/declaration/document/ rough.htm.

FEDERALIST 44. Confidence, Money, and Debt

1. See http://www.mercurynews.com/ci_24406734/california-oregon-washing ton-and-british-columbia-sign-climate.
2. See http://www.bloomberg.com/visual-data/best-and-worst/most-underfund ed-pension-plans-states.
3. See http://illinoisissues.uis.edu/archives/2010/02/pension.html.
4. See http://www.chicagotribune.com/news/local/breaking/ct-chicago-debt-rat ing-met-20150227-story.html.

FEDERALIST 50. Maintaining Constitutional Fidelity

1. See http://www.washingtonpost.com/wp-dyn/content/article/2006/09/28/ AR2006092800824.html.

FEDERALIST 51. Designing Institutions for Devils (Who Organize Themselves into Political Parties)

1. See Immanuel Kant, *Perpetual Peace: A Philosophical Sketch,* available at https://www.mtholyoke.edu/acad/intrel/kant/kant1.htm; for quotes from the "First Supplement" see https://www.mtholyoke.edu/acad/intrel/kant/firstsup.htm.
2. William Ossipow, "Research Note: Kant's *Perpetual Peace* and Its Hidden Sources: A Textual Approach," *Swiss Political Science Review* 14, no. 2: 357–389, available at http://onlinelibrary.wiley.com/doi/10.1002/j.1662-6370.2008.tb00106.x/pdf.
3. Daryl Levinson and Richard Pildes, "Separation of Parties, Not Powers," *Harvard Law Review* 119, no. 8 (June 2006): 2311–2386, available at http://papers.ssrn .com/sol3/papers.cfm?abstract_id=890105.

FEDERALIST 54. Who Counts as Worthy of Representation, and for How Much?

1. Though attributing the term to Garrison, the *Yale Book of Quotations* gives as its specific source the resolution adopted, no doubt at Garrison's instigation, by the

Massachusetts Anti-Slavery Society on January 27, 1843. The term is a paraphrase of Isaiah 28:15: "We have made a covenant with death, and with hell are we at agreement."

2. Avishai Margalit, *On Compromise and Rotten Compromises* (Princeton, NJ: Princeton University Press, 2009).

### FEDERALIST 55. Does Size Matter, and If Not, What Does?

1. See http://economix.blogs.nytimes.com/2013/12/31/the-size-of-state-legislatures/. The Alaska state Senate has only twenty members.

2. See the invaluable "population clock" maintained by the United States Census Bureau, in which the number of estimated residents literally changes before one's eyes, given that there is a net gain of one person every fifteen seconds as one computes the new birth every eight seconds, a death every twelve seconds, and a new immigrant every thirty-three seconds. See http://www.census.gov/popclock/.

### FEDERALIST 56. "Local Knowledge" and Representation

1. Seth Barrett Tillman has argued that neither the president nor vice president comes under the constitutional prohibition because, as noted above, they did not receive their positions through presidential appointment. Though this raises interesting, highly theoretical questions for the legal professoriate, it is, for obvious reasons, spectacularly unlikely ever actually to be tested by a "real" case.

### FEDERALIST 57. Does "Representation" Mean "Mirroring"?

1. See http://www.gallup.com/poll/5392/trust-government.aspx.
2. See http://www.electionstudies.org/nesguide/toptable/tab5a_2.htm.

### FEDERALIST 61. What Is a Propitious Time to Choose Representatives?

1. See Heather K. Gerken, *The Democracy Index: Why Our Election System Is Failing and How to Fix It* (Princeton, NJ: Princeton University Press, pbk. 2012).

2. See Posner's dissenting opinion in *Frank v. Walker,* available at http://media.ca7.uscourts.gov/cgi-bin/rssExec.pl?Submit=Display&Path=Y2014/D10-10/C:14-2058:J:Posner:dis:T:op:N:1433281:S:0.

3. See http://www.nytimes.com/2014/07/08/us/08northcarolina.html?module=Search&mabReward=relbias%3Ar%2C{%221%22%3A%22RI%3A10%22}.

### FEDERALIST 62. On the "Lesser Evil"

1. Rick Perry, *Fed Up!: Our Fight to Save America from Washington* (New York: Little Brown, 2010).

2. See http://www.salon.com/2012/08/16/repeal_the_17th_amendment/.

3. Pauline Meier, *Ratification: The People Debate the Constitution, 1787–1788* (New York: Simon & Schuster, 2010), 284.

### FEDERALIST 66. The Past Is a Different Country

1. Azar Nafisi, *Reading Lolita in Tehran: A Memoir in Books* (New York: Random House, 2003).

2. Jeff Shesol, "Did History Win in Noel Canning?" *New Yorker*, June 26, 2014, available at http://www.newyorker.com/news/news-desk/did-history-win-in-noel -canning; or http://perma.cc/7CYL-CPVW.

## FEDERALIST 67. A Monarchical President?

1. See http://www.nytimes.com/2014/06/10/opinion/does-royalty-still-have-a -meaningful-role.html?partner=rssnyt&emc=rss.
2. See http://press-pubs.uchicago.edu/founders/documents/v1ch8s10.html.

## FEDERALIST 68. Selecting the President

1. L. Paige Whitaker and Thomas Neale, *The Electoral College: An Overview and Analysis of Reform Proposals* (Washington, DC: Congressional Research Service, 2004).
2. The FairVote proposal is set out in considerable length in *Every Vote Equal: A State-Based Plan for Electing the President by National Popular Vote*, available at http://www.every-vote-equal.com/.
3. See Ian J. Drake, "The Constitution and the National Popular Vote Interstate Compact," *Publius: The Journal of Federalism* 44 (Fall 2014): 681–701.

## FEDERALIST 69. Comparing the President with the/a King

1. See http://www.cbsnews.com/news/the-truth-of-truthiness/.
2. J. R. Pole, ed., *The Federalist* (Indianapolis: Hackett Publishing, 2005), 368, note to lines 35–41.
3. See http://www.politico.com/news/stories/0710/40299.html.

## FEDERALIST 70. Unity in the Executive

1. Richard Neustadt, *Presidential Power and the Modern Presidents: The Politics of Leadership* (New York: John Wiley and Sons, 1960), 31.
2. See http://www.cbsnews.com/news/bush-the-decider-in-chief/.

## FEDERALIST 72. You Can't Get Too Much of a Good President

1. As a technical matter, President Truman was exempted from the amendment, but he was sufficiently unpopular that there was no question about his running for a de facto third term in 1952, when he made way for Adlai Stevenson to carry the Democratic banner.

## FEDERALIST 74. The Presidential Prerogative to Pardon

1. See http://www.huffingtonpost.com/2012/09/08/esteban-nunez_n_1867393 .html.
2. See http://www.washingtonpost.com/opinions/haley-barbour-on-his-pardons -of-mississippi-prisoners/2012/01/17/gIQAtOuG9P_story.html.

FEDERALIST 76. The Appointment Power

1. See, e.g., Helene Landemore, *Democratic Reason: Politics, Collective Intelligence, and the Rule of the Many* (Princeton, NJ: Princeton University Press, 2013).

2. See http://www.senate.gov/artandhistory/history/common/briefing/Nominations .htm#10.

FEDERALIST 78. Is the Judiciary "Above Politics"?

1. One might wonder, incidentally, exactly what practical expectations underlay the notion of "life tenure" in 1788 as against those in the twenty-first century. Historical "life expectancy" tables prepared by the U.S. Census Bureau go back only to 1850, though it is unlikely that expectancies diminished over the previous sixty years. In any event, white males—the only relevant group in 1788—who survived to 60, in 1850 could expect to live another 13.7 years; 70-year-olds could look forward to living another 8.6 years. By 1998, analogous expectancies for white males were additional 19.7 and 12.8 years, respectively; white women (who are now relevant with regard to judicial appointments) can expect to live an additional 23.3 and 15.5 years, respectively. Nonwhite men who were 60 in 1997 had a life expectancy of 18 more years, while 70-year-olds could look forward to living another 12 years. Nonwhite women, like their white counterparts, were expected to live longer, 21.8 and 14.7 additional years, respectively. See *Historical Statistics of the United States* (Millennial ed.), vol. 1, table Ab656–703: "Expectation of Life at Specified Age, by Sex and Race, 1850–1998" (New York: Cambridge University Press, 2006), 442–445.

2. Paul Angle, ed., *The Complete Lincoln-Douglas Debates of 1858* (Chicago: University of Chicago Press, 1958), 57–58.

3. See Jack M. Balkin and Sanford Levinson, "Understanding the Constitutional Revolution," *Virginia Law Review* 87 (2001): 1045–1109.

FEDERALIST 79. Fixed Salaries—but What about Inflation?

1. See http://www.uscourts.gov/JudgesAndJudgeships/JudicialCompensation/ judicial-salaries-since-1968.aspx.

2. See http://www.bls.gov/data/inflation_calculator.htm.

3. See http://www.businessinsider.com/one-percent-state-map-2014-9.

4. See http://www.nytimes.com/2007/01/01/us/01scotus.html?_r=0.

FEDERALIST 80. The Importance of Federal Courts

1. See http://press-pubs.uchicago.edu/founders/documents/v1ch8s13.html.

2. See http://press-pubs.uchicago.edu/founders/documents/a3_1s10.html.

3. See http://www.gallup.com/poll/171710/public-faith-congress-falls-again-hits -historic-low.aspx.

FEDERALIST 81. Disciplining Judges by Threatening Impeachment?

1. See *Yale Book of Quotations* (New Haven, CT: Yale University Press, 2006), 282, citing "Remarks in House of Representatives" on April 15, 1970.

## FEDERALIST 82. A Judiciary for the Whole

1. See R. LaFountain, R. Schauffler, S. Strickland, and K. Holt, *Examining the Work of State Courts: An Analysis of 2010 State Court Caseloads* (National Center for State Courts, 2012), 45, available at http://www.courtstatistics.org/~/media/Microsites/Files/CSP/DATA%20PDF/CSP_DEC.ashx.

## FEDERALIST 83. Trial by Jury

1. Sanford Levinson, *Constitutional Faith*, 2nd ed. (Princeton, NJ: Princeton University Press, 2011).

2. See Title 28 United States Code § 1332(a).

## FEDERALIST 84. The Limited Importance—If Not Outright Dangers—of Bills of Rights

1. See Sujit Choudhry, ed., *Constitutional Design for Divided Societies: Integration or Accommodation?* (New York: Oxford University Press, 2008).

## FEDERALIST 85. "A Nation [with] a National Government"

1. See http://www.mlive.com/lansing-news/index.ssf/2014/03/michigan_petitions_congress_fo.html.

# Index

abortion, 77
Achean League, 68
Ackerman, Bruce, 242–243
Adams, John, 174, 175, 264, 293, 304, 325
Adams, John Quincy, 174, 192
Allen, Woody, 103
Amar, Akhil Reed, 162, 312
Ambassadors, public ministers, and consuls, 158–159
amendment by new convention, 328–329
American Revolution, 10, 24, 52–53, 62, 86–87, 102, 103, 105, 150, 168
Amphictyonic Council, 68, 69
Anthony, Susan B., opposition to Fourteenth and Fifteenth Amendments, 197
Arizona, attempt to regulate undocumented aliens, 19–20, 70
armed citizenry, importance of, 173
Articles of Confederation, 9, 30, 50–52, 106, 140, 163; Article XIII and amendment, 149–150, 162; defects (and "imbecility") of, 57–63, 75, 78–79, 100, 159, 224; exemplifying weaknesses of alliances and confederations, 22–23, 48
Athens, 39

"bad man," 75–76
Bailyn, Bernard, 86
Bankruptcy Clause (of Article I, Section 8), 165
Barber, Sotorios, 168
Barbour, Haley, 281
Beard, Charles, 164
Bill of Rights, inadvisability of, 323–327
Blackman, Harry, 111
Bolman-Pozen, Jessica, 63, 131
Bolton, John, 258
Bork, Robert, 290
Brennan, William J., 257, 300
Breyer, Stephen, 74–75, 259

"Brutus," as critic of federal judiciary, 308–309
Bush, George H. W., 113, 268, 290, 294
Bush, George W., 29, 70, 195, 229, 239, 256, 294; as "decider," 270; and election of *2000*, 260; frequency of veto overrides, 278; unpopularity of, 274; use of recess appointment power by, 258; withdrawal of Kyoto Protocol by, 286
*Bush v. Gore*, 260, 310

Calhoun, John C., 122, 144
Canadian Charter of Rights and Freedoms, 325
capital punishment, 111
Caro, Robert, 295
Carter, Jimmy, 284
census, 208
Chase, Samuel, 312
"checks and balances," 177, 191–196
Cheney, Dick, 291
China, as potential student of Publius's lessons, 46
Choudhry, Sujit, 327
citizenship, definition of, 157–158, 159
Clinton, Bill, 11, 174, 268; use of pardoning power by, 281; use of recess appointment power by, 258
Clinton, Hillary, 174, 237, 271
Colbert, Stephen, 266
commerce, importance of, 45, 47
compromise, 205–206, 237–238
Condorcet Jury Theorem, 289
"Constitution of Conversation," 116, 122
"Constitution of Settlement," 116
constitutional convention, 2
Coolidge, Calvin, 290
Council of Censors, 186–187
"coup of 2012." *See* Dunlap, Charles
Cover, Robert, 111